I Was Born Cold Blow Lane

Barrie Stradling

The Parrs Wood Press
Manchester

First Published 2004

THE PARRS WOOD PRESS
St Wilfrid's Enterprise Centre
Royce Road, Manchester, M15 5BJ
www.parrswoodpress.com

© Barrie Stradling 2004

ISBN: 1 903158 55 9

Printed and bound by Biddles Ltd of King's Lynn

Contents

Dedications

I'd like to dedicate this book to all my numerous home and away Millwall companions past and present - Roy Munro, Colin and Bob Briden, Paul White, George and Peter Webb, Steve Kimberley, Peter Gibbons and Peter Desmond.

Jim Stephenson, Bob and the boys, 'Striker', 'Win or lose have a booze' Jason, Dave Murray, Simon Watson, Phil and Trevor, Mick and Eddie, Big John and Laupie.

The Essex contingent of Paul and Gavin Huish, Andy and Mark Bell, Glyn Kerry, 'Millwall Youth Boy' Lawrie and John Brown.

The East End contingent of Simon, Patrick and Lisa Barrett; Dave, Paul and Nathan Simms; Lois, Aaron and Clive 'Thunderclap' Whates, Johnny Lynch, Micky and Steve Fisher and last but not least Ted 'Mayhem' Mayhew.

My apologies to all those I may have forgotten to mention.

To Millwall fans everywhere.

Introduction

This book is one man's experience of a lifetime following Millwall home and away. It shows the love, devotion, blind faith, stupidity and money that are required to support a team for over three decades.

It's Millwall as a Sixties-style kitchen-sink drama, with grim, bleak locations, down-to-earth industrial language and violence, but without the sex. Truly, football for the working class common man and you don't get more working class than Millwall, after all how many other teams mention beer and jellied eels in their club song?

It includes personal memories from the Old Den days through to today's modern New Den era and features a guide to the real joys of away travel from London to points North, South, East and West.

Cataloguing the good and bad times, the characters, chants, wit, wisdom and mentality of a Millwall crowd and the strange things encountered on the way.

It incorporates all the joys and pains that you could wish for from following a football team.

With the modern era ranging from the lows of life in Division Two, to the joy of winning the Division Two Championship in 2000/01, to the low of losing a Division One Play-Off and the subsequent riot in 2001/02 and the fraught season that followed in 2002/03, through to personal recollections from 2003/04, a season that was to turn into one of the most exciting in the club's history. Culminating in the heights of an FA Cup Final and qualification for Europe for the first time ever.

Barrie Stradling is in his forties and has been following Millwall nationwide for too long to see sense now.

Millwall is for life - as they say, the first 38 years are the worst.

1.

Love, Devotion, Pariah

THE TITLE OF THIS BOOK comes from an Old Den chant from many moons ago, which can be found in the chants chapter later on. Obviously, I wasn't literally born under the Cold Blow Lane, that would have been a bit uncomfortable for my mum, I was really born in the London Hospital, Whitechapel, but the title just seemed to sum up my lifetime's affinity to Millwall. From my days at the Old Den to the New Den version of today.

For the benefit of those of you who have not read my other Millwall book *Tuesday Night In Grimsby*, I'd like to start with a brief note about how my Millwall allegiance came about - Stepney in the East End where I grew up is considered to be in West Ham's heartland; consequently, people have often asked me why I support Millwall. Well in truth, even though there's a river in between East and South East London, Millwall is my nearest team.

West Ham, although considered the local club, are miles away and not remotely in my thoughts. I had a couple of West Ham-supporting cousins and Hammers-supporting friends in primary school, several of whom even had trials for West Ham; thankfully, I wasn't one of them because trying to get me on to a hallowed Hammers' pitch would have been like trying to get Damien into the church in *The Omen*. However, I also had a cousin, uncle and three neighbours who supported Millwall during my formative years.

My first visit to the Old Den against Brentford in the League Cup on 29/8/1966 helped to cement my affinity. Once I had tasted the Old Den's unique atmosphere as an impressionable 8-year-old I was hooked, there really was no place like it. Every other London ground that I subsequently went to in my childhood years paled in comparison to it for passion, atmosphere and of course hostility.

I WAS BORN UNDER THE COLD BLOW LANE

From this first Millwall game onwards my cousin Roy regularly took me to the Old Den and my dad, who was a Spurs fan, frequently took me to White Hart Lane, as well as occasionally taking me to other London grounds. Consequently, from a young age I went to football almost every week. I suppose most boys and girls get their choice of team from their fathers in the main and I'm sure that my dad wanted me to follow Tottenham; however, despite seeing numerous Spurs games, I chose Millwall. This was partly due to my secondary school which, even though it was in the East End, had many boys from South East London and Millwall E.14 version.

As a result it was far more Lions--friendly than my primary school which had been predominantly West Ham-oriented. In my teens I went to Millwall games with my Lions supporting secondary schoolmates, several of whom also still go to this day. As the years have passed, my Millwall support has grown into a condition of personally having to be at as many home and away matches in the flesh as I possibly can, so that I can suffer it all manfully.

To me being a true fan means having to be there come rain or shine and nationwide, only then can you truly relish the joys and suffer the pains that the real fan in the real world outside of the Premiership money machine has to go through week in week out: the promotions, the relegations and the missed opportunities with the Holy Grail in sight. Not forgetting the added Millwall fan ingredients of ground closures, away travel bans, travel restrictions, trouble-inspired all-ticket matches, living in a police state and of course financial disaster.

I have developed a couple of philosophies over my years of following the 'Wall. The first has helped to keep me sane (ish) and the second has enabled me to feel that I'm doing my bit.

These philosophies are:

1) **Have no expectation or delusion that success is here to stay**. You cannot then be disappointed. Cynical it might be but it has worked to protect me from all the years of under-achieving and yo-yoing about the Leagues that my Lions-supporting era has witnessed.

2) **Always get behind Millwall at games.** This was something that was drummed into my psyche since my early years at the Old

Den. I have always sung at games since a child and I'm not going to change just because I'm older, if not wiser. If anything, I'm getting worse as the years go by, there's no escape - see Grandad! I have to feel that I'm playing my part at games; it's the ethos of a hotbed crowd like ours. In my opinion if you're going to a game you should be as vocal and ideally as positive as possible, why go if you act like a monk that has taken a vow of silence or all you're going to do is to slag Millwall off?

It's a waste of time and cash if you ask me.

I know we pay our money and we all moan from time to time, it's only human nature, and whilst everyone is entitled to their opinion, booing and getting on the team's backs is hardly going to encourage them, is it? For me supporting Millwall is all about passion and giving the other team and fans a good ear-bashing, not acting like you have Laryngitis and/or a grudge.

That's what I think anyway and I'm sticking to it.

As anyone who support the 'Wall will confirm, it isn't easy. To envisage what it's like being a normal Millwall fan; imagine a pot of tar, one big brush and all of us, hooligans or otherwise, being tarred with it. For anyone considering Millwall as their team, it's important to realise what you're letting yourself in for by association. You will have to accept things from all angles, true or otherwise; some examples:

1) You must accept that you personally are a pariah and the sole cause of all of society and football's ills and consequently you will be an object of hate.

2) You will be on the wrong end of all manner of scurrilous media coverage, much of which borders on a witch-hunt, whereby any Millwall-related incident is normally blown out of all proportion or at best subject to wildly inaccurate reporting presented as fact.

To add to your persecution complex other club's fans similar or more serious misdemeanours will be totally ignored.

3) The most flimsy or tenuous of Millwall links will require the Luton/Birmingham riot footage to be shown, because naturally there's no other footage available of any other team.

4) Your club's fans will often be mentioned when talking about other clubs' misdeeds, implying somehow that it was Millwall's fault; you must therefore accept that non-involvement in an event does not prove innocence, think of it as a sort of 'Millwall until proven innocent' policy.

5) Due to our real misdeeds and reputation, you will see your club's fans appear in every other club's 'Hoolie' books and on any football hooligan-related TV programmes.

6) With your club affiliation you will be perceived as a dangerous, rabid and racist thug and will have to endure 'serious' questions like 'You must be a hooligan then?' and 'You must be a racist then?' plus 'humorous' Hooligan comments like 'I thought I'd ring to make sure you hadn't been nicked at the game!' and 'Watch him, he supports Millwall!'.

7) You will have your club held up as a watchword for hooliganism and anti-social behaviour. I'm sure if Millwall appeared in the dictionary the definition would simply say 'Hooligan' and vice-versa.

8) You will often have to watch a person's facial expression change to one that they would usually reserve for someone who they have just witnessed punching their grandmother as soon as you say that you support Millwall.

9) On the technology front, you will have the dubious pleasure of keeping abreast of all the latest police/security equipment and video/CCTV technology, as you will undoubtedly get to see so much of it home and away during the course of the season. It is a boon for anyone wanting to appear on the likes of *Big Brother* though as being on camera for hours at a time is nothing to a Millwall fan.

All of the above are just a brief taster of what it's like to be a Lions fan. It's no wonder that we've developed a 'No One Likes Us'/'F... 'Em All' siege mentality, is it?

I know that Millwall have been involved in several high profile incidents over the years, but then so have a lot of teams' fans. I suppose I should be used to being a scapegoat by now but sensitive soul that I am, it still irks me as I'm sure it does every other true Millwall fan.

LOVE, DEVOTION, PARIAH

As a child, supporting a team with a violent fan reputation gave me a perverse pride and an air of reflected menace - no one liked us but everyone knew us, that was for sure. However, over the years it has become a millstone, especially with a modern pre-conceived media image that makes a trip to Bermondsey look about as appealing as a fortnight in Baghdad.

My Lions-supporting life now stretches to more than three decades so I've had to endure all the emotions and changes I could wish for, including the traumatic upheaval of the move from the Old Den and various threats of extinction.

What I've tried to portray in this book is my own personal view. It's an honest account of the Millwall experience, warts and all, the wit, wisdom, characters, chants, banter and the violence that I've personally witnessed and experienced at both Dens and up and down the country. It encompasses a 'Wish you were here' style travelogue of two eventful seasons, 2000/01, 2001/02, the interesting incidents from 2002/03 and my memories from the surreal season that was 2003/04.

I hope that you enjoy it.

2.

Home Sweet Home 1
The Old Den

Location, Location, Location

FOR THOSE OF YOU TOO young to have experienced the Old Den in the flesh, it was in Cold Blow Lane, London SE14, in a mostly residential area, with a school positioned just a short distance from the left hand corner of the ground and industrial yards opposite the turnstiles and adjacent to other parts of the stadium.

Two of the terraces - the Cold Blow Lane and Halfway Line - had entrances in the above road, as did the South Stand seats. More bizarrely, there was latterly an away fan alleyway on the same road, which over the years was the site of numerous violent clashes. Alternatively, you could enter the stadium at the Ilderton Road end of the ground, via a path that in the 60s/70s was close to the entrance for the New Cross Greyhound/Speedway stadium.

The approach roads to the Cold Blow Lane end of the ground, my most usual haunt, either wound through the residential streets from New Cross Gate station or via the park and railway tunnels from New Cross station. These dark railway tunnels were none too welcoming, as you can imagine, especially with 'Abandon hope all ye who enter here' type of graffiti adorning the walls, which must certainly have gladdened the hearts of any away fans as they arrived at the old ground.

When I first started going to matches in the mid -1960s football was a far less glamorous thing than it is today and all the grounds countrywide were of a very primitive nature as anyone who had the pleasure will confirm. You could still find their like in the last few years at places like Oxford, Cambridge, Colchester and of course Fulham.

Prior to the Taylor Report new grounds explosion of the modern era, the Old Den was pretty much industry standard. There was only one section of seats in the ground located in a 'grandstand', which consisted of a small upper and lower tier that ran the length of the South side of the pitch. In my early years there was terracing on the lower section until the club replaced it with seating. It had a roof that completely covered its length; unfortunately, from a restricted viewing perspective, this was held up by metal posts. In later years, it also had the added intrusion of a pitchside perimeter fence.

The grandstand was connected to the Cold Blow Lane end (aka 'CBL') and the Ilderton Road (aka 'Dog Track End') terraces behind each goal and you had the ability to transfer into it via turnstiles on the terraces inside the ground for an additional fee. The terraces at each end had a roof covering that went along most of their width but only covered the rear of the terrace. These two terraced ends behind each goal were also connected to the Halfway Line/North terrace, which itself had a central roof section that again only covered the middle portion at the rear of the terrace. The Halfway Line side terrace was the largest in the ground by far and its connection to the two end terraces effectively created what amounted to a continuous terrace on three sides of the ground. This was only broken up by the iron railings between the sections, the old style raised floodlight pylons in the four corners and the fact that the North terrace tapered down in the corner between the Ilderton Road and the Halfway Line, where one of the floodlight pylons stood. This was the only large gap on the continual terrace and was one of the locations for a collection of large broken clocks that graced the Old Den over the years. It was through this opening that you could see the ethereal glow of the dog track's floodlights at night matches and it was the gap that allowed the Jews' Hill community to flourish, more of which later.

From the Cold Blow Lane end of the ground, entrance on to the CBL terrace was via a staircase with yellow crush rails that led up to the back of the middle of the stand. Those heading to the

Halfway Line via this end had to take a path to the right of the CBL stand and go by way of the lower side terrace or via a passageway that ran along the back of the terrace. This passageway had openings that allowed people on to the side terrace, with its main opening leading straight into the Halfway Line shed section itself in the centre of the stand.

For my first ever visit to the Old Den, and for many subsequent games, Roy and I stood to the left of the Halfway Line shed. This meant that we frequently used the passageway to get to and from the turnstile. As a young child this alleyway, with its narrow width, high walls and crowds of large adults, meant that it was like being in the land of the giants, a none too pleasant experience for a small boy. Prior to the stricter segregation policies, save for the iron railing fences between the home sections, the ground was unsegregated and you had the ability to go totally around the terraced parts from one end of the ground to the other unimpeded.

The terraces themselves usually had crumbling steps, which were allied to yellow-painted and rusty crush barriers that were often themselves less than well maintained. What you've got to remember though is that the 1960s/1970s was an era when a pre-season lick of paint, a spraying of Weedol on the terraces to prevent the grass poking through and a bit of step and roof making good, was deemed major and radical refurbishment.

Completing the ground layout, the players came on to the pitch via an entrance slightly to the left of the goal at the CBL end; apparently, The Den was one of less than half a dozen league grounds to have a player's tunnel behind the goal. This entrance had a low roofed no man's land area around it and was surrounded by metal rail fencing to keep the natives out.

In later years, they added an additional extended tunnel covering as well, largely because we pelted West Ham players with coins at a game in the old First Division in the 1980s if memory serves.

No Mod Cons Gov!

As with most other grounds of the day the amenities at the Old Den were basic to say the least. They would appal anyone who was only used to the modern era, were they confronted with them today.

Believe it or not, in the 60/70s the executive box didn't exist and the big knobs had to slum it with the rest of the stand dwellers! There were a couple of bar and refreshment stalls at the back of the stands and burger and hot dog stalls inside and outside of the ground, some of which were a bit too close to the loos for Health and Safety purposes for my liking. The only other food option was buying unshelled roasted peanuts in small paper bags from the Percy Dalton men. The peanut sellers outside the ground would often implore us to buy their nuts with a cry that sounded to me like 'Peanuts - Almost Dead!'. I'll wait until they are dead if it's all the same with you.

There was a small ticket office inside the CBL forecourt that had a downstairs window and latterly they added a tiny upstairs ticket office atop a narrow staircase that ran up the side of the original office. You have to bear in mind that the 60s/70s were very much 'pay on the day' eras, with all-ticket matches being like hen's teeth so there wasn't actually any need for vast ticketing facilities. In this era there was also no such thing as overt club sponsorship, blatant advertising, pitch-side hoardings or merchandising, unlike today's 'if it moves, whack a sponsors name on it'.

There was a very small club shop on the corner of the CBL close to the Halfway Line side section and, in later years, they constructed an additional small shop inside the ground at the back of the CBL. You could buy items like metal badges, rosettes, mugs, plates and scarves etc, but it was very low key. I cannot recall actually being able to buy a complete official club kit, although in the 70s you could buy a white shirt and sew the club badge on yourself or get your mum to do it for you; if you could find a badge anywhere, that was.

In later years the club installed a betting stall near the turnstiles and close to the open-air urinals, or walls if you prefer - a real joy in the summer, smell-wise. The Gents' WCs were located close to the seated area in the CBL to the extreme left of the forecourt as you entered the ground; these also had extra troughs and, luxury of luxuries, a roof. The women's facilities were limited, but in truth, this was a time when not too many women attended, so a Ladies was deemed an extravagance,

I WAS BORN UNDER THE COLD BLOW LANE

The late 60s/early 70s was an era before crowd segregation and with far less stewarding or crowd safety requirements, it was possible to cram crowds into grounds up to levels that would be considered dangerous today. As I was at the mercy of my dad or cousin as to what games I went to, I wasn't taken to the biggest game of the mid-60s at the Old Den, an FA Cup 3rd round tie against First Division Tottenham Hotspur on 28/1/1967, a match that finished scoreless and attracted a crowd of 41,260. Consequently the biggest crowd that I was personally in at the Old Den was for an FA Cup 4th round game against First Division Leicester City, a 1-0 defeat on 25/1/1969. This game attracted a crowd of 31,480, which was crammed into the old ground.

The size of the expected crowd prompted Roy and I to make sure that we got to the ground at about 1pm, an hour and a half earlier than our usual arrival time. It also meant that as a ten-year-old boy I had to stand on the raised ledge at the back of the Cold Blow Lane end in order to see anything, my only other options being the indignity of being passed overhead by the adults to the front or not seeing anything at all. When you consider that the Old Den crowd record was some 17,000 more than the Leicester gate, God alone knows what it was like then. I remember the winning Leicester goal in this game scored by Allan 'Sniffer' Clarke when a John Gilchrist back-pass stuck in the mud and he pounced. Funny why some games and goals stick in your mind.

The Roar!

It was my experience in my youth that Millwall's players were urged on by a crowd unlike any other. No one could generate an atmosphere like the Old Den, a ground famous for its 'Roar' and continual singing. The noise was generated by the continuous nature of the terraces and the partisan mentality of the crowd. I may be biased but personally speaking give me 10,000 diehard Millwall fans over 30,0000 fans of another side any day. That said, having a passionate hotbed crowd could also be a double-edged sword. In the main the Old Den 'Roar' served Millwall well, hence the 59 home game unbeaten run in the 1960s. However, it also frightened our own side on some bigger occasions, prompting them to freeze or underperform in several important matches over the years, with panic sometimes setting in when they attempted to appease the baying home crowd.

As the Old Den was such a passionate ground it was a very rare occurrence that you could actually hear the away fans singing, even after the segregation was in place and they were no longer incognito. If you could hear them it meant that Millwall were in a slump and we had our 'we're doomed' heads on. This certainly wasn't the norm as the usual scenario was that an Old Den crowd in full flow would frighten the opposition and fans into submission, especially at night matches with the added 'fear of the dark' factor.

The compact nature of the ground, with its close proximity to the pitch and hostile, fervent home fans, made for an uncomfortable afternoon or night for any opposition fans or players. It would prompt many an away player to be only too glad to get off the pitch and shoot off home to give their ears a rest from the continual din. See Eamon Dunphy's book *It's Only a Game* about the Millwall experience as a player.

The normal ritual at Millwall, still prevalent to this day, was for the Lions to kick towards the CBL in the second half. Pre-segregation this would prompt a half-time crowd migration, as fans nomadically came from the Dog Track end, picked up more fans from the Halfway Line en route and then converged on the usually already heaving CBL via the alleyway. This would concentrate the 'Roar' even more with everyone wound up to the hilt and it would lead to a very highly charged second half as Millwall attacked this end to encouraging chants like 'Attack Attack, Attack Attack Attack!'. If we went behind, we would pump up the volume to urge Millwall to get back on level terms pronto. The hyped-up nature of the home support meant that any home goal was greeted with crowd hysteria with everyone jumping about like excited Mexican jumping beans.

If for some reason the opposing skipper won the toss and decided to play mind games with us, it was never quite the same if we had to attack the Dog Track end in the second half. However, it did mean that some people would migrate in the opposite direction to the norm, in order to be standing behind the goal that the Lions were attacking in the second half. This mobile support walkabout policy, with the added ingredients of ground layout, shed-like roofing to sing under and the crowd's mentality, enabled us to turn the Old Den into a fortress.

Pre-segregation, the atmosphere was formidable, with the 'Roar' echoing all around the ground, especially between the CBL and Halfway Line covered sections. It always sent a shiver up my spine anyway. When the authorities decided that we needed to be put behind cages, the segregation tempered the volume initially, though it wasn't helped by being an experience akin to standing behind fences in a concentration camp 'For you, Tommy, the war is over' style.

When the segregation policy took hold it restricted the ease of movement by our Bedouin community, and whilst it did affect the atmosphere, in my opinion it was only when the club broke the CBL and Halfway Line flow by putting in a seated and partially covered Junior Enclosure between them that the atmosphere was really adversely affected. Especially when the junior section had kiddies' entertainers, puppet shows, etc, not very Old Den like!

Having said that the atmosphere wasn't as good, perhaps this was just a case of 'Nostalgia ain't what it used to be', because after the junior enclosure was installed, I met some Norwich City fans in an East End pub who had stopped off on their way back from a match at West Ham. I was with mates Micky and Steve Fisher and we had just returned from a match at the Old Den. We got talking to the Norwich fans and told them we were Millwall; they said that they had been at Millwall for the live TV spectacular 3 - 2 defeat on 22/1/1989. They told us that they travelled the country with Norwich and the Old Den was by far the noisiest place that they had ever been to, including Old Trafford 'pre-prawn sandwiches' and Anfield, so maybe it's just my 'Now in my day!' mind.

Welcome To The Den - Hotbeds/Hard Battles

A visit to the Old Den must have been very high on any visiting fans 'I really must go there!' list, I'm sure. It certainly wasn't a welcoming place for away fans to visit either from an aesthetic point of view or from the crowd hostility perspective. It had some unwelcoming home fan rituals, for example the younger fans would stand on any vantage point, including the turnstile roofs, outside the Cold Blow Lane terrace scouring the streets for any 'enemy' among them. Any that were spotted would then be identified and their presence broadcast via the jungle telegraph to the older home fans, so that they could be 'dealt' with inside the ground. Pre-segregation it was definitely advisable for any away fans either to remain anonymous or not to come to the Den at all. If away fans chose to turn up, they had to keep their wits about them. The best policy was to stay quiet and try to blend into the background and thereby remain undetected. Consequently, away fans that did turn up would usually go to the Dog Track End corner, presumably deeming it preferable to standing on the CBL or Halfway Line; mind you, I saw fights in the posh seats on occasion, so nowhere was really safe.

Pre-segregation, away fans wearing colours, chanting or celebrating a goal wasn't too sensible, because the continuation of the home ritual meant that one of two things would invariably then happen. Occasionally, the home fans went across the pitch to get to the away fans to save time. Usually though the home fans would mass in the CBL, walk around behind the terrace onto the passageway leading behind the Halfway Line to gather up with other like-minded souls and then continue onward to the Dog Track end to gather even more troops. They would then steam straight through any away fans that they had identified, who would invariably get on their toes in a manner Linford Christie would have been proud of and dive through the nearest exit. These evictions were normally accompanied by encouraging chants like 'Hello, Hello Millwall Aggro!' and 'We Are The Hardest In London!' from us young fans as we roared on the home warriors until the enemy were vanquished.

From our CBL vantage point, we had a perfect panoramic view of these unfolding away fan assaults and their impending doom; aptly it was very like Lions stalking their prey. Whether the away fans were expecting this I don't know. We certainly were, as it seemed to happen practically every home game. With the 'It's All Going Off!' scenario now over, resulting in yet another successful Millwall victory, we would then return our attention to the game.

I WAS BORN UNDER THE COLD BLOW LANE

I do recall some foolhardy souls who ignored the 'blend in/act like a local' option and who paid the inevitable price for their lack of common sense and camouflage. I especially recall Sunderland and Notts Forest fans in the late 1960s/early 1970s standing conspicuously in their red and white scarves among the home fans, for a short while at least, as the home fans did a double take, cartoon-style eye rubbing in disbelief, just prior to showing the visitors the error of their ways, as it were. Their red and white scarves came in handy to mop up the blood discreetly, which was some consolation I suppose.

One game that especially sticks in my mind in this lack of commonsense category was when some particularly daft Barnsley fans turned up at the Old Den for a League Cup game in midweek in September 1968, a first round replay game following a 1-1 draw in Yorkshire. Roy and I went to this game and as we walked towards the CBL some chanting, scarf-wearing Barnsley fans passed us. A helpful London Bobby approached this small idiotic band and advised them that this wasn't the best policy at the Den, saying that they would be wiser to be a little less conspicuous; he added that they should avoid the main home terraces. Unfortunately, with bluff Yorkshire pig-headedness they chose to ignore him and once again found their red-and-white scarves coming in useful.

I especially remember this game as it also highlighted another football lesson. We were winning 1-0 when Roy and I decided to leave early to beat the traffic. It was only when we arrived back home that we found out that Barnsley had equalised at the death, sending the game into extra time, with Millwall eventually running out 3-1 winners.

A lesson learnt there; stay to the bitter end.

The Joys Of The Terrace

To explain the joys of standing on the terraces week in week out, to anybody too young to have 'enjoyed' the experience first hand. In the old days you had to be fairly fit because you were standing up for hours on end and it took a while to get acclimatised each season, with the early games often resulting in aching legs. The only relief from standing was being able to sit on a crush barrier or the terrace steps and hope that nobody knocked you off or tripped over you during the pre-match and half time sit-ins.

Terracing necessitated having the following abilities:

1) Being able to stand on tiptoes like a ballerina for hours at a time in order to try to clear the sea of heads in front of you, especially when you were young.

2) Being able to bob and weave like a professional boxer from side to side in an attempt to see around anyone moving about in front of you.

3) Being able to stretch your neck like Stretch Armstrong or Twizzle (ask your dad), thus enabling you to crane your head above the sea of bobbing heads in front of you.

Having climbing ability also helped because, in the early years, you could gain some height by standing on the raised portion at the back of the CBL, by scaling a crush barrier or climbing up the floodlight pylons before they put a fence around them.

Bombarding the goals with toilet rolls was a 60/70s favourite nationwide, leaving the goalmouths looking like an Andrex puppy's ultimate fantasy. If you didn't have a bog roll you could always use a bus ticket roll, as long as you remembered to take it out of the ticket machine first!

Terraces also meant that it was best to avoid the following -

1) Standing behind any extrovert crush barrier gymnast, this policy could come unstuck however if you were in front of a barrier and they fell off during their crush barrier balance beam performance only to then land on top of you.

2) Being crushed by any latecomers or the second half Bedouin invaders.

3) Being in the path of the frequent CBL human avalanches, caused by the crowd surging in anticipation of any 'nearly' goals and by the kids who used to tumble down from the back for a laugh, thus creating a tidal wave of humanity. On these occasions, you'd find a place on the terrace and think 'This will do', only for an avalanche of people to come crashing down from behind.

I WAS BORN UNDER THE COLD BLOW LANE

What this meant was that if you were in its path you could be standing near the back of the stand one minute only to find yourself 20 steps further down the terrace the next, much to the annoyance of anyone who you unwittingly careered into. You were then obliged to abuse and shake your fists at the excitable kids at the back who had caused your plummet. It was therefore usually advisable to get a position away from the aisle and ideally in front of a crush barrier.

Terraces did however give you an excellent opportunity to go ever so slightly loopy when a goal was scored, hence the 'Let's Go F...ing Mental!' type of chants. They also gave you a good opportunity to empty the contents of your pockets unwittingly all over the floor as you jumped around and ejected your change, keys, etc in your jubilation, onto the hard concrete floor. Luckily, there was no such thing as a mobile phone at the time to shatter.

As I said it was an Old Den terrace tradition to sit down on the terracing steps before the game and at half-time; this was a practice that had its risks, for example whilst sitting on the terrace you could -

1) Drown in a sea of peanut shells or at least cut your arse on them.

2) You could encourage haemorrhoids in winter by sitting on an ice-cold step without your Daymart thermal long johns on.

3) Your seated position also meant that your legs and body acted like a human tripwire as you were sprawled out in front of people trying to weave their way through the forest of feet.

4) You could then be drowned or scalded by someone carrying a drink and coming a cropper over you, as they were concentrating more on not spilling their drink than looking where they were going.

5) You had the dubious pleasure that if somebody standing in front of you didn't sit down the only view you had was of a bloke's rear end, a joy for some obviously, but not my idea of a good view.

6) Finally, if you were drunk or advancing in years, trying to get up unassisted with any grace and your dignity intact was a bit of a problem.

Jews' Hill - A Freeloader's Paradise

In the good old days we had the otherworldly glow of New Cross Stadium's floodlights illuminating the night sky in a gap between the Ilderton Road end and the Halfway Line until the Dog Track/Speedway stadium was demolished in the mid-1970s. This viewing area then became the grass verge known as 'Jews' Hill', a freeloader's paradise whose numbers rose or fell depending on the enormity of the game. This hill community would sometimes consist of hundreds of individuals at big games. It comes to a pretty pass when you can become a freeloading glory hunter doesn't it?

I recall one game when another team's 'Firm', Leeds I believe, came charging over the grass hill and appeared on the horizon like in *Zulu* only to find themselves in the midst of our buckshee fans and not our 'Boys'. Quite what you could see from this vantage point I have no idea, but you could hardly complain about a free view could you? Millwall must have lost thousands of pounds over the years, why they didn't either put up a brick wall to obscure the view or sell opera glasses and food to them I don't know, at least that way they would have got something back from the tight buggers!

I Can See Clearly Now!

When I first went with my cousin in the mid-1960s, it seemed that we always ended up standing behind a fence, be it on the CBL or next to the Halfway Line. For my first ever game against Brentford we stood next to the Halfway Line shed, just by the entrance to the alleyway at the back, leaning against a brick wall. This meant that we had a partitioned fence to the side of us, running from the top to the bottom of the shed and obscuring the view. When I started going regularly the normal position that Roy and I took up was in the far left-hand corner of the CBL next to the turnstiles from where you could transfer into the seats; we therefore stood behind a fence that divided the CBL from the seats. In latter years, we reverted to a position to the left of the Halfway Line to stand with a gang of Roy's mates, again standing to the right of the dividing metal fence, just beneath a police observation box. Therefore, my seminal years found me in positions that all had restricted views for some reason. I don't actually think that I had a clear view of a game unhampered by fences until I took up a new position in the middle of the CBL with my schoolmates in the early 1970s. So at least I had a few years' grace before the pitch-side perimeter fences went up and, once again, my vision was impaired.

From the early seventies onwards the CBL was to become my permanent home for the rest of the Old Den's natural life. Obviously, over the years I had call to stand or sit in other parts of the ground. Colin, an old school friend who is now a New Den season ticket-holder even though he lives in Dorset, initially used to stand on the South Lower Stand terracing with his dad Bob before being forced by the installation of the seating on to the Dog Track end and I occasionally stood with them on this terrace.

I also stood under the shed on the Halfway Line a few times, a very good spot to lambast any hapless TV commentators and their chums who sat high on the makeshift rickety gantry that used to be erected above this section for any televised games. In all my 27 years ago at the Old Den, I only sat down twice, both in the lower section.

Don't Fence Me In

In the early 1970s matches nationwide were awash with pitch invasions. However, even though the Old Den pitchside wall was low, unthreatening and climbable, away fan invasions didn't happen at Millwall. This was because we had a 'Tony Martin dealing with a burglar' type of mentality and anybody who went pitchside to confront us would find half the home crowd joining them.

The Old Den native rituals combined with the 'riot' at the much publicised Ipswich Town FA Cup Quarter-Final 1-6 defeat on 11/3/1978 led to the enforced erection of the Old Den perimeter and segregation fencing. This game had a Wild West shoot-out show as entertainment, no wonder there was trouble! I don't recall the Ipswich trouble being that bad; mind you I was in the comfort zone of the CBL. Nevertheless it prompted the FA to close the Old Den from 26/3/1978 to 9/4/1978, with one game against Bristol Rovers on April Fool's Day being played at Portsmouth.

FA Cup games had to be played away for an initial two-season period, which was reduced on appeal; additionally the club were fined £1500 and banned from selling alcohol in the ground. It also led to the Ilderton Road end becoming an away-fan-only area, with the smattering of away fans now snug as a bug in a rug in their total exclusion zone accompanied by a policeman each, with home fans nowhere near them. Perimeter/segregation fences were naturally an attempt to keep rabid hordes like ourselves out or in, whichever you prefer and whilst this fencing was obviously boom-time for fence erectors, it meant that we fans were now effectively in cages. It became an era when live football-watching was a real restricted view, often a claustrophobic experience at best, particularly on a crowded day. It was also obligatory to drape the pitchside fences with country and club flags; consequently, even if you could originally see through the fence, you now had to try to peer through a flag as well. This meant that the old policy of passing kids to the front for a better view was now pointless as the closer you got to the pitch the worse the view got.

The new pitchside barriers had to be approved for severity by the football League; as a result, over the years the Old Den had various nasty types of fencing tried. From what I saw at other grounds Millwall probably had the worst of these type of fences, some just shy of a middle-age torture chamber's Iron Maiden. Not the band, that would've been too much punishment! The ever-lovely rotating spikes were my particular favourite, why they didn't just put up razor wire or broken glass and be done with it I don't know.

In addition to nasty perimeter fencing we had the added intrusion of the football League-sponsored CCTV cameras, fairly primitive at the time I'd imagine compared to today's state-of-the-art equipment, where it's probably more like the film *Sliver* with a naked and soaped-up Sharon Stone... sorry, wandered there for a minute. The matchday programmes from the mid-1970s onwards would carry photographs of the all-new CCTV systems with dire warnings about coin throwers, etc, now being captured on the 1984-style cameras and being banned from the ground.

I WAS BORN UNDER THE COLD BLOW LANE

As the years passed they constructed segregation fencing/cages on the Dog Track end to allow the home fans back on to this terrace. The away fans were then given a corner terrace section situated next to their posh chums who sat in the away corner of the grandstand. Leicester fans attempted to sue Millwall for their away cage restricted view, bloody cheek. I recall one particular game when there were Millwall fans next to the away fans; this was against Bristol City on the 27/10/1984, when two Millwall fans attempted to scale the fences to get into the away section, prompting the City fans to flee like lemmings looking for a cliff. I assume that they expected a large-scale assault or perhaps the two assailants were rabid and frothing at the mouth? We couldn't see from where we stood at the opposite end. This was the infamous CB radio game when Millwall ambushed Bristol's coaches. This two-man assault and the subsequent Bristol evacuation was quite comical to watch, it certainly made the away return fixture interesting.

The whole of the Dog Track end was given over to any team with either a very large turnout or a trouble reputation. For these games home fans were once again not allowed on to this end. The police used this isolation tactic for the visit of Leeds United on 9/11/1985. Even so, there were missiles, including lumps of wood, thrown from the Halfway Line into the away section and there was mayhem outside. The aggro at this game prompted the FA to impose an 'all-ticket' policy, whereby we had to buy tickets for home games in advance, up to a maximum of two per person.

It was this palaver that prompted me to get my first ever season ticket, as it made it much easier to go to the games without having to go to the bother of having to get an advance ticket. This ticket policy was in place post-9th November until mid-March 1986 and meant that our crowd plummeted as a result. Moving forward in time to 2002/03 - plummeting crowds and ticketing problems, does this sound familiar?

You can understand the numerous restrictions I suppose; mind you what do you expect from a club whose fans initially had East End roots and later a South East London following? The working-class dockside environment was the main source of Millwall's fans, hence the docker mentality being well to the fore; please remember that the Docklands actually used to contain docks years ago.

Travel

My early days of going to the Old Den would consist of Roy and me making a mad last minute car dash from Stepney through the Rotherhithe Tunnel, more often than not after 2pm. Anyone who drove to the ground invariably had to park their car in the surrounding streets because a football ground car park wasn't exactly pre-requisite at the time, so we would usually park up on the road that wound between New Cross station and Southwark Park, often on a grass verge. We would then have to bomb along past the student flats behind the railway lines and through the always-welcoming dark railway arches before emerging on the Halfway Line side of the Cold Blow Lane. Never was there a more evocative and apt name. We would then dash to the turnstiles to take up a place on the terraces a few minutes before kick-off.

At one match on a wet rainy day, we parked on the grass verge and went to the game. When we returned to the car after the match we found that our attempts to dismount the verge, which was now sodden, led to a comedy-style wheel-spin routine. The more we tried the more entrenched we got and the more mud we were spraying in all directions, but mostly all over a once-pristine white car next to us. This resulted in this car bearing all the hallmarks of a damned good mud dashing. Luckily, we managed to eventually dislodge ourselves and drive off before the car owners returned. If this was your car in the late sixties, now you know, sorry!

Roy stopped going in the mid-1970s after professing not to return until they stopped playing Harry Cripps, I think it's safe to come back now! Even so, he's not been back to Millwall since. When Roy stopped going I went by tube, I preferred this to driving because you then got a steadily building atmosphere as you meandered through the winding residential streets that led to the ground, especially from New Cross Gate station. As you got closer to the stadium, you could hear the gradually increasing crowd noises and the PA announcements would become clearer, serving to heighten your sense of anticipation. The route via New Cross

I WAS BORN UNDER THE COLD BLOW LANE

Gate also led you past the weirdest graffiti of all time, on a wall at the top of Brocklehurst Street it said 'Lesbians Ignite'. I'm sure they would if their vibrators short-circuited. I imagine the residents in the houses that we passed must have longed for match days. I'm sure that their location so close to the Old Den must have made their properties highly sought after, I don't think.

There were a few interesting Tube-related incidents over the years. We played Arsenal in a second leg League Cup tie in the 1990s, a trip which led me into direct contact with a contingent of Arsenal's 'Boys' at Whitechapel. Despite my Millwall insignia, they seemingly had bigger fish to fry, as I was able to stand amongst them waiting for my mates outside the station unimpeded; my main reason for mentioning it though was a return journey that bore all the hallmarks of the '*Keystone Cops* meet *The Thin Blue Line*'.

The first game at Highbury had finished in a draw, as did the Old Den game; consequently, the game went in to extra time and eventually penalties, which we lost. Irrespective of the delay in the time the match finished, the police had their travel plans set in stone and that was that. Their idea was to ferry the Gooners from New Cross Gate non-stop to Moorgate. With the Arsenal fans being held in the ground, we Millwall fans naturally arrived first, without an Arsenal fan in sight. We obviously thought that once we informed the police of the situation they would revise their travel plans, let us go on our usual Whitechapel route and run the Moorgate special when the Gunners actually arrived. Sadly unfazed by the now nonsensical nature of their original travel plan, they bundled a platform load of Millwall supporters on to the train, which then sped off across the river, sailed through the East End and didn't stop until it arrived at Moorgate. We all then had to cross over to the eastbound platform to get a train back to where we had just whizzed through. police intelligence? I rest my case.

It was a regular occurrence to head eastwards, with a large contingent of Millwall 'Boys' heading to the mainline stations to kick it off with any returning London Clubs or homebound away fans whose team had played in London. This East London Line Hoolie tube trip had the added bonus of a more than likely tear up with West Ham's 'Boys' en route to the selected terminus.

In December 1987, during our championship season, I got locked on New Cross Gate station to allow a Manchester City 'special' to empty out and be taken to the ground in safety. We gathered Lions were held behind closed doors while the Mancs got preferential treatment, which we were none too pleased about as you can imagine. It all went off outside the Cold Blow Lane away alley, so that was a bloody waste of time, wasn't it?

Finally, I was waiting on Shadwell Station for my southbound East London line train for a game against Kevin Keegan's Newcastle United. The train pulled in and it was crammed to the gunwales with pissed--up Geordies. As the doors opened the fumes from the mobile Newcastle Brown Ale Brewery overcame me. Now I like a drink, God alone knows, but just inhaling the fumes that emanated from this Toon Army pisshead express meant that I didn't need a drink myself. I declined their kind offers to join them on board largely because I was now too mullered by their fumes to be able to find the train doors.

Drink!!

Before they brought in football ground prohibition it was possible to buy an alcoholic drink at the Old Den, more often than not to top-up the booze that many people had already had in the pubs near the ground. In the CBL, there was a bar at the back of the stand where you could get a beer in a plastic glass, if that makes sense? There were no real glasses as that might have been a bit dodgy. If you bought a drink you then had to try to get it back to your position intact, good luck.

This was a real adventure as a plastic glass is quite squeezable in the first place and therefore liable to spill its content with the slightest tightening of your grip. If you combine this with the people sitting on the terrace, hidden amongst those who remained standing, you then certainly needed your wits about you in order to get back to your place; it was a bit like a challenge on *Don't Try This At Home*. The usual result of this navigation through the human obstacle course was that you'd get back to your spot shaken and needing a drink only to find that you now only had half the contents left if you were lucky, the rest having been spilt in transit.

I WAS BORN UNDER THE COLD BLOW LANE

Someone who had obviously managed to get enough booze on board prompted the following scenario-

In the 1980s, I used to go to home and away matches with schoolmate Steve Kimberley. At one game at the Old Den, we stood minding our own business on a sweltering hot day when we heard the following conversation behind us: 'You all right?', 'Yeah!' followed by 'HUGHIE!'. As the respondent spewed up all over our backs, doing a bloody good impression of Regan in *The Exorcist* and her projectile vomiting. You cannot beat a hot day with a steaming pavement pizza on your back in my book.

If, like our sick chum, you managed to get enough beer inside, or outside, of the ground, you then had the necessity of taking your full bladder on a toilet trip. The usual scenario was that you may get out of the ground to the open-air toilets but, with the inevitable feelings of relief of having done what a man has to do, you now had to get back to your spot. This was usually accomplished with the assistance of a chorus of 'Excuse me mate' accompanied by a gentle hand on the shoulder. Even so it was still like trying to negotiate a bargain hunt at the January sales in an effort to get back to your mates.

If you didn't fancy this scenario you could always adopt the 'Stand and Deliver' alternative, the rolled-up newspaper method, which was great for those in front of you, especially at the very front as a tidal wave of piss headed their way to cries of 'Surf's up!'. Just joshing, it was more likely that some people in front of you would end up with a suspiciously damp back of the leg. If you did use the newspaper method you also had to try to explain to the wife or girlfriend why you had black ink all around your old chap come lurve time.

PS. the newspaper method should not be used in an all-seater stadium. Another alternative I suppose was that you could ask a nearby policeman if you could borrow his helmet for a bit - perhaps not.

The Old Den Old Bill

The emergence of violence at the Old Den, and nationwide, seemed to put the police totally on the back foot. In the early days their shambolic unreadiness for what was gathering apace around them, in a football sense, meant that initially the bovver boys had carte blanche to run amok at will. It was an era where ill-prepared coppers seemed to be fighting the Hooligan tide with a 'Hello, hello what's all this here then?' attitude and with only a trusty whistle, truncheon and a shiny helmet for company. In an attempt to combat the 'early in ground' Boot Boy traditions, the police formed snatch squads, a source of great fun in the early days.

Before the segregation fencing went up the snatchers used to do a comical 'Will they? Won't they?' ejection tug-o-war game across the low pitchside wall with the home fans, who tried to pull the ejectee back. This happened on a regular basis in the CBL and was always a joy to watch. Once the nasty perimeter fences went up the police merely walked the offenders down to the front of the terrace and took them out through the emergency evacuation gates or via a back exit - where's the fun in that? It became a frequent sight at the Old Den to see a steady stream of ejectees paraded around the cinder track, ejection walk-pasts met with either mass abuse or praise, depending on who the ejectees were affiliated with. Often the crowd chanted 'Naughty Boy, Naughty Boy, Naughty Boy!'. Ejections were always a good time to watch the different personalities of the offenders, who were usually being held in an arm lock or led by the arm by a couple of constables.

However they were restrained you'd then see them either:

1) Go quietly, head bowed and ashamed.

2) Give it the big one and try to wrestle several burly coppers to escape, invariably in vain.

3) Treat an ejection as though it were a parade and wave to their friends in the crowd.

Having completed their cinder track walk-pasts, the poor soul who had been nabbed by the Fuzz would either be bundled back into their correct end or more likely be marched out of the ground to the waiting Black Mariah, in the back of which they could enjoy a spot of some 'Honest Sarge he fell down the stairs!' treatment.

In the last decade or so of the Old Den, I stood at the centre back of the CBL close to the exits, just to the left of the usually boisterous but non-violent kids. They would often bounce about, sway and surge forward, creating the human avalanches that I referred to earlier, to accompany their singing. It seemed that it was police policy at the time to nick or eject as many of these kids as possible, presumably to top up their figures and thereby justify their presence. It seemed that they had an 'easy pinch' policy whereby they only ejected kids, sometimes merely for over-exuberance after we had scored a goal.

The usual state of play in the CBL was that after any bouncing or surges had taken place, several hefty policemen would arrive and wade through the crowd as if they were in pursuit of a criminal mastermind. They would then emerge with a youth who was about eight stone, wringing wet. Obviously, these *Chitty Chitty Bang Bang* childcatcher-style ejections elicited a less than favourable response from us adult home fans. We invariably responded with sarcastic applause and ironic comments like 'Well done officers, you're a credit to us all!'. We used to question why it appeared that the police only ejected what looked like soft targets, whilst leaving us big lump adults alone, especially strange because we had been acting in much the same manner. We never got an answer but it seemed that ejecting someone who might resist was just too much bother, so kids it was.

Outside the ground, police started using horses for crowd control and they quickly found that they had to equip the poor creatures with protective goggles to prevent damage from flying missiles. However, this didn't prevent people rolling marbles underneath them to bring them down or tossing fireworks at them to scare them.

The introduction of police cavalry brought a bonus for any gardening enthusiast who lived near to the ground though - as a by-product the horses would invariably leave a street full of horseshit in their wake. Any budding Alan Titchmarsh merely had to listen out for the horses clippety clops, come out of their house and simply follow the steaming swishy horse tails, armed with a bucket and a shovel, to gather up their plippity plops. They would then have enough manure to keep their prized begonias in tip-top nick for weeks.

The first real technological police innovation that I can recall was the 'Hoolievan', the work of a genius. It was impervious to marbles underneath it, that was for sure. Apart from the all ticket roadblocks in the 1980s, I don't ever recall the Old Den reaching the saturation police levels of today, even at the height of the Boot Boy era, although we did have probably the most high-visibility police box in the League.

'You're The Referee At The Den!!'

Being chosen to officiate at Millwall must have been seen as the shitty end of the stick, as it were, imagine the sheer terror of a referee hearing the phrase 'You've been picked to referee at Millwall'.

A referee was an Old Den favourite, as you probably well know, sharing bottom billing along with the Linesmen and the police in any popularity poll. Referees were about as popular as traffic wardens, an unpopularity due to several factors:

A) Anti-Millwall bias.

B) Having a chip on their shoulder.

C) Incompetence (a phrase that covers a multitude of sins).

D) Physical imperfection.

E) All of the above.

Naturally, over the years we were treated to all that refereeing had to offer; we had the short, the bald, the old, the ginger, the fat, the 'F... the rules, let's get on with it!' types, the overly fussy or officious and the just plain useless. Many also arrived with an attitude of 'They won't intimidate me!'. This led to Millwall at home having a vast collection of 'Away Town Harrys', in complete contrast to, say, Manchester United or Liverpool's 'Home Town Harrys'. We had very few refs who did the 'good' refereeing trick of not being noticed and using common sense.

Due to their ineptitude, referees invariably had to face a barrage of ironic cheering and clapping for any decision that went our way accompanied by a deluge of noises and finger pointing for any throw in or free kick positioned incorrectly, as highlighted by the Old Den crowd's irate response that greeted any attempt by the opposition to steal the merest inch (sorry, 2.54 cm) at a throw-in or free kick. If allowed to pass this would be seen as the referee letting them get away with murder and was confirmation that the officials were all part of a League-wide conspiracy against us. This would lead to 'No One Likes Us' welling up with gusto to show our solidarity against the referee's injustice - isn't paranoia wonderful?

What I used to hate at the Old Den was the wall of sound, whistling crescendo or the deluge of 'Oi, Oi, Oi's' that greeted any controversial refereeing decision or away goalie's goal kick. The whistling would sound like a thousand old style kettles all coming to the boil at once. This would also be used to complement the 'Blow Your Whistle, Blow Your Whistle Referee, Time's Up' type chants. The indignant 'Oi's' and 'Arghs!' would continue on and on and end up sounding like the collective voices of the damned, probably very apt. Both of these events did my ears no good whatsoever. During my youth I used to go to numerous heavy metal and rock gigs and as such was prone to a decent bout of tinnitus already. I was a little like 'I heard that, pardon?' anyway without this additional eardrum assault.

With a Millwall Crowd's in-built sense of injustice, persecution complex, overall passion, siege mentality and 'They are all out to get us' attitude, I can't imagine being an official was or is too easy. Just ask referee Norman Burtenshaw against Aston Villa in 1969 or Gerald Colyer, a linesman against Cardiff City in 1975, both of whom were 'hands on' victims of the crowd at the Old Den.

The best documented case of what it was like to be an official at the Old Den was shown on Channel 4's *Football Stories - The Man in Black*, a documentary about top referee and public school housemaster David Elleray and his experiences of running the line or refereeing at the old ground. If you can get a bigger contrast than a public school and the Old Den I'd like to hear about it.

Elleray said that as an Old Den linesman it was always advisable to wear your spare second kit to run the line as you'd invariably be spat on and have drinks thrown at you all afternoon. He said that it was like running a gauntlet up and down the touchline for the whole of the match, especially in front of the Halfway Line. He told a story about a game when a bloke followed him up and down the touchline saying something like 'Look at me, linesman; I want you to remember my face because the next time you see it's when you die!'. That should get him on our side! A less violent tradition carries on to this day with the modern penchant for booing the officials as they warm-up pre-match home-and-away.

Elleray was also the experimental guinea pig chosen for a miking-up experiment when we played Arsenal in 1989 in the old First Division and he was wired for sound and filmed. The C4 documentary showed him conversing with Arsenal players after he'd waved play on following what look like a perfectly good 'over the line' Arsenal goal after a goalmouth scramble. The ensuing discussion saw Tony Adams run past him and call him a 'F...ing cheat!', prompting David to go into full public school housemaster mode. He blew his whistle, called Big Tone over to him and admonished him like a small schoolboy, telling him to stand up straight while he spoke to him and rebuking him for his 'Cheat' accusation. He did end with a brutally honest phrase - 'We may be useless but we don't cheat!'

Well at least he admitted they were useless.

Another Millwall practice at the Old Den to pacify and encourage referees was to inquire as to who was having their evil way with the referee's wife while he was busy making our lives a misery, hence this olden day chant - 'Referee, Your Old Lady Is A Whore!'

The usual adulterous suspects were -

A) The ref's best mate.

B) The milkmen.

This always helped to keep them on their toes and eased back on the injury time that they added on, because they were keen to dash home to find out what their missus was up to. For further examples of the high regard that referees are held in at Millwall see the 'Who's The Wanker In The Black?' in the 'Karaoke Dokey' and the away sections later on.

Kick, Bollock And Bite

Generally the Millwall crowd's mentality was and still is, give a hundred percent, sweat blood and you've no problem, fanny about and beware - it's Phil Barber time! Our crowd's favourite players over the years have generally consisted of a certain type, those that epitomise the title and who reflect the fans wholehearted (Mad) approach.

The Old Den crowd would cheer to the echo the type of player who perfectly reflected the crowd's mentality. I thought I'd list some of my favourites some of whom spanned both Dens.

Harry Cripps aka 'Arry boy, or as we used to know him 'Put Him In The Stand 'Arry!' which he used to do frequently when faced with a hapless nippy winger. To me he was also memorable for his frantic forward forays, his red-faced and puffing return trots back to defence and *The Ballad Of Harry Cripps* single.

My secondary school was essentially a basketball and rugby school, it was a grammar school albeit in the East End so we couldn't be too grand. Nevertheless, football was considered a bit low coarse and vulgar by the school, so it was difficult for us to have an official team.When we did have football practice at Fairlop in Essex we were often coached by 'Arry Boy and Dennis Burnett combined, both of whom played for the Lions at the time.

In fact, Harry once refereed our self-selected school side in a schools' Cup game. This was when we had picked the team ourselves from the house sides and asked for permission to enter a local schools Cup competition. In this particular game, I played in goal and Harry allowed any number of highly dubious opposition goals to stand. That's boyhood heroes for you. We lost something like 5-2 so that's my excuse anyway.

R.I.P Harry Cripps.

Barry Kitchener: Millwall to the bone and the best-uncapped centre-half that I've ever seen. Sadly, I'm old enough to remember his debut, which does date me somewhat. In addition to his 'Ra, Ra, Zigger Zagger Kitchener!' chant Barry also used to have a Hare Krishna style chant 'Barry Kitchener, Barry Kitchener, Barry Kitchener, Barry Barry!' It was a shame that people didn't form a Kitch Cult; they could then have marched around the West End dressed up to look like Barry instead of poncing about in orange robes with tambourines.

I recall a couple of Old Den incidents that summed up Barry's mentality perfectly. In 1978/79, we played Preston North End at home in the last game of the season and needed to win something like 20-0 to avoid relegation. Barry decided to lead the line by playing up front in a typically gung-ho performance. Unfortunately, despite his valiant efforts, we lost 2-0 and went down to the then Third Division, a game played out in front of only 2,833 fans.

The other on-field incident that I recall was a night match at home in the late 60s/early 70s when Barry kicked Sheffield United's goalkeeper from the edge of the six-yard box into the net. He wheeled away to claim the goal only to find that the referee had disallowed it. Appalled that the ref had seen some infringement Barry said something like 'But the ball was loose, ref!' to which the ref probably replied 'I think that you will find that was the goalkeeper's head, Barry!'.

Bloody referees, or in this case bloody Alan Hodgkinson, it looked like a good goal to me at the time and I'm not even remotely biased. We bumped into Barry after the Auto Windscreen Final outside Wembley and we got talking to him and what a nice bloke he was too. He used to run a souvenir shop in Caister-On-Sea, selling 'Kiss Me Quick' hats, lilos, buckets and spades, etc, that one of my mates Clive once went into it when on holiday there.

Now Barry either had no customers, a thing for blondes, which Clive is, or a great memory because he remembered Clive from this visit. That's customer service for you. To my mind, his only fault is that his first name is spelt wrong.

Terry Hurlock aka 'Terry's Gonna Get Ya!'. Despite his curly locks and the fact that in his non-Millwall games he was roundly Gypo'd by us, I don't remember him being subject to any 'Cooeing!'

Terry was so hard that he could play in a pink Tutu and with ribbons in his hair and I for one wouldn't have mentioned it. Hard but fair, usually, and much underrated to my way of thinking, forming what I consider my Millwall-era best midfield partnership with Les Briley, another largely unsung Millwall hero of mine. They invariably played outnumbered week in week out, especially in the old First Division, where they more than held their own.

Terry inspired the 'Hurlock: Just When You Thought It Was Safe To Go On A Football Pitch' T-shirts with 'Feed Them To The

Lions' on the back, widely sold at the Old Den. He frightened the life out of Wimbledon's 'Hard Man' Vinnie Jones when we played them. Terry should be a Hollywood star, not him! He was also responsible for uttering a phrase that I had never heard before or since - 'That's two weeks up me ribs!' Pardon? This was in a post-match interview after he'd received a club fine for being sent off early in his New Den return against Leicester. The epitome of a Millwall player and a true reflection of us fans.

Keith 'Rhino' Stevens aka 'Rhino's Gonna Get Ya!', who got his name from his habit of attacking Range Rovers. A man who was another perfect example of our fan mentality, a sort of fans' representative on the pitch. It was he who along with Alan McLeary brought Millwall back to life post-Nicholl, Bonds, etc. In my opinion, he should still be at the club in some capacity.

Worship for the cult of Rhino did prompt one loony to wear a rubber rhino suit in an executive box close to the CBL at the New Den a few years back; rather like the furry Lion suits on the Blackburn promotion day and the Old Den's final day this must have seemed like a good idea at the time.

Rhino - Millwall through and through and one of us.

Some other players who were Millwall personified:

Alf Wood, mad as a loon, 'tasched up and in where the boots were flying, for a slightly more modern reference see 1980s player Kevin Bremner. Not forgetting John 'Fash The Bash' Fashanu.

Ooh Bop! Fashion

My Old Den life encompassed the terrace fashions of the skinhead/suedehead era - Ben Sherman's, or Brutus, Jaytex and Stradbroke if poor. Dr Marten boots, rolled-up Levi's, braces and Harrington jackets, with the winter collection containing a Crombie overcoat, set off by a natty silk pocket-handkerchief as the obligatory accessory. If required you could also add a trilby hat for that added bit of style.

There were also donkey jackets, the more fashionable of which had the orange plastic back/shoulder sections ideally with a local council's initials on them; this was the height of workman chic at the time. Following the original Hoolie era we had the suedehead then casual era, the latter prompting the wearing of Lacoste and Pringle, etc. One thing you used to see years ago at the Old Den, were people who had presumably been on holiday in the States wearing Detroit Lions merchandise. You still see this in isolation today,

The most bizarre fashion was the emergence of white butcher coats. I wonder who first thought that writing your club affiliation all over a white coat was a good idea? It certainly made the old 'Got the time mate?' quiz irrelevant, as your club affinity was written all over the bloody thing. Talking of blood, these white coats could end up looking like a real butcher's coat after the wearer had suffered a Stanley attack. Equally bizarre was who decided that a meticulously buffed, lovingly polished pair of Ox blood/Black Dr Martens would now look better customised with an aerosol and spray-painted in gold or silver?

There was one bonus to this fashion during the Bovver Boy era. The newly-decorated 12-lacehole boots, steel toecap variety or otherwise, could naturally still be used for a good kicking. However, they now also had the added benefit that if that wasn't painful enough, the lead in the paint would now give the victim lead poisoning as well, so that was good.

There was a game when Millwall's 'Boys' wore blue surgical masks in the Ilderton Road end and another game when they appeared to be wearing something like Bulgarian Army hats. They were in truth deerstalkers, worn by Millwall's boys, presumably the South London branch of the Sherlock Holmes appreciation society. There was also a period when ski hats were all the rage. Whilst technically superior in knitting technology to bobble hats, they still left the wearer looking like a complete pilchard no matter how hard they tried to manipulate it in to a fashionable shape. I must admit that I still have one; I bought it outside Palace many years ago when it was pouring with rain and I stood on the open Holmesdale away terrace. I ended up with a blue head from the bloody thing; still, it served me right for buying it.

Millwall ski hats carried a Millwall logo, with a Union Jack or a Scottish club badge, usually the Old Firm. Strangely, no Queen of the South. Showing an Old Firm affinity on your hat led to a

CBL practice. On dull no-opposition days the crowd would chant 'Celtic' or 'Rangers' depending on hat affiliation and then steam into each other, keeping up their combat readiness.

A Few Old Den Era Memories

Here are some Old Den memories, in no particular order:

There was our East End-based Scottish jam workers birthright, which led to our adopting the rampant Lion flags and looking like the Tartan Army many years ago.

There was our olden day motto 'We Fear No Foe Where E'er We Go', which you still see on baseball caps today, and the more recent motto 'No One Likes Us '.

There was the time when we used to play midweek home games on Monday night and frequently played pre-season friendlies against Scottish sides in the 1960s.

There was the day that the victorious Millwall Lionesses paraded their trophies, as it were!

At the Old Den, sarcasm was rife. For example, whenever a policeman, linesman or ball boy showed more skill when kicking the ball back into play than the players on the pitch did, i.e. during the reign of Peter Anderson, we would often sing 'Sign Him Up!'.

There were the Sunday markets.

There was the time when we moaned about a lack of ambition at Millwall especially in the 1970s, when the phrases 'We've Found Our Level' and 'They Don't Want to Go Up!' were much bandied about, especially prevalent in the Fenton/Purser era. An impression not helped by what looked like a 'Help Thy Neighbour' policy, whereby if we were safe in mid-table going nowhere and neighbouring Londoners were struggling, we often seemed to roll over rather conveniently, gifting them very useful points with an especially inept performance, most noticeably away at Leyton Orient and Fulham. It happened too frequently to be accidental.

It also always seemed during this era that Millwall had one of two types of season - either we would start the season very well, coming in like a Lion, only to end it like a Lamb or we would come in like a Lamb and finish like a Lion. This seemed to be the way of the 'Wall; we were consistent in our inconsistency, hence the frequent wrecking of chairman Micky Purser's car showroom.

Following the 1985 riot we were obviously banned from Luton, so our next game there was beamed back live to the Old Den. This was on a particularly sunny afternoon with the video screen showing our victory on the surreal Astroturf. I went to the game to do my rant at the TV for the first and only time. Sadly, due to the sunny conditions, size of the screen and its far away positioning in the farthest corner from the CBL in front of Jews' Hill, it meant that you practically had to guess what was happening.

There was the emergence of the first black players at Millwall - Trevor Lee and Phil Walker in 1975/76 when we also conversely gained a racist reputation due to monkey chants and banana throwing. In truth, this sort of thing was the norm at the time and was happening nationwide; it merely mirrored a social trend. However, it wasn't helped by the presence of National Front and The League of St George activists at the Old Den trying to tap in to Millwall's perceived racist feelings by selling their literature like *National Front News*, *Bulldog* and *Phoenix* openly outside the ground. The presence of fascist groups at football grounds was certainly not only a Millwall thing it was widespread in both London and at many inner city clubs. This was an era when these groups considered a football/hooligan crowd as ideal recruiting grounds. Even so it was this period of time that probably earmarked Millwall as a racist club, a perception that will probably perpetuate forevermore, even though we were, and are, no worse than many other sides. Still, give a dog (or Lion) a bad name and all that. Anyway, for people of my vintage, 'Tiny' was black, wasn't he?

To continue my ramble there was German ace Karl-Heinz Rummenigge's career highlight when he visited the Old Den with Swiss side Servette, when we were in the old First Division.

There were the regular occasions at very crowded games when PA man Les said 'Please move along inside, there are many more waiting to come in'. This was just what I wanted to hear as I was already going blue in the crush. These latecomers were usually the post-pub brigade.

I WAS BORN UNDER THE COLD BLOW LANE

There was seemingly a tradition at crowded games to announce mathematically bizarre attendance figures. It was packed to the gunwales only for a low crowd then to be announced, to the amazement of everyone packed in the ground. There were also the customs of bunging the turnstile man, bunking-in and those that used to stroll in for free when the gates opened with 10 minutes left, presumably having walked around from Jews' Hill. All of which naturally had no bearing on the crowd count. A good example of eccentric crowd counting was exhibited by the crowd at our 4-1 Championship day celebration defeat by Blackburn Rovers on 7/5/1988. For this game I stood on the CBL on my own, as my then Millwall companion Steve Kimberley for some reason didn't want to go. I decided to stand near to the front to avoid being behind the masses of flags being waved about and I was standing next to a middle-aged bloke who said to me 'Blimey it's crowded, I've been here when the crowd was 40,000 and it wasn't this packed!' Naturally, the crowd was then announced as 15,467 plus flags! Mind you, the era that this man was talking about was pre-segregation.

This was the same day when during the post-match celebrations Johnny Doc said 'Sing Ya Bastards!' to the players as they gathered in front of the CBL to take our acclaim, as shown on the club video. According to Tony Cascarino, the whole team apparently played this game pissed following a celebratory night on the town, which explains a lot.

There was the time when we used to play 'throw the ball back' to try to knock a copper's helmet off at games.

There was the time when they switched the intro theme from *Let 'Em Come* to the olden days *Shoeshine Boy*, a Bing Crosby song from something like 1936, which naturally didn't work as you had to be at least 60 at the time to remember it.

There was the time when they switched 'Bye For Now Les' for a plummy voiced Bob Danvers Walker-type, who used to say things like 'So at the Vetch Field it's the Swans from Swansea nil and the Hornets from Watford one'. This was just too much information, it was like a geographical 'Name the grounds tour'. He didn't last long and Les returned.

There was the time in the early 1980s when they used to produce the *Pride* newspaper with forewords by the likes of Des O'Connor, Tommy Steele, etc.

There was the annual ritual of end-of-season pitch invasions that very often ruined any laps of honour by the team. These invasions often led to the players being surrounded, manhandled and sometimes stripped down, often ending up in only their jockstraps. On celebratory days, if the invasion spoilt the party, the invaders would be told to get off in no uncertain terms. The most famous modern(ish), pitch invasion was the 29/4/1972 Preston 'Promotion' one. As per usual the jungle drums got it wrong when they said that Birmingham had lost, way off the mark, sadly. However, we didn't know this so cheering and premature hysteria crept around the ground.

Many people spilt from the terraces over the low pitch sidewall and on to the cinder tracks. As more people gathered behind the goals the nets were being strained to the limit by the pressing weight of all of the fans behind them, which prompted a 'F... This I'm Off!' decision by the referee, whose final whistle led to a mass pitch invasion of jubilation. I clambered over the low wall and on to the muddy pitch to join the swarm, my first and only time.

We had our euphoric 'We're In Division One!' bubble burst by the pinprick of reality as the truth emerged that Birmingham hadn't lost and we eventually finished third. This was at a time when it was only the top two that gained automatic promotion, with no second chance via the play-offs.

There were the games played around Bonfire Night that inevitably heralded a glut of loud bangs and mini explosions, with each one greeted with a cheer from the home fans.

There was the period in the early 1970s when we had to play games on weekday afternoons during the three-day week when electricity rationing, caused by the coal miners, power and electricity strikes, meant that the floodlights couldn't be used. My most memorable game during this period was the League Cup Quarter-Final against Norwich City, a 1-1 draw on 19/12/1973, when Canaries goalkeeper Kevin Keelan put on a one-man 'They Shall Not Pass' performance to gain a draw and take us back to

Carrow Road, where we lost the replay 2-1. In order to attend these afternoon games instead of going to school and doing games, it was necessary to get a note from my mum/dad along the lines of 'Barrie cannot come to games today because...' I then had to remind them not to write 'He's going to Millwall' to end the excuse.

There was the first game in the old Division 1 against Derby County when free plastic commemorative key rings were handed out, which I naturally lost on a drunken night out.

There was the fancy-dressed climbing display by the loony known as the 'Lion on the Roof' for obvious reasons.

There was the game when ex-Chairman Alan Thorne handed out hot drinks to away fans as a peace gesture.

On the football front I saw two 6-1 home defeats to Ipswich Town and the mighty Grimsby Town and I saw Bobby Charlton's management career at Preston North End crash to earth with a bang when we beat them 5-1 on 22/10/1973. Not forgetting Saturday 1/10/1988, the famous day that we beat QPR 3-2 to go top of the old Division 1.

Last but not least, many thanks to Wrigleys for enabling me to buy hundreds of packets of chewing gum over the years. I have sampled the full range from Juicy Fruit through to sugar-free Orbit. I worked on the principle of the more high-pressure the game the more packets I'd require. This theory enabled me to get through my agitated CBL-induced state much easier. How I wished for Valium-flavoured gum to calm my Old Den 'whipped up into a lather' nerves at times.

Goodbye Old Friend - 8th May 1993

My own personal association with the Old Den ended after almost 27 years at the last ever game against Bristol Rovers. A premature euthanasia of the old place, according to many at the time. Whatever the cause, we had to move and the final day was a truly emotional one for anyone who had seen the Old Den as a second home for any length of time.

For me the day started as my mate Simon and I made our usual trip to New Cross Gate station. On the tube we got talking to some Bristol Rovers fans, who seemed very apprehensive about the likely outcome of our forced eviction fearing a 'Watch it come down' demolition derby. We tried to calm them saying that we thought it would be more of a carnival atmosphere, although in truth we didn't know if it would be a Carnival Of Horrors or a joyous, if tearful day. We told them that it wouldn't matter if we won or lost, as the event was much bigger than the game. They took our word for it and, like gatecrashers at a party, they headed for their away pen to watch it unfold. It seemed on this day that everyone had taken up their usual most favoured position wherever possible, in order to watch the Old Den die and to contemplate what life would be like at the new place. Simon headed to his spot and I myself took up my customary CBL location.

The day itself had flags, balloon releases, a parade of old heroes and an inevitable defeat. It was also a day when there were numerous people in fancy dress, all now sweating profusely. Putting on a thick heavy Lion costume must have seemed like a good idea at the time but they must have regretted their decision when these suits turned into a furry sauna.

The game flew by and the end came with the customary turmoil of pitch invasions and a primitive style de-turfing, culminating in a mud and grass-slinging frenzy, with the pitch eventually looking like it was suffering from galloping alopecia. In the frantic scramble to find something to take as a memento before Uncle Reg's 'Everything Must Be Sold/One Careless Owner' car boot sale came into play, the impromptu house clearance continued unabated. My own favourite memory of the day was when a bloke standing near to me at the back of the CBL decided to steal the ground regulations sign. I said to him 'If you look on there mate, I'm sure that there must be a regulation that says "Do not steal this sign!".'' When the mayhem abated it was time to gaze upon the old place for the final time and to let your Millwall life pass through your mind. In many cases grown men stood in silence and wept before heading to the pub for a post-Old Den wake.

When I arrived at the pub it seemed that there were an awful lot of keen gardeners all of a sudden. It was like an Alan Titchmarsh returf your lawn day, where everyone seemed to have bags full of Old Den grass or turf. Those who didn't have a bag seemed to be utilising a ripped out seat as a carrying aid for their turf. What the people who took the goal posts did with them I have no idea, they must look great in the front room I'd imagine. Pack your bags, we're leaving!

3.

Home Sweet Home 2
The New Den

THEY SAY THAT MOVING home is one of the most stressful things that anyone can do. It's bad enough having to endure what being Millwall really means without the added pressure. It's surprising that we're not all in a nuthatch; mind you, some would say that at the New Den we are.

The move to a new ground experience is a big wrench, like any house move except that you personally don't have to get Pickfords in, worry about getting new curtains or whether your furniture will fit. All you really have to worry about is if your arse will fit into the new plastic seats of your new home. That said, if you've been a regular at a ground for any length of time, it really does become like a second skin, a real home from home as comforting and reassuring as your own front room, especially if you're from a dysfunctional family. You therefore have to get used to any new location and its surroundings initially, even allowing for the fact that the two Dens are only a couple of hundred yards apart. The site of the Old Den is now a residential estate. Some lucky soul must have the old centre circle underneath their living room floorboards, we should organise pilgrimages to this sacred site. In truth, the New Den isn't too different in surroundings from its predecessor.

Once again situated in a mostly industrial area, featuring in its case the towering red-lighted chimney of the incinerator/recycling plant. The obligatory dark railway arches and railway lines once again surround the new ground; it also has skip hire companies and car repair lots in its locality. Like other big city areas, many of the approach roads show the signs of urban decay with dumped cars, some burnt out and used as makeshift skips, rubbish bins or for fly-tipping. Although conversely some of the more rundown housing close to the South end of the ground has been demolished and rebuilt in more recent times. That aside, as with most inner city clubs, a Millwall fan's character is merely a reflection of their surroundings. Personally I'm glad to say that today we still possess a 'call a spade a spade 'mentality, nothing racial intended. I think I can honestly say that as much as the powers-that-be try to gentrify football, they'd have had a job radically changing us.

football grounds and their fan base are still in the main drawn from the less well-to-do urban areas, with all the accompanying influences that go with it. Perhaps clubs building new grounds in out-of-town locations is an attempt to negate the inner-city influences? The initial attempts at anonymity on the club and local authority's behalf, led to the street signs, around the South Stand entrances at least, saying 'New London Stadium' or merely 'Stadium'. There was no mention of Millwall and equally for quite a while after its opening the New Den itself was also naked of any Millwall connection. Do you think that they were trying to hide something, or were they just ashamed of us?

It's all singing and dancing now at the ground and amazingly, it now even says 'Millwall Football Stadium' on a sign in Ilderton Road, incognito no more.

First Night Nerves - 4th August 1993
Millwall v Sporting Lisbon

For the inaugural match at the initially monickered 'New London Stadium' against Bobby Robson's Sporting Lisbon, Luis Figo and all, I rang the club to see if as a South Stand season ticket-holder I'd need to get tickets in advance and was told 'No'. So naturally, I turned up on the night to find a packed South Stand and queues for tickets aplenty. Obviously there were no tickets left except in the North Stand Lower, due to a large 'Crawl out of the Woodwork' contingent, more of which later.

I had arranged to meet my mate Micky Fisher outside the ground and I set-off via the East London line to the nearest station, Surrey Quays, nee Docks, to launch my adventure to try to find the ground, a search that wasn't helped by the lack of street signs. I wandered about aimlessly until I met another long-suffering Lion, John from Brentwood. As neither of us really had a clue where the ground was, we did the classic 'scan the sky for the glow from the floodlights' routine, joining the other lost souls doing exactly the same thing. Once we had eventually navigated our way to the ground John headed for his own seat and I looked for Micky. Having found him we got our tickets and headed to our positions in the North lower i.e. in the stand that was to become a wasteland in the years to come and might as well have been covered in dustsheets for all the use it's got. Micky and I sat down and I took a few minutes to look out at the stadium around me. I thought to myself that this is pretty swish, nice and compact. The atmosphere was good and 'No One Likes Us' echoed around the ground, cheerleaders gyrated in front of us as then Labour Party leader John Smith cut the tape. Thankfully, it hadn't been John Smith gyrating about in front of us and the cheerleaders cutting the tape, that would have been too bizarre!

It was an emotionally charged big crowd debut for the New Den, despite Millwall losing 2-1, like the Old Den's last game, it was of little consequence. The result didn't matter, it was a New Home Sweet Home. One good thing about the evening was that as we were playing a Latin side we had the pleasure of seeing lots of hand wringing, pleading and rolling about on the pitch in customary mock-injured fashion up close. Marvellous, I like a bit of live theatre myself.

The big game hunting aspect of the opening night's large crowd was put into perspective when the following weekend's match against Honved, another defeat, saw a crowd of about a quarter of the opening night's inaugural game. This gets me on to a pet hate of mine: 'Big game-hunting' fans, or as I prefer to call them 'The Carpentry Club', the sort of people who emerge from the woodwork for any big game and then slip back under the skirting board until the next Bertie Big Bollocks affair. I could never be a big game hunter or a TV only fan, whose only involvement in a game is to plonk their arse in front of Sky, decked out in club merchandise on their sofa like Buddha with the remote control. Probably in some cases never actually venturing to a game in the flesh, where is the fun in that? Until you've frozen your nuts off at the likes of Barnsley in February, you've not lived. To me a big game or armchair fan professing a love for their side in the flesh once in a blue moon or from indoors is a bit like a holiday romance or a young girl's devotion to a Boy Band, a fleeting encounter or an unrequited love from afar. For me football supporting has to be an emotional ride and you must have a firm bond with your side to truly enjoy a game and to get full value for any success. Without this, I cannot see the point. I need to endure the mental and physical anguish of following the Lions all over the country, through both the thick and thin times; as they say 'No pain, no gain'.

The first 'Real' match, a Sunday afternoon league fixture screened live by LWT, saw another defeat, this time a 4-1 coshing by the mighty Southend United, so off to a flyer then!

I Love A New Den With A Happy Atmosphere

To my mind, it's the nature of the club's fans and the atmosphere that they create that really attracts you and solidifies your loyalty to a club, far more than any football on display. Let's be honest, the players, managers and directors will move on or retire, but a loyal fan doesn't have this luxury. It is the sense of being on the same wavelength with your fellow home fans, of being one that draws you in, especially with a partisan passionate crowd like Millwall. Quite how a fan becomes attached to a club whose crowd display all the passion and hostility of an afternoon nap, Palace for example, I couldn't tell you.

Prior to the move the main topic of conversation, aside from what the new ground would look like, was how we would react to our new surroundings. It's the same for any new ground club I'd imagine, but with our 'hotbed' reputation, it was mentioned ad nauseam especially as we were moving from a mostly terraced environment to a seated one. After all, most people prefer to sing standing up, unless they're Val Doonican of course, ask your dad. We were obviously the same people, merely transported to a different location; but would we retain the Old Den's unique atmosphere? Would we lose the 'Roar'? That was the question; the answer is yes and no. It does seem that most all-seater grounds suffer to some degree from a reduction in atmosphere when seated, look at Liverpool's 'Kop'. Whilst I haven't been there recently it does appear from the television coverage that I have seen and heard that it's certainly not the 'Kop' of old. Obviously even such a volatile crowd such as ours takes time to recover from the initial disorientation of a move. One problem was that the whole crowd was now sitting down so there was probably a mixture of Old Den stand dwellers mixed in with their more volatile terrace counterparts, thus watering down the atmosphere overall.

Another problem was not having the ability to congregate with your friends in the ground ad-lib as you could on a terrace. Initially, we often found ourselves scattered all around the ground due to ticketing confusion. It took a while to sort this out and for us to stake out our territory. Obviously in a terrace environment everybody would know roughly where their friends would be standing and you could merely arrange to me up in a general area. After a season's bedding-in we made sure that those that wanted to sit together got season tickets in the same stand/block and for any Cup game we used to get all of our tickets at the same time, a similar operation to an away match in effect. Everyone has gradually gotten used to the New Den over the years and you now see the same people more or less in the same positions week in week out. I suppose it just takes time to adjust to your surroundings.

Home or away, I'm not a lover of reserved seating. I prefer it to be a block or stand allocation only, with seats taken up on a first-come first-served basis, particularly if the crowd has been swelled by any success and they don't understand the Millwall ethos of sit where you like. It only makes it more complicated to my mind to have to get all of your tickets together in a seat specific stand. Especially in the case of home season tickets - what if you don't like your neighbours or, perish the thought, they don't like you. You're lumbered with each other for the season come what may, fraught with problems as it is.

Whilst we've recently entered the realms of pre-match rabble-rousing, mega mixes and choreographed clapping, I still prefer the old spontaneous unprompted crowd way. As my mate Simon once said 'Who needs a rabble-rousing? All we used to need to get us going was the opposition, their mouthy fans and a crap Ref!' How true. Thank God that we haven't had to resort to the disgrace of having to call in the assistance of a brass band or, horror of horrors, having to mike us up to enhance the atmosphere, ye gods! I'd die from embarrassment if this ever became necessary. Whilst the atmosphere was initially patchy it still managed to frighten Dave Sinclair, Jimmy Nicholl era, hard man my arse! if you will pardon the expression.

The atmosphere since our move to the New Den hasn't been helped by play-off failures, financial Armageddon and relegation. However, it has improved and in my opinion, at volatile games at least, it's now almost up to Old Den proportions in terms of volume and hostility - sorry, hospitality - or at least it was prior to our pre-2002/03 problems. One thing that did improve the atmosphere was the formation of the 'opium den' section in the East Upper. What this did was to mimic the Old Den's layout, with the East Stand contingent a breakaway faction from the South Stand, creating an area like the old Halfway Line near to the away fans and with the South Stand becoming the CBL, both in name and nature. I used the drug reference about the East Upper because whenever my CBL chums and I have occasionally sat up there it was like being at a Howard Marks Convention. The Old Den was special because it didn't have just one end, it was the whole ground that sang, and so it is now at the New Den. Even the often libraryesque West Stand also join in the fun on occasions, and quite right too.

The more passionate Den games have prompted some very descriptive press comments, for example 'The Theatre Of Screams'/'Den Din' and '15,000 Screaming South Londoners'. These descriptions were used specifically for our long overdue win against Wigan in 2001/02, 'The Theatre of...' reference was a play on Manchester United's 'Theatre Of Dreams', 'Den Din' is self-explanatory and 'South Londoners' isn't strictly accurate; don't forget we have mouthy tourists from the East End, Essex and Kent.

Numerous visiting clubs have also acknowledged the New Den as a loud, hostile place in their fanzines, even such anti-Millwall sides as Gillingham, Palace and Manchester City. This is music to my ears. Who wants opponents to feel cosy? I know I don't. With the Old Den 'Roar' in mind, it always pleases me when the New Den crowd is at full tilt; it gives me a warm glow and an 'Ah! The real Den's arrived, that's better' sensation. I want it to be rabid, hostile, loud and ever so slightly partisan, but that's just me, I'm afraid. Millwall have always had a 'hotbed' crowd reputation and long may it continue.

All Mod Cons Gov!

The 'why move?' questions led to the many negative aspects of the Old Den, and the problems in making it into an all-seater stadium, being forgotten. These were replaced by a rose-tinted spectacles version, which created a beautifully romanticised dreamy experience of the old place.

Don't get me wrong, I loved the Old Den with a passion as much as the next Lion and I wouldn't have missed it for the world, but the new ground is better, if now a bit rusty. The New Den itself and its immediate environs are a million miles away from its predecessor in terms of facilities. My initial impression of the new stadium was favourable, it was a good, compact, if a little spartan ground at the offset, due to its lack of Millwall identity and anonymous status. At the time it was state of the art and a forerunner in implementing the Taylor Report. Personally, I'd have preferred a closed-in ground with possibly only the away stand unconnected. this would have retained the all-round 'Roar', but you can't have everything, can you?

In truth, I'm happy at whatever ground I'm in as long as Millwall are playing. Save for its original anonymity, bare internal grey concourses and the lack of the promised McDonald's and Pie and Mash shops, which were an initial bone of contention, the ground is a modern edifice with all the modern norms. It's obviously been outstripped by every new ground built since but that's the problem with being a trendsetter. Still, its all-seater - which is far better than an open terrace, that's for sure - has unrestricted views, numerous refreshment points, concourse TVs and indoor toilets! Including some for women! Whatever next? There is also the Lions Leisure/Community Centre, the Lions/'Arry's bar, Kitchener's restaurant and of course the modern corporate pre-requisite of executive boxes, banqueting suites and function facilities. The club shops are a vast improvement on their Old Den counterparts, although the positioning of the main one close to the away stand is a tad odd especially as it's often shut at the end of the match for safety reasons. The ticket facilities, away travel, Lottery windows, etc are a vast improvement on the Old Den. One thing that I do like is the recent addition of the memorial plaques in the ground and the garden of remembrance for deceased supporters outside the ground, albeit that it's a fairly basic affair, it shows that many people are dedicated for a lifetime to the club. Last but not least, there's the other modern pre-requisite - the video screen, in our case the inappropriately named 'Jumbotron'. It's just as well that they say that size does not matter, as my TV at home is as big. It's also a shame that Lions TV/Lions World isn't really called 'MTV' as 'Bye For Now Les' once called it, I was looking forward to a load of soft porn girlie pop videos myself. One question though - Why doesn't it have subtitles? I personally can never understand a word that anyone says from the screen; this was especially true when Mark McGhee was the manager.

The Executive Experience

If you said executive box in my Dad's day he'd have been totally mystified - 'What's that, a groin guard for a Director?'. Not today, when every ground must have these posh areas so that the local bigwigs can entertain and the big knobs can hang out away from the unwashed masses. I have personally only been to one executive day at the New Den when another Millwall mate, Dave Murray, won one for the day against Plymouth Argyle, Bruce Grobbelaar and all, in a Second Division match on 12/4/1997. Dave and his posse of freeloaders trooped along to the box, which was located in the East lower right hand corner, close to the away fans in the North upper tier. This was at a time when the East upper wasn't the hostile thing that it is nowadays.

Unfortunately I had another engagement on the evening of this match so I couldn't get stuck in to the beer with my usual gusto. I gave the sandwiches a good 'Buntering' though, it would have been rude not to. The box itself was comfortable with a TV, seats in front, beer, food and all the comforts of home. However, I couldn't get into the match in my usual rabid partisan fashion at all; whether it was the lack of booze or having the ability to wander in and out during the game that did it I'm not sure, it was a bit like having deja vu, whereby the New Den looked familiar but somehow wasn't quite right. Personally, I prefer to be in the thick of it amidst the singing and abuse, in my case in the South Stand/CBL upper tier. This was highlighted by a friend of mine, Helen, whose first ever visit to a football match was as a corporate guest at our home game against Manchester City in 1998, a wise choice.

This infamous night match saw the New Den at its hostile best. She sat in her seat in the East lower executive boxes and was amazed, not to say alarmed, by the bear-pit/Roman Coliseum-like atmosphere that this particular match had. It was just as well that she didn't see the home fans attempt to 'converse' with the City fans, post-match, that culminated in large-scale clashes with the riot police outside the ground. I spoke to her a couple of days later once the initial culture shock had worn off and she said to me 'Is it always like that?' and 'Was I in the wanking hand signals section behind the goal?'. 'Yes' and 'Yes' I said proudly. The by-product of this game was that the 2001/02 clashes were restricted to home fan only affairs, something that we had to get used to in 2002/03.

'Your Name's Not Down
You're Not Coming In!'

Even before the Birmingham City play-off problems we had draconian police restrictions due to Millwall's reputation. In my opinion, it's a ground more rigorously policed than other sides of a similar persuasion such as Birmingham, West Ham, Stoke, Wolves or Cardiff to name a few. Millwall also have the police turning up en masse for the least likely trouble games. For example, we've had policing like the May Day Riots, for games against such notorious sides as Wycombe and Crewe. This despite the fact that violence is invariably saved for other trouble clubs and usually only happens at games that stand out a mile off. In 2002/03, we even had mass Old Bill turnouts at home-fans-only games.

I WAS BORN UNDER THE COLD BLOW LANE

We're not exactly lacking in stewards either, so you could say that we're well bouncered hence the reference in the title. Serves us right for being passionate and volatile I suppose. As we've mostly been in the lower Leagues recently the customary isolation policy for away fans has often led to the North Stand resembling the post-Ipswich FA Cup riot Dog Track End at the Old Den, frequently resulting in the ludicrous situation of oceans of empty seats with a small turnout of away fans stuck in one block on the upper tier surrounded by stewards and police.

On various occasions, the away end has had both home and away fans on it, against non-hostile opposition, where Millwall fans have been allowed onto the away North Stand. Naturally there had to be a huge no man's land separating us from them. It was also given over to Millwall totally for Oldham in 2001/02 and Bradford City in 2003/04 when the away fans were relocated to the West Stand Upper beneath the police box. All of these instances went off without a hitch. However, as there sometimes is trouble, it means that the police normally deem this policy unworkable so financially disastrous segregation, total away fan bans and radical ticketing policies it invariably is.

I can't see why the North Stand cannot have a permanent dividing wall/fence so that it can be split into two sections if required, one for home fans, one for away fans. It worked for the games that I mentioned above and it's a tactic that works perfectly well at other volatile grounds around the country. Even since we've been in Division One and more away fans have turned up they still aren't allowed on to the lower tier as a rule, so more often than not it results in the absurd situation of both teams having to kick towards what looks like an empty stand; which is particularly embarrassing when viewed on television.

Unfortunately, Millwall are invariably seen as a special case with the police perceiving us home fans as especially dangerous, prompting the building of a mega-expensive walkway from South Bermondsey station to the away North Stand to allow the police to try to get the away fans in and out of the ground safely without being attacked by the locals. It was first used for the Sunderland home game on 17/1/2004 and, by the police's own admission, it was a complete nightmare on the day. Its opening before the 2003/04 visits of Stoke, West Ham and Cardiff was no coincidence.

On top of the heavy Policing already deemed necessary for a Millwall match, there was a slight infringement of civil liberties proposed for the New Den a couple of years back. This idea would really have really heralded the arrival of George Orwell's Thought Police. The proposal was to put bugs under the seats or secrete microphones in the home stands, so that the police could eavesdrop on any home fans' conversations of a conspiratorial nature, especially those that appeared to be about aggro-planning. Naturally, police paranoia and Machiavellian tendencies didn't come into this idea. I thought that it was a real oddity; a few things sprang to mind - many areas at the New Den are unreserved seating, so how would you know who was sitting where, who you were bugging and who was talking? Also, consider exactly what they would have got if it was a Graham Rix 'sex offender' seats-slamming night, bang goes the bug and the eavesdropper's eardrums. As a matter of course they would get wall to wall, no pun intended, effing and blinding, surround-sound farting and inane banter, and that's only me. When you consider the fact that at the New Den most people are already heavily monitored on CCTV cameras anyway, it is almost like Big Brother (Orwell or Channel 4 versions) already without this thankfully aborted (I think?) idea.

The CCTV does work, after a fashion, as another of my home and away chums Ted found a few years ago when he was unceremoniously dragged out of the CBL upper by the long and numerous arms of the law for allegedly being in possession of a laser pen, which they said he was flashing in the opposing goalkeeper's face. This prompted the normal pre-requisite 50-strong police invasion on to the stand to apprehend Ted in a Public Enemy Number One fashion. He was then led away still pleading his innocence and, after the obligatory strip search, genital electrodes and anal probe interrogations had failed to discover any pen, let alone a laser one, they let him back in. The police suspected that he had given it to one of us, which he hadn't. He still claims he is innocent to this day so God knows what the CCTV saw. Still, it gave the Old Bill a bit of step aerobics exercise so that was something I suppose.

To Sit Or Not To Sit?

For any fans of my vintage, sitting at a football match isn't the norm. I used to sit at Spurs with my dad when I was a small child but that was only because he deemed it safer than standing on the packed terraces. As an adult it would always be the terraces for me given the choice. However, times have changed and whatever the shortcomings of our newish ground, I now feel after a decade that I'm now truly at home. I have my feet firmly under the table as it were, especially now that most away grounds are now all-seater as well; today it's a novelty to stand up at a game.

Nowadays you don't have the leg weariness or dangers that we had from standing on terracing. Your only real danger at an all-seater ground; apart from getting a flying seat in the bonce, is arse-ache, cramp or DVT from sitting down for too long. I try to avoid this by behaving like a cat on a hot tin roof, or a baboon with piles if you prefer. I'm usually in and out of my seat at the drop of a hat, so arse ache isn't a problem for me. Earache from the people behind telling me to sit down, yes, arse-ache, no. There's one other disadvantage and that's plastic seats, beautifully described by Simon as 'Thermos' seats because they give you Michael Miles by remaining icy in the depths of winter and an arse like a greenhouse by retaining the heat during the warmer months. A lovely image, I'm sure you will agree.

Whilst the return of the terraces is often mooted I can never see them returning in their old form, especially not at a ground with a reputation like Millwall. I must admit though that when I listed the joys of the Old Den and its terraces it did make me pine for the good old days; nostalgia, eh? Still, it does give us older Lions a chance to bore to death - sorry, pass down - our Old Den mythology and folklore to those poor unfortunates who were too young to have had the pleasure. The Old Den was a great place as a Lions fan to watch football, but times change and that's that.

HOME SWEET HOME 2

A Few New Den Memories

To complement the 'Old Den Memories' I thought I'd close this chapter with just a few new ground ones. In no particular order:

There was the relief that the ground wasn't called 'The Reg Burr Stadium'. There have been three disastrous home play-off semis, resulting in the Derby County and Birmingham City play-off 'Riots'. There has been a relegation, a Division Two Championship and the Auto Windscreen Final, not forgetting financial administration and salvation. There was the C... who shouted out during Harry Cripp's minute's silence. There's the new 'Ministry of Sound' PA pitchside. There's DJ 'Bye For Now Les' seemingly having to play *Love Shack/Sit Down/House Of Fun/Living Next Door To Alice* (Who the F... are Palace? stylee) and more recently *London Calling* at every game. Not forgetting the *Hi De Hi* style ear-splitting safety announcements. There is Mr Den who, rather like Elvis, enters and then leaves the building.

There's the modern phenomenon of playing 'Let 'Em Come' as the teams come out complete with out of time clapping which, speaking as a music lover, always makes me cringe and there's the 'EIO' air pumping goal celebrations now allied to the 'Let 'Em Come' goal time music. There were the demonstrations after yet another hapless display in the car park against Jimmy Nicholl and Peter Mead during our financial doom period. There was BBC2's *Back to the Floor* with Theo and its behind-the-scenes revelations.

There was the day when the club decided to give free entry to Albanian asylum seekers and the resulting furore. There was the strange sight a few years ago of Stoke City's turnout being augmented by Dundee fans, who then had to be segregated from the Stoke fans themselves, which was very bizarre, as is seeing foreign football fans like Dutch, Italians and Germans at some home games complete with their own home club scarves on. There were the games when rogue fans confronted away players on the pitch prompting the standard response of 'Somebody could have been killed! What if they had a knife?' and calls to bring back perimeter fencing by the 'National Service, That's What They Need/ Bring Back The Birch/Put Them in the Stocks/Send Them to the Colonies!!' brigade. I think if someone did stab a player in front of a football crowd, on CCTV and possibly live on TV as well, there would be such a cast iron prosecution case that even if Johnny Cochran teamed up with Rumpole of the Bailey, Kavanagh QC and Perry Mason as the defence lawyers they still wouldn't be able to get them off.

There was the half-eaten pie Lino assault against Birmingham in 2001/02.There was the Graham Rix 'Sex Offender' night against Pompey. There was Yuran and Kulkov's money-grabbing act and their crowd swelling high hopes introduction against Port Vale. There was the West Ham era of Billy Bonds, Kenny Brown and Paul Allen, how did that happen? There was renaming the South Stand to a more appropriate Cold Blow Lane aka CBL. There's the mystery of having a 20,000 capacity ground that appears to hold only 18,500 when full to capacity. There was the 'We don't need a groundsman' season when the pitch looked like a cabbage patch and the time when the area in front of the West Stand looked like a ploughed field due to lack of sunlight.

To close, a few CBL characters:

Grandad, or John as he's known, is the New Den's CBL spiritual leader. He's become a main character in the upper tier in the last few seasons and is a regular at the away matches. At away games, his song-starting antics usually draw quizzical looks from the local stewards and police, especially when he does his usual routine of standing up, taking off his baseball cap and using it as a prop to lead the singing. He has the habit of responding to 'Grandad, Grandad What's The Score?' by standing up and shouting '1, 2, 3 (Etc.) and 'F... 'Em!' accompanied with Italian-style 'Up Yours' gestures of a 'Get stuffed' nature. He also responds to mouthy away fans by going into a mock parental grandad admonishment mode, standing up and saying 'If I Have To Come Up There!'. This goes to prove my earlier theory that you do get worse as you get older; it's what a lifetime following Millwall does to you.

There has been the recent emergence of crowd favourite, the big boned junior goalie 'Tank' and his half-time penalty shootout heroics. Finally the 'Lion on the Roof', a great British eccentric, a big bloke with a deep booming voice reminiscent of Linda Blair in *The Exorcist* who has been known to appear on a CBL upper stairwell shout out 'Zigger, Zagger, Zigger, Zagger!' only to disappear and then reappear on another stairwell, as the CBL chant 'Who's The Lion On The Roof?'.

4.

Karaoke Dokey –
The Best Wit and Wisdom
From The Dens

APART FROM THE TEAM itself one of the things that first drew me to Millwall was the crowd's mentality and the chants. In my opinion, Millwall fans are and always have been the biggest bunch of piss takers to be found anywhere in football. This book is proof positive of that. I have listed many chants in my other book and this chapter is a selection of chants/comments not listed there, chosen from a vast collection that I've compiled over several seasons.

They are mostly from the CBL New Den although there are some from the Old Den as well. It's a world of funny, abusive, racist, sexist and just plain odd chants, I make no apologies for any of the language or sentiments, whether I agree with them or not, as it's an honest, true reflection of a Millwall crowd's mentality and sense of humour. Beware, you are about to enter a Parental Advisory zone.

Golden Oldie Chants

To start a charming Old Den classic that prompted the title of this book:

**'I Was Born Under The Cold Blow Lane, Oh! I Was Born
Under The Cold Blow Lane,
Boots Are Made For Kicking, Kicking In The Head,
I Won't Stop F...ing Kicking Until The Bastard's Dead,**

Oh! I Was Born Under The Cold Blow Lane, The Cold Blow, Cold Blow Lane.'

There was also a verse that went **'Knives Are Made For Stabbing!'**. It was sung to the tune of Lee Marvin's mumbling classic *Wanderin' Star*. Not that I agree with the sentiments but this version could be used if John Woo ever remade the musical of *Paint Your Wagon*.

Another golden Old Den favourite sung to the tune of *Do Ya Ken John Peel* went something like:

'Bertie Mee Said To Bill Shankly, Have You Heard Of The North Bank Highbury?
Shanks Said "No I Don't Think So, But I've Heard Of The Millwall Cold Blow".'

Or **'Aggro'**, your choice, I think that there was a longer version of this that included The Shed and the Stretford End among others, but I'm afraid that I've lost too many brain cells to recall it all, sorry.

A few chants that seem to have disappeared of late -
'The Lions, The Lions, Da, Da, Da, Da, Da, Da, Da, Da, Da, Da Roar! (War!)' accompanied at the Old Den by surging and 'on the pitch' gestures, sung to the tune of *The Vikings* horn line, an old favourite, as were **'Come On You Lions!'/'We Are The C B L!'** and **'We Are The Millwall, Etc; We Are The Millwall Cold Blow Lane!'**

To close, a couple of bizarre old chants:

'Millwall Boys We Are Here, Wow Oh! Wow Oh! Millwall Boys We Are Here, Wow Oh! Wow Oh!
Millwall Boys We Are Here - Shag Your Women And Drink Your Beer, Wow Oh! Wow Oh! Ah!'

'We're The Boys Who Make More Noise Ooh! Ah! Ooh! Ah! Ah!'.

You explain them!

Grandad

The CBL (and away) choir leader is held in high regard and usually gets-

'He's Old, He's Grey, He's Millwall All The Way, Grandad, Grandad!'
'He's Old, He's Blue, He's Millwall Through And Through, Grandad, Grandad!'

'He's Here, He's There, He's Every F...ing Where, Grandad, Grandad!'

Even so. he's still had a few disrespectful chants, for example the ageist **'Get Your Teeth Out For The Lads!'** and, on a cold day:

'Grandad's Got His Long Johns On, Do Da, Do Da, Grandad's Got His Long Johns On Do Da, Do Da Day!'

So much for respecting your elders.

Grandad's Guide To London

Some sweeping non-PC generalisation London chants, courtesy of Grandad again apart from the East End one, that's as old as the hills:

North London: **'Oh! North London Is Full Of Yids, Etc, It's Full Of Yids, Yids And More Yids, Oh! North London Is Full Of Yids!'**

West London: **'Oh! West London Is Full Of Poofs, Etc, It's Full of Poofs, Poofs And More Poofs, Oh! West London Is Full Of Poofs!'**

East London: **'Oh! East London Is Full Of Shit, Etc, It's Full Of Shit, Shit And More Shit, Oh! East London Is Full Of Shit!'**

To close on a positive note, South London:

'Oh! South London Is Wonderful, (Is Wonderful), It's Full Of Tits, Fanny And Millwall! Oh! South London Is Wonderful!'

Self-Mockery

A couple of chants now from the CBL to the West Stand, which can be quite sedate, and to the much more vocal East Stand **'West Stand, Give Us A Song'**.

There was no reply so **'West Stand Are You Dead?'**.

To the East Upper we sang **'East Stand Give Us A Song.'** Again, there was no reply so **'Are You West Stand In Disguise?'**.

There's nothing like taking the piss out of each other, I say.

You're So Hurtful - Players

Shaun Goater MBE got **'Goater You're An Ugly C...!'** Not so much racial abuse as facial abuse, this was the first airing of the chant, since adapted and sung to all and sundry.

He also got **'Have You Ever Pulled A Bird?'**.

Peter Crouch the 6 ft 7 in (!) beanpole got the following sizeist abuse: **'Freak, Freak, Freak!'/'You're Just a Freak Of Nature!'/'You're A Freak And You Know You Are!'** Not forgetting the classics **'There's Only One Rodney Trotter'** and **'There's Only One Olive Oyl!'**.

Adi Akinbiyi was greeted with a real piss take: **'You're Worse Than Akinbiyi!'** Is it possible to be worse than yourself?

Ex-Leicester player Trevor Benjamin hadn't been able to get in to their side ahead of Akinbiyi so he moved to Palace where he got the usual **'You're Worse Than Akinbiyi!'**. Which, technically speaking, he was.

Iwan Roberts got the following dental abuse: **'One Tooth, He's Only Got One Tooth!'**

Tommy Mooney's bald domehead prompted **'You've Got A Head Like A Baked Bean!'**.

Luke Chadwick, the acned missing Bee Gee, got the obligatory

'Ugly C...!' chant in a couple of games. He also got 'Clearasil, Clearasil, Clearasil!'.

Former Pompey star Paul Merson got 'You're A Coke Head Merson!' Not forgetting the much more specific 'You're Just A Wife Beater Merson!'. After he ripped us to shreds at home in 2002/03, he quite rightly got a standing ovation from we home fans, respect where it's due. It was an ovation that he later said meant a great deal to him because it came from real football fans.

Robert Earnshaw obviously got the obligatory 'Ugly C...!' and various variations on a theme: 'You've Got A Face Like A Beaver's Arse!'/'Earnshaw, You're An Alien!'/'You've Got A Face Like A Donkey!' and 'Eey Ore!'.

Paul Williams was greeted with the big bum jibe 'J Lo Wants Her Arse Back, J Lo Wants Her Arse Back, La, La, La, La La, La La, La!'.

Blackburn Rovers' Andy Cole had to endure 'You're Not Wanted Anymore!'/'You'll Never Play For England!'/'Oh! Teddy Teddy Etc, Teddy Sheringham!'/'Ruud Van Nistelrooy Na, Na, Na, Na, Na!'/'Andy Cole, Etc When He Gets The Ball He Does F... All! Etc!'. Naturally, he scored the winner, right at the death.

That's All Folks

A few players have been compared to cartoon characters. Julian Gray played in day-glo orange boots, now that's confidence for you. He also wore an all-black kit, which gave him a cartoon character look, so we sang 'Daffy Duck! Daffy Duck! Daffy Duck!' When he went down injured he got 'Shoot The Duck! Shoot The Duck! Shoot The Duck!'.

Returning to Robert Earnshaw he also got 'There's Only One Bugs Bunny!'/'What's Up Doc?' and 'Earnshaw You're a Goofy C...!'.

Ed de Goey was greeted with the bizarre 'Ed The Duck, Ed The Duck, Ed The Duck!'.

'I'm Sure I Should've Brought Something?'

Walsall and Gillingham both turned up at the New Den without a kit. It's not the first time it has happened but is very confusing, especially for an away traveller. We sang **'Shit Team - No Kit!'/'Shit Team - No Strip!'/'Are You Millwall In Disguise?'/ 'Nice Shirt - Shit Team!'** and **'You're Not Fit To Wear The Shirt!'**. Gillingham won, as usual; shouldn't this count as an away win to us?

These kit cock-ups are probably why we've seen so many day-glo yellow, green and orange away kits of late. Kit-men have probably instigated them, after all, it's not easy to forget a kit hamper that's pulsing and glowing in the dark in a corner.

Oh Wisey!

Some chants about Dennis Wise and his breaking of Callum Davidson's jaw:

> **'Oh, Wisey Wowo! Oh, Wisey Wowo!**
> **He's Only 5 Foot 4; He'll Break Your F...ing Jaw,**
> **Oh, Wisey Wowo, Oh, Wisey Wowo! '**

> **'Dennis, Dennis Break His Jaw, Etc!'.**

Chants aimed specifically at Davidson at the New Den were **'Callum, Callum How's Your Jaw?'** and **'Does The Doctor Know You're Here?'**. To highlight Wise possibly bankrupting Leicester we sang **'He's Gonna Take All Your Money!'**.

Millwall Players

Robbie Ryan wasn't exactly a goal machine - there, I've said it - and after he scored his first ever goal he got this classic:

> **'You Can Stick Roberto Carlos Up Your A...! Etc**
> **You Can Stick Roberto Carlos, Stick Roberto Carlos, Stick**
> **Roberto Carlos Up Your A... - Sideways!'**

Tony Craig replaced Robbie for one game and scored his first ever goal, so we sarcastically sang **'You Can Stick Robbie Ryan Up Your A...!'**.

In the great tradition of the old Terry Hurlock/Keith Stevens chants, Kevin 'The Most Hated Man In Football' Muscat gets the following sung to the tune of *Skippy The Bush Kangaroo*: **'Muzzy, Muzzy He'll Kick The F...ing Shit Out Of You!'** That should improve his profile.

Noel Whelan had an on-pitch fracas with Tim Cahill in the first half of the Coventry home game in October 2003, resulting in 'Johnny Come Lately' Whelan receiving the less than complimentary **'F... Off Whelan!'**. He was also booed each time he got the ball. Before the second half, there was a very public kiss and make up display

In homage to his hairdo, Darren Ward got **'There's Only One Peckham Beckham!'** and **'There's Only Two David Beckhams!'**.

Finally, to finish, a bizarre Bobby Bowry chant from a few years back, **'Bobby Bowry Is An Ethiopian!'**.

Millwall Managers

Just a few anti-manager chants. When Mick McCarthy was our manager his shouts to the players from the dug out always used to sound like the foghorn of a boat in distress to me, very apt at some games. As we languished in Division 1 we used to sing this ditty to the tune of *Merry Christmas Everybody*:

'So Here It Is Mick McCarthy, No One Here Is Having Fun, Look To The Future Now, Stuck in Division 1!'

Mark McGhee was never truly accepted at Millwall following Lions legend Rhino into the job and intermittently during his reign got **'We Want Our Millwall Back!'** and **'You're Worse Than Mick McCarthy!'**. Not to mention the slanderous **'You're Worse Than Jimmy Nicholl!'**. I'd have sued if I were McGhee.

Just prior to his departure, during a 1-0 home defeat to Preston, he got **'One Nil To Mark McGhee!'/'F... Off McGhee, etc, F... Off!'/'F... Off Mark McGhee, Oh! What Can It Be To A Sad Scottish B......, Etc'/'McGhee Must Go!'/ 'McGhee Out!'** and **'We Want The Sweaty Out!'**. For any non-Londoners out there Sweaty = Sweaty Sock = Jock = Scotsman. I hope that has clarified it. There was also the sarcastic, I think, **'Grandad For Manager!'**.

A Voice From The Crowd

Leicester City's Jordan Stewart gave a dying swan display and a bloke behind me in the CBL shouted **'Get Up! You're Only Gary Lineker's Sausage Jockey!'**.

Spurs player Stefan Iversen was the target of a very bizarre comment regarding his Scandinavian connection and his love of Ikea (?) at Rhino's testimonial game; **'Iversen You Flat-Packed Mother F...er!'**

Wolves' keeper Matt Murray, whilst in front of the CBL, was getting the customary fat tosser abuse when one bloke at the back of the upper tier shouted out the classic **'Murray You've Got An Arse Like Dawn French!'**.

Brighton's Tesco-bag-shirted away fans continually sang **'Seagulls'** on their last visit, at which point a wag behind me at the back of the CBL kept shouting out **'Seaweed!'**. The same man also said of the 'Gay' side **'They Don't Like It Up 'Em! Oh Sorry, They Do, Don't They!'**.

Watford manager Gianluca Vialli got this Italian wartime reference - **'Oi Vialli! Why Don't You Just Put Up Your Hands And Capitulate As Usual You Eyetie!'**

Medical Diagnosis

Due to Joe Kinnear's heart problems, when he returned as manager of Luton Town he got **'Dodgy Ticker!'** and **'You're Going To Die In A Minute!'**.

Kevin Keegan at the New Den got our psychiatric opinion of **'Keegan Runs From Pressure!'**

Serenading Mr Plod

In our case 'Serenading Mr Riot Plod', his more aggressive brother, always popular with we Lions. A couple of original recent chants; after yet another police incursion onto the CBL upper Grandad sang the Baha Men classic **'Who Let Pigs Out? Oink, Oink, Oink, Oink, Oink!'**. There was also this questioning chant: **'What's It Like To Have No Mates?'** Oh, what it is to be popular. Speaking of popularity;

Who's The Wanker In The Black?
(Cheat, Cheat, Cheat!)

Referees are a set of people guaranteed to get 'nil points' in any Millwall popularity poll; they and their trusty assistants are about as welcome as Farmer Giles on a bumpy car ride.

Years ago the Millwall programme used to print where the officials come from, so you could play a geographical guessing game to try to deduce just how close the officials lived to your opponents and whether they had in fact come to the game on the away team's coach. They don't do this today so you can no longer ascertain if their performance is down to regional bias or just good old incompetence.

Before I start I'd like to say, Phil Prosser - the perfect rhyming slang name for a ref!

The following is just a sample of the home abuse -

Mark Cowburn - Bore a marked resemblance to Jerry Springer and got **'Jerry, Jerry, Jerry!'/'There's Only One Jerry Springer!'** and **'Jerry Springer Is A Wanker!'** and the alternative piss take **'There's Only One Oprah Winfrey!'**.

Mark Warren - In the first half of one night match Warren didn't dismiss an opposing player so we sang **'Where's Your Bottle Gone?'**. He then failed to appear for the second half. Following a long delay his replacement arrived to finish the game and got **'Who Are Ya?'** and **'Who The F...ing Hell Are You?'**. To conclude the night's fun one of the linos was called J. Beadle! So that was what was going on, some bearded twat will come on to the pitch and say 'You Thought You Were At A Football Match But...'

Mark Cooper - Cooper got the ball straight in the vitals in a game against Colchester United on Boxing Day 2000. He eventually rose to his feet and immediately booked the player that had kicked the ball, deeming it an attempt to ruin his chances of fathering a family. Ever the most sympathetic of grounds he got **'Let Him Die, Etc!'** and **'You've Only Got One Ball!'**. Then when he made his first bad decision after his ballbag bashing, he got **'Are Your Bollocks In Your Eyes?'**. He was lucky enough again to be the referee on pancake night in 2003, now bald as a coot and looking like he'd spent all day eating pancakes. By now he bore a remarkable resemblance to the Addams Family uncle and received **'There's Only One Uncle Fester!'**. Following a crap decision, he got **'Uncle Fester, Is A Wanker, Is A Wanker!'**.

Paul 'Stumbling' Allcock - Got the obvious **'You Ran From Di Canio!'** and **'She Fell Over!'** plus the less obvious **'Allcock No Balls!'**.

David Elleray got a classic case of misidentification when he made an error and got the ultimate insult of **'Are You Rennie In Disguise?'**. An easy mistake to make, a 6 ft-plus, black karate expert and a short white, bald school housemaster, from a distance they could be twins.

Andy Hall - My mate Clive took Lois, his then 3-year-old daughter, to the 2002/03 Notts Forest home game. Referee Andy Hall had a nightmare and as we told him so, she sat there cheerfully going **'Wanker! Wanker!'**. It's difficult to convince a child that it's naughty to call the nice incompetent twat a **'Wanker'** when we're all saying it isn't it?

Eddie Wolstenholme - Wolstenholme's final performance was against Coventry City in May 2003. To commemorate this Theo Paphitis awarded him a presentation shirt as a memento; I thought I was imagining things when I heard Millwall fans applauding this. The day I applaud a ref is the day I give up going to football. As the ref had a customary crap performance, we sang **'You're Not Fit To Wear The Shirt!'**. One bloke in the CBL shouted out **'It's A Pity You Didn't Retire Yesterday, You C...!'**. That's more like it!

Any dodgy linesman decision (sorry, dodgy assistant referee/referee's assistant or whatever the bloody hell they're called) gets the following : **'There's Only One Stevie Wonder!'** and **'You Can Stick Your F...ing Flag Up Your A... - Sideways!'**. A tricky manoeuvre and one that I doubt would improve their performance any.

The twitchy flag-happy lino against Birmingham City, who got missiles including a half-eaten pie thrown in his direction, shot away from the touchline quicker than any red-blooded man would if they saw a naked Julian Clary approaching them from behind in an excited state. From the CBL we couldn't tell what had been thrown from the East Upper, so we sang **'You Ran From A Paper Cup!'**.

This pie-lobbing incident did prompt future linos to be asked what pie they preferred. Most seemed to find it humorous, unless they were hit with one of course, particularly one of those cook in the tin efforts that was still in the tin. To conclude, why don't officials have names on their shirts like the players? Perhaps their criminal performances qualify them for anonymity under the witness protection programme. Just an idea, but the ref could have 'Wanker' or 'Bastard' emblazoned across their shoulders, whilst their trustee assistant has **'Referee's Nark'** or **'I'm With That Idiot!'**.

Celebrity Spotting

Coach: Preston's coach a few seasons back looked like Jimmy Saville, so he naturally got **'There's Only One Jimmy Saville!'** and **'Jimmy, Jimmy Give Us A Wave'**. Which the miserable bugger didn't.

Player: Walsall's quiffed-up Latin striker Jorge Leitao in the FA Cup 3rd round tie in 2004 was sent off after scoring, so we sang **'Bye, Bye Elvis, Etc, Bye Bye!'** and **'Where's Your Elvis Gone?'**.

Stewards: There's a steward on the CBL who bears a remarkable similarity to JK Rowling's wizard who has received **'There's Only One Harry Potter!'/'Harry, Harry Give Us A Song!'/'You Can Stick Your F...ing Wand Up Your A... - Sideways!'** and **'Harry Takes It Up The A...!'**. Not in the films he doesn't.

A very fat steward (I'm not thin but he abused the privilege) in a Sumo wrestler/King of Tonga fashion was guiding a police incursion on to the CBL and got **'Waller, Waller Give Us A Song!'** followed by a piss-take high-pitched rendition of *I Will Always Love You* in homage to his likeness to Rik 'Flop Idol' Waller and his single at the time.

Regional Stereotypes

Men Of Harlech. Enter the land of song, with its close-harmony singing, shut-down coalpits, cottage burning and sheep molesting - Wales. The usual chants to the Welsh clubs are **'Always Find The Welsh Shagging Sheep!'/'Get Your Sheep Out For The Lads!'/'You're Welsh And Your Mum's A Sheep!'/'You Sleep**

With Your Sister's Sheep!' and **'What's It Like To Shag A Sheep?'**.

Northern Monkeys Enter a land of big frothy-headed pints, clogs, cloth caps, dark satanic mills, bizarre accents, meat and potato pies and cobbled street - The North. The usual chants for any northern club are about social deprivation; **'You Live In A Factory!'/'You're Going Home To Your Ferrets'/'You're Going Home To Your Pigeon Lofts!'/'We've Got A Job You Ain't!'/'Sign on, With A Pen In Your Hand And You'll Never Get A Job!'** and **'There's Only One Job Between Ya!'**.

Local Yokels Enter a land of sheep, wellies, muck-spreading and cow shit - the country. The usual chants for any country team are **'Ooo Ar, Ooo Ar! Etc'** and **'Ooo! Ar Ya?'** the last one giving a rustic twist to usual **'Who Are Ya?'**. Not forgetting **'The Wheels On The Tractor Go Round And Round, Etc All Day Long.'** Not when the bloody things are sitting in front of you on a country lane they don't.

Caravan Dwellers Gillingham are perceived as caravan dwellers so they get Gypsy stereotype abuse. A small selection here;
    'Going Back To Your Caravans!'/'Does The Fairground Know You're Here?' and **'You Only Sing When You're Thieving!'**.
    There are many more regional chants in the away sections later.

Everybody Needs Good Neighbours

Just a few chants about our three nearest neighbours:

West Ham United: There was of course the 'Bobby Moore - Robin Hood' song and the anatomically impossible chant of **'You Can Stick Your F...ing Hammers (Bubbles) Up Your A... - Sideways!'**. I bet you any money that they can't! A couple of golden oldies;

I WAS BORN UNDER THE COLD BLOW LANE

'If I Had The Wings Of A Sparrow,
If I Had The Arse Of A Crow (?),
I'd Fly Over West Ham Tomorrow,
And Shit On The Bastards Below, Below
And Shit On The Bastards Below!'.

Not forgetting **'Chim, Chiminey, Chim, Chiminey, Chim-Chim-Cheroo, We Hate Those Bastards In Claret And Blue!'**. Excuse the spelling, I was away the day we did Dick Van Dyke at school.

Crystal Palace: Always get **'Ooo Ah Eric Cantona!'** and **'Palace, Palace? Who The F... Are Palace?'**. Until 2003/04, when the latter was banned after they complained. Ah! bless. They also get **'You Only Sing When You're Posing!'/'East Croydon Is Full Of Shit!'** and **'We Hate Croydon, Etc We Are The Croydon Haters!'**. Not forgetting the pre-Selhurst renovation reference **'F... Off Back To Sainsbury's!'**. See the diary section later on for many more.

Charlton Athletic: Charlton get plenty of anorak/trainspotting references but there's only one real chant: **'When The Red, Red Robin Comes A Bob, Bob Bobbing Along, Shoot The B......, Shoot The B......, Shoot, Shoot, Shoot!'**. This was a reworking of their theme tune and was very popular with the RSPB.

Respecting Opponent's Managers

Manchester United and England captain Bryan Robson got due respect for his Captain Marvel status at the Old Den when we serenaded him with both gay and sexual disease innuendo chants; **'Robson Takes It Up The A...hole, Robson Takes It Up The A...hole, Robson Takes It Up The A...hole, Cos He's A Northern C...!'** What about Jerome?

'U.N.I.T.E.D, Bryan Robson's Got V.D, With A Nick Knack Paddy Whack, Give A Dog A Bone, Northern B...... F... Off Home!'. This is almost the perfect player abuse - personal, sexual, and regional.

Patently untrue but we at Millwall have never been respecters of national treasures. Gary McAllister, Coventry's ageing and balding player-manager, got various ageist chants including **'Are You Grandad In Disguise?'**.

West Ham's terminally bewildered manager got this observational chant: **'Roeder Is A Gerbil!'**

Steve Bruce during his wanderlust phase got **'He's Here, He's There, He's Every F...ing Where Stevie Bruce!'/'You'll Never Last Three Months!'** and **'You're Going To Leave In A Minute!'**.

Neil Warnock, to highlight his 'spat' with Liverpool's Henchoz, got **'We're Gonna Spit On The Warnock!'**.

A Bit Fishy

Grimsby Town, the old fishy sea dogs, got the full range of abuse: **'We Can See You Sneaking Trout!'/'We Can Smell Your Fish From Here!'/'You're Going Home to Your Lighthouse!'/'There's Only One Captain Birdseye'/'Captain Birdseye - Sex Offender!'/'You Sleep With Your Sister's Fish!** and **'You're Shit And You Stink Of Fish!'**.

The Boat Race

Cambridge United got the following University Boat Race chants: **'You Only Sing When You're Rowing (Sinking)!'** We sang the above and another Boat Race chant, this time to Oxford United: **'You Always Lose To Cambridge!'**

A Bit Of Politics

Political observation is a good area for piss taking whether you agree with the politics or not. With the foot-and-mouth crisis in full swing, any country team got **'Foot And Mouth, Foot And Mouth, Foot And Mouth!'/'Dodgy Cattle!'/'Where's Your Cattle Gone?'/'Shit Team, No Sheep!'** and **'What's It Like To Have No Sheep?'**.

To any mining side after Thatcher had crushed the miners and shut the pits, we sang **'There's Only One Maggie Thatcher!'**.

I WAS BORN UNDER THE COLD BLOW LANE

When their local car plant was in danger Luton Town played us, so we gave them the following: **'Where's Your Vauxhall Gone?'**

We played Bradford City during the war in Afghanistan; there were reports in the media of possible attacks on Iraq so to any Muslims among them we sang **'Bomb Saddam, Bomb Saddam, Bomb Saddam!'**. No **'You're Shiite And You Know You Are!'** yet, though.

Finally, Grimsby Town again got this chant about their fishing fleet's decimation - **'You're Not Fishing Any More!'**.

Ethnic Stereotyping

To show our European Union affinity Italian Gianluca Vialli got the following stereotype chants; **'You Work In An Ice-Cream Van!'** and **'There's Only One Mr Whippy!'**.

We sang a classic collection when Pompey had Japanese goalkeeper Yoshikatsu Kawaguchi in their side. He got all manner of Asian references Japanese - **'Ah! You Jap Tosser!'/'Sumo, Sumo, Sumo!'** and **'Ah So, Ah So, Ah So!'** to the Chinese restaurant stereotype chants **'Sweet and Sour Chicken Balls!'/'Can We've A Takeaway?'/'One Chip No Pea!'** and **'What You Wan'? What You Wan'? What You Wan'?'**.

Not forgetting the Korean food classic **'You Eat All Your Neighbour's Dogs!'**. Racist I suppose but very funny nonetheless, a very inventive collection, wasted on his level of English. I think.

Sarcasm

The CBL once sang **'Stand Up If You Love Millwall'**. As most people were still sitting down, we sang **'Sit Down If You Hate West Ham'**. Same response, so success!

The following West Ham chant from a few years back was sarcastic, I think; **'They've Got Di Canio - We've Got Mark Birchio!'**. Not any more they/we haven't. I know who I'd rather have had playing for us and, as a clue, he wouldn't now be at QPR or a Canadian. Di Canio himself got **'Paolo Di Canio, He's Going Downio!'**.

In response to an **'Is That All You Take Away?'** chant to our 700 fans at Port Vale in November 2000, when Port Vale played the return game with a turnout of less than 200 we sang **'You Must Have Come On A Skateboard!'**.

The home Manchester City game in December 2001 led to an empty North Stand. Sarcastically we sang **'Is That All You Take Away?'/'North Stand Give Us A Song!'/'Shall We Sing A Song For You?'** and **'Can You Hear The North Stand Sing?'** etc. Ex-Lion Darren Huckerby obviously scored against us and then did a piss take goal celebration to the non-existent away fans in the North Stand, cheers.

Cardiff City in the Second Division at the time played us in the League Cup and got **'What Division Are You In?'**.

A fat shirtless Wolves fan a few years back got **'Is Your Wife As Fat As You?'** and **'We Can Smell Your Pits From Here!'**.

The **'You're Just A Small Town In...'** phenomenon led to the following geographical classic sung to Walsall - **'You're Just A Small Town In Poland!'**. Finally, I could have been mistaken but I thought that the CBL sang the following to Burnley fans recently - **'You're Just A Small Tony Blackburn!'**.

Sexual Section - Denzil's Equipment!

Due to Tony 'Denzil' Warner's alleged whopper chopper he got **'Denzil's Hung Like A Donkey!'** and **'He's Got A Hosepipe Down His Pants!'**, the last one sung to the religious strains of **'He's Got The Whole World In His Hands'**. It sounds like he sure has!

Sexual Connotations - Homosexual

Sorry PC people but Millwall's crowd is very homophobic I'm afraid; consequently this section isn't exactly 'Sing If You're Glad to Be Gay', far from it. Practically the only thing that we have not sung is 'Any Old Iron?'.

Sunsequently Elton John always has to endure the slanderous - **'Elton, Elton How's Your A...?'** Surely, that should be **'Sir Elton, Sir Elton How's Your A...?'** A bit of respect for the knighted, rug-wearing, Ivory Tickler. **'He's Bald, He's Bent, His A... Is Up For Rent, Elton John!'/'He's Fat, He's Queer, He Takes It Up The Rear, Elton John, Etc!'/'Oi Elton! Leave His A... Alone!'/'Stand Up If Your A... Is Sore!'** and **'Elton Shags Vialli, Etc La La, La**

La, La La, La La!'.

Gianluca Vialli himself got **'Are You Shagging Elton John?'** and Peterborough's manager Barry Fry got **'Barry It Takes It Up The A...!'**. I bloody don't!

West Ham sing **'Come On You Irons'** so just how many gay players do they actually have?

In a pre-season friendly in 2003/04 Southampton's 'Gay?' player Graeme Le Saux was wolf whistled, waved at and cooed mercilessly every time he touched the ball. He also got a rendition of *Y.M.C.A.*

To finish this section -

Brighton: I have listed many gay chants. sung by us against Brighton previously; here are just a few of the less obscene new ones. **'There's A Queer Boy Up Your End (Ring), Tra La, La, La, La!'/'You're Just A Town Full Of Pooftahs!'/'You Only Sing With Your Boyfriend!'** and **'You're Bent; You're Queer, You're Sitting Over There, Brighton, Brighton!'**. Finally their fans sang **'We Hate Palace More Than You!'**. I doubt it! In response we sang **'We Hate Pooftahs More than You!'**.

The FA is thinking of making gay abuse an offence like racist abuse. Let's hope it isn't in force before we play Brighton in 2004/05!

Sexual Connotations - Paedophiles

Convicted sex offender Graham Rix, manager of Pompey in December 2001, got a deluge of abuse including **'Sex Case Give Us A Wave'/'Sex Case What's the Score?'/'Gary Glitter Is Your Friend!'** and **'Graham Rix Is A Paedophile!'**. Not forgetting the chant **'Graham Rix Is A Sex Offender!'** accompanied by seat banging which went on all night.

Wolves' Dave Jones got similar to Rix although he only had allegations made against him, of which he was found innocent, but as you know shit sticks, I'm afraid and innocent or not it made no difference to us. He got the above and **'Oi! David, Leave Those Kids Alone!'/ 'You're Going Down With The Nonces!'** and **'You're Supposed To Be In Jail!'**.

Stockport's Carlton Palmer also got similar abuse, which I think was news to him.

Sexual Section - Flashing And Brothels

There was a girl in the Burnley section at the February 2004 home League game who responded to **'Get Your Tits Out For The Lads!'** by doing just that, bravo!

At one game the CBL sang **'You Couldn't Score In A Brothel!'**. My mate Simon's young son Patrick turned to me and said 'Bal, what's a waffle?'

I said 'It's a sort of fried pancake thing, why?'

He said 'Why are they singing you couldn't score in a waffle?'

I said 'No, they're saying brothel!'

He said 'What's a brothel?'

I said quickly 'Ask your dad!'

He sat quietly for a few moments and finally said:

'Is it a place with naked ladies? Like a strip club?'

I said 'Erm! Yes, sort of!'

I then tried to get him off the subject, Simon said to me 'Thanks for telling him it's a brothel, he's been calling it a waffle for two years!'

Glad to be of service.

The Fashion Conscious

The classic abuse of a fashion victim was ex-Wolves and Aston Villa player Paul Birch at the Old Den. His lush and blonde (sic) curls attracted so many 'Cooes!' and wolf-whistles that it was like a building site workers' convention outside a girls' school. So distracting was it to the peroxided, permed (?) one that his manager had to pull him off, as it were. This was a few years back. A couple of modern players have been the target of fashion abuse.

Firstly Efetebore Sodje who played in a bandana for Crewe got the following Ali G comparisons - **'He's Got A Tea Towel On His Head - Aiii!'/'One Ali G, There's Only One Ali G!'** and **'Bling, Bling!'**. As we took the lead he got **'Tea Towel, Tea Towel What's The Score?'**. He was sent off in the game and got the customary **'Bye, Bye Tea Towel! F... Off Tea Towel, Etc!'**.

Secondly in 2004 Bradford had a 70s Blaxploitation throwback Robert Wolleaston sporting an afro. He naturally got the full treatment of **'There's Only One Lionel Richie!'/'Lionel, Lionel Give Us A Song!'** and **'Hello, Is It Me You're Looking For?'**.

Goalies Go A Wandering

My favourite goalie story was when Hull's keeper Tony Norman, unfortunately pushed the ball into his own net from a cross right in front of the CBL at the Old Den, in a manner that Gary Sprake would have been proud of. To comfort him we sang **'Tony Norman Is Our Friend, Etc, He Drops Crosses!'**. He was also subjected to every chant that we could think of: **'We're The Famous, The Famous Norman'/'We Love You Norman Oh! Yes We Do'/'Give Me An N. O. R. M. A. N, Etc.'/'We're Proud Of You Norman!'** and **'Norman, Norman, Norman!'**. Both the clapping and *Amazing Grace* versions to name just a few. As you can imagine, he wandered further and further up the field as the sarcastic abuse behind him continued unabated.

Who Ate All The Pies?

The olden day chant of **'You're Shit Ah!'** has been replaced at the New Den with **'Ah! You Fat Tosser!'**. Just a sample of the other type of abuse cuddly goalies get **'Fatty, Fatty What's The Score?'/'You Fat B......!'** and **'You Fat C...!'** (Who I thought was a Vietnamese politician?).

Peterborough once had a skinny goalkeeper who got **'You Should Eat All The Pies!'/'You Skinny C...!'** and **'Who Had All The Slimfast?'**.

Wimbledon's goalkeeper got **'You Fat Squatter!'** and **'You Fat Womble!'**.

At a Boxing Day match in 2002 Gillingham's Jason Brown got **'You're Just A Fat Little Pikey!'**. He also got the post-*Only Fools And Horses* 2002 Christmas special illegal immigrant reference **'Gary, Gary, Gary!'**.

Kevin Pressman is a fat goalie who played for a team sponsored by 'Chupa Chups'. When I first saw the logo, I thought it said 'Chubby Chops' on his shirt, which I thought was a bit harsh. He used to get **'Sumo!'/'Pressman's On The Slimfast!'/'There's Only One Billy Bunter!'** and **'Belly's Gonna Get Ya!'**.

Grimsby's goalkeeper Danny Coyne got chants to highlight Grimsby's fishy heritage; **'Who Ate All The Fish Pies?'**, the usual **'Ah! You Fat Tosser!'** chant became **'Ah! You Fat Kipper!'** and classically, **'Dodgy Keeper'** became **'Dodgy Kipper!'**, marvellous.

We played Burnley on pancake night and their keeper Marlon Beresford got the topical **'You Fat B......, You Fat B......, You Ate All The Pancakes!'**.

There you have it, Millwall home abuse in a bloody big nutshell, you'll find many more chants in the away match sections later on. To close, a few chants from our guests.

The Best From Our Visitors

There were a couple of observations aimed at Wigan's usual piss poor turnout - **'You've Only Got 10 Fans!'** and **'What's It Like To See A Crowd?'**, to which they replied **'Where's Your 40,000 Gone?'**. To highlight the return to the woodwork of our Auto windscreen glory hunters, touché. I noticed in a Millwall programme from the 1980s that Wigan used to be sponsored by 'Bulldog Tools'. Now, if that's not another way of saying 'Dog's Bollocks' I don't know what is!

Walsall beat us 3-0 at the New Den, a week after Scotland nearly lost to the Faroe Islands so they sang **'Are You Scotland In Disguise?'**.

West Brom were flying high in 2003/04 and sang the sarcastic **'Top Of The League - We're Having A Laugh!'**.

To finish this chapter, a classic; Cambridge United sang the following to a fat bloke in the East Upper, an adaptation of **'Who Ate All The Pies?'** and a dig at their local rivals Peterborough's manager - **'You Ate Barry Fry!'**.

I'd like to leave one thought with you - it's not the winning that matters, it's the taking the piss that counts.

5.

The Continuing Diary
Of A Masochist

Season 2000/2001 Division 2

In this chapter, I have completed my diary of travelling away in 2000/01 and added a few home games to complete this very eventful season. It starts from my fifth away game; the other four games appear in more detail in *Tuesday Night In Grimsby*. To précis them -

Notts County, 19/8/2000, won 4-3. At Meadow Lane, a steward asked if he could frisk me by saying 'Hello ducks can I just search you?'. Silly me, I must have forgotten to take my Orville costume off. Certainly, the strangest steward's inquiry I've ever had. The PA announcer had whistling dentures, we won the game 4-3 with a glorious late winner and the homeward-bound train went all around the Midlands to get back to London due to an on-track suicide.

Brighton, Tuesday 22/8/2000, League Cup 1st round 1st leg, won 2-1. Withdean a trip to the posh area of Brighton, a match played in a weird athletics stadium inside a park, with an away stand like a bouncy Meccano kit topped off with wooden planks.

Brentford, 16/9/2000, drew 1-1. There was missile throwing from our section and the home fans to the side of us were moved away whilst chanting 'We're Supposed To Be At Home!'. It was also the game that we barracked Rhino and McCleary prior to their departure.

Ipswich Town, Tuesday 26/9/2000, League Cup 2nd round 2nd leg, lost 5-0. Following a 2-0 home win we faced a referee-induced Alamo-style onslaught with Millwall down to 7 men at one point.

THE CONTINUING DIARY OF A MASOCHIST

Peterborough United, 30/9/2000, won 4-1. Paul Simms drove his brother Nathan, Mad Ted, Simon and I, some of the usual East End group, to Peterborough. We parked in a pub car park and headed towards the town centre in search of food. It was my third visit but the first time I had been driven there and I had never seen the Olde Worlde town centre before. Walking around we noticed that every pub was heavily bouncered and had police cars parked outside. We bought some food in Burger King and sat on a monument's steps to eat it.

Almost the instant that we sat down all hell broke loose outside the pubs. Ted hared off to join the fray, he's partial to this sort of thing and isn't called mad for nothing. The rest of us preferred to eat and watch the police race past us towards the skirmishes. Once it had died down Ted rejoined us and we set off towards the ground. As we walked, we were flanked by some decidedly dodgy looking locals, shaven headed, shirtless and gypsyesque. We had Millwall shirts on and expected an attack at any moment, bugger the 'We don't attack the shirts' policy. The main threat was a monster with tattoos on his shaved dome; now, that has to hurt, Neanderthal skull or not.

We made our defence plans. My brilliant idea was to attack the monster, not too sensible and something that even Ted wouldn't consider, he's mad not daft. My excuse is that I've been whacked on the head over the years playing in goal and doing Karate. We continued on battle stations but thankfully, nothing happened. I for one wasn't too sorry. We bought a programme that had a picture of Jason Lee on the front with a crop, having dispensed with his trademark 'Pineapple'. The programme notes by Barry Fry were odd; they consisted of him saying how good Millwall's team were and how passionate we fans were, a strange way to inspire his own side and fans I thought.

The game was supposed to be all ticket. Annoyingly, when we got to the turnstiles you could also pay on the day; this turnstile had no queue whilst our advanced ticket turnstile had a bloody great queue. The away Moys section consisted of a shallow covered terrace behind the goal and we also had a side section of seating to our right, in total 1600 fans.

I WAS BORN UNDER THE COLD BLOW LANE

Pre-match, 'Boro's chairman walked along the front of our terrace extolling us to have a nice family club time. I think he had the wrong end. I only recognised him from the programme; everyone else must have thought he was a loony because he got a 'nutter on the bus' response.

Before the kick off the hundred or so Lions in the seats were joined by a 30-strong Boro 'Firm' in the adjoining block. In time-honoured fashion, midway through the first half they suddenly stood up and announced themselves. This elicited a less than cheery response from the Millwall ranks and we broke into 'Is That What You Call A Firm?'. In response one bright Posh 'Boy' with a crop and a bright red shirt sitting close to the front decided that he wasn't conspicuous enough so took off his shirt and waved it around his head. Let's just say that his six-pack owed more to the local pubs than the local gyms. His shirt-waving was like a red rag to a bull, or in this case a red shirt to a Lion. Having made himself the prime target his only option was to front it out, he got 'Fat C... - No Hair!'/'Fat C... - Cheap Shirt!' and 'Cheap Shirt - No Hair!'. As our second half goal tally rose, he got a 5-minute barrage accompanied with the appropriate gestures - 'Fat C..., Fat C... What's The Score?'. I think he now realised that his actions might have been a mistake.

Before the end of the game the home Firm tried to leave. This prompted a couple of hundred Millwall to attempt to get out to have a 'chat' with them; luckily for the home fans the gates were locked. We cruised to a 4-1 win with our team and fans living up to Barry Fry's programme billing. Contentedly we drove home, as happy as Larry with new dentures.

Luton Town, Sunday 8/10/2000 Noon, won 1-0. I have been to Luton so many times that I have lost count, it's always a treat (sic). Kenilworth Road is essentially in an Asian ghetto with the Oak Road away entrance in the middle of a residential street. The facilities could most kindly be called a f...ing disgrace, a throwback to an era long since discarded, which no one should have to put up with nowadays. Having negotiated the rickety stairwell on to the all-seater stand, inside it is particularly claustrophobic with a low roof and posts - a restricted view at best.

THE CONTINUING DIARY OF A MASOCHIST

The ground has improved over the years. The away end used to be a home stand for a start; however, it's still a real curiosity. Especially the greenhouse executive boxes, more akin to a garden centre than a football ground, topped off with high netting, presumably to stop the agricultural-type defenders whacking the ball clean out of the ground. Whilst I wouldn't especially put Luton in the trouble club category, it's not exactly peace and love either. The Home 'Boys' usually position themselves behind the fences to the right of our stand giving it the big 'un. It can be a volatile atmosphere, riot notwithstanding, and there have been town-centre skirmishes and pub clashes in the past.

Today's match followed the pattern of all of the recent games. Paul, Nathan, Ted and I drove the 30-odd miles, parked up, walked to the Eric Morecambe Suite, bought a programme, the away following exchanged niceties with the locals, we picked up three points and drove home, job done.

The only thing of note was that they had a bearded steward who got 'There's Only One Kenny Rogers!'. Or two Dolly Partons, if you prefer.

Stoke City, 21/10/2000, lost 3-2. The minor skirmishes at Peterborough were merely a taster to the main course at Stoke, which is always an 'interesting' trip. Paul and Nathan were due to pick me up with Ted making his own way to the ground to get the 8.30am coach. Unfortunately, the two brothers overdid it on Friday night and were still in bed when they should've picked me up. I woke them with my panicky phone call and they set off from Chingford, like Michael Schumacher with a rocket up his Jacksy.

Ted was already on the coach and was having kittens and consequently I received numerous agitated calls to my mobile. I told him the situation and said that if the coach left, we would drive up to Stoke. Fortunately, Billy Neill had made a ricket and booked the coaches as per the previous visit, which had kicked off at 1pm, so although we arrived late they hadn't left. We had an easy trip up with the highlight being a very dodgy video of *Nutty Professor 2 - The Klumps*, which had Chinese subtitles.

Like many new grounds, the Britannia is close to the motorway and well away from the town centre. We arrived and went onto the left side of the Signal Radio Stand behind the goal; there were 1100 of us on the lower portion of a stand that had netting across it, creating a 'No man's land' between the home fans to our left and us. Pre-match, Ted spoke to a Stoke steward who confirmed what I already knew; that trouble was a frequent occurrence, with seat throwing a speciality; he also said that there had been trouble in town Friday night with several arrests. Just before kick off a sizeable Millwall 'Firm' arrived surrounded by a large contingent of riot police.

The game started and Neil Harris scored after 20 seconds. Stoke pulled a goal back and then went in front all within the space of the first 12 minutes. Stoke's Victoria Ground was one of the best for atmosphere and despite being all-seater the Britannia still retains a hotbed volatility. With the atmosphere already tense, this added excitement prompted an escalation in the pleasantries. Several home fans to our left motioned to get onto the pitch naturally, Millwall followed suit by clamouring over the segregation netting in an attempt to meet them. The riot police quickly moved in, forming a barrier around the players' tunnel to the left hand of our stand. Unable to get at each other, the verbal insults continued but didn't escalate. Thankfully Neil Harris made it 2-2 just before half-time. During the half-time period, all was calm.

In the second half, the game appeared to be set fair for a draw. The PA announced an injury-time Stoke substitute Chris Iwelumo, who'd only been drafted into the squad because another player was injured in the warm-up. His name was met by howls of laughter and I said to the others 'He sounds like an African Teletubby!' Typically, he scored Stoke's winner with practically the last kick of the game. This late goal prompted their fans to jump about wildly and our fans to unleash a barrage of broken seats at them across the player's tunnel. The whistle went and the players, etc headed for cover. Humorously, the salvo ceased whenever a Millwall player went into the tunnel, because everyone stopped to applaud them prior to relaunching the bombardment. When all was calm, the announcer said 'Would all the people going on a London-bound train please remain in the ground'. Everyone ignored him and headed outside, quite why they didn't lock us in I don't know.

THE CONTINUING DIARY OF A MASOCHIST

To the left of the away section runs a fence adjoining the side home stand. Since my previous visit, they had replaced the original wire fence with a metal railing one. As before, Stoke's fans had taken up a position above this fence and proceeded to throw anything that came to hand at us; bricks, wood, bottles, traffic cones, etc. Naturally, everything that landed on our side was thrown back and a medieval battle ensued. As the police tried to disperse the home fans and Millwall fans tried to batter down the metal fence, someone tossed tear-gas into our section, police or home fans, I don't know. Whoever it was it worked because those at the fence retreated with their eyes streaming. A large group of Millwall then broke off and tried to attack the home fans being moved on by the police. Skirmishes broke out in various parts of the wide-open car park, mostly with the police. After a while, the team came out to get onto their coach. This distracted people sufficiently to allow the situation to calm down. In all the fun, I had lost track of the other three so I thought it best to go back on the coach and wait for them there.

Steward Larry suddenly declared that, even though half the passengers were in the car park, we were leaving. He and I then had a discussion along the lines of 'You're not leaving my mates in the F...ing car park!' to which he replied 'The police have told me to go!', prompting my response of 'F... the police, you're not leaving them here!'. He saw the logic in my argument and waited for the absentees to return before leaving. The trouble was largely ignored in the media, unusually there was no sign of the normal 16-page full-colour 'Hoolie' special. I suppose I should be grateful for small mercies.

Swindon Town, Tuesday 24/10/2000, won 2-0. Swindon is a family club of an unthreatening nature and a huge culture shock following the previous weekend's fun and games. Paul and Nathan's dad Dave drove to this game in his minibus with his sons, Ted, Simon, Pat and me.

A 90 mile trip is what we seasoned travellers call a 'Just up the roader', which it is once you're doing 70mph-plus on the motorway. We arrived early and joined the ritual Millwall occupation of Burger King, wasting time until the turnstiles opened. We eventually went into the ground and onto the Upper Arkells Stand with around a 1000 Lions fans. I once sat in this stand, the fire alarm went off and nobody took a blind bit of notice. Early on, they played a pre-recorded female voice saying something like 'Swindon is proud to be a family club, so no swearing, abuse, racial or otherwise. In fact, if you could manage to generate no atmosphere whatsoever we would be much obliged.'. Nearer to the game, the PA announcer extolled the home fans to sing 'Come On You Reds!'. He proceeded repeatedly to chant this. I got the impression that this particular idiot was doing his DJing from a nice padded room free of sharp things, with the microphone as his only friend. I have a theory that if a crowd sing songs like 'Come On You …!' etc, it's either because they don't sing as a rule or are glory hunters who don't know the songs; that's my opinion and I'm sticking to it. Although there were only a few home fans in the ground at the time of both of the above, they somehow managed to obey the requests. Save for a big bass drummer, they gave a performance like Harpo Marx. We barely got a peep out of them all night except for a barely audible bee in a jar sound every now and then.

Something that has often puzzled me at the County Ground was who decided that the away-seated section behind the goal is in the Mediterranean and therefore doesn't need a roof? They are not the only ones with this tropical delusion. The idea of having an open end in sunny Wiltshire was put into perspective as we sat freezing in our stand, which had a roof, and Pat turned to Simon and said 'Dad, where are we?'. I said to Simon 'Tell him Spartak Moscow, it's bloody cold enough!'.

The game was unusual in that for once in my life we had a referee who was an 'Away Town Harry' who proceeded to give most of the decisions in our favour. They had a player sent off for diving; his second yellow card, at which point their manager Steve McMahon lost the plot and was also sent off. We won 2-0 largely thanks to the referee, which certainly made a nice change. We left the ground and within an hour and a half, we were in Kensington. The police had shut a main road due to a murder, so we tried to take a detour via Olympia. We passed a cab whose driver said 'They're working on a bridge up there mate, you won't get that thing through; it's only a 6 ft 6 inch clearance!'. I was riding shotgun in the front and said to Dave 'How wide is the van?'. He said that he didn't know and we had visions of getting stuck and blocking West London for days. Luckily, with a gnat's helmet to spare, we got through.

Port Vale, 4/11/2000, drew 1-1. I went to this game with Paul, Nathan and Puff Teddy on a 9am club coach. This particular Ted nickname was very apt for this particular trip because the New Den car park reeked of wacky baccy, a bit bloody early I thought. The journey to the Potteries was uneventful.

We arrived at Vale Park for my third visit and inside we met up with my cousin Paul and his Essex mates. As we stood chatting by the food counter there appeared to be a 'joint' police/refreshment stall operation going on, along the lines of the New Den spliff smoking. They appeared to be pumping marijuana through the air vents on the concourse around the food stall - the air was full of it. An ingenious policy if you ask me, with a double benefit -

1) It would lull us volatile Lions fans into a more manageable mood.
2) It would give everyone the munchies, boosting food sales as well.

Increasing food sales and sedating the rabble at the same time, marvellous! I'm amazed that no one had thought of it before.

The ground itself had changed markedly since my last visit in the 1990s, when I had stood behind the goal on an open terrace; we were on the same end as before, however, it was now an all-seater stand with a roof. Work appeared to be underway on a new stand to the right of the away section to complete the 'Wembley of the North' as some nutter once called it. I also noticed that one of the home stands was called the Mizuno stand, presumably to pay respect to Burslem's Japanese community?

Twenty home fans in a side stand sang this hilarious chant to the 700-plus away fans - 'Is That All You Take Away?'. Irony is obviously lost on them. We laughed at them and sang 'Is That All You Have At Home?'. Other than this there was no atmosphere whatsoever, which for some reason draws everyone in the ground into lethargy, even volatile fans like us; mind you, that could have had something to do with the earlier police policy. The game finished 1-1 and there was very little to report in truth.

The only things of note were that the home side's large dog Muppet kept on showing us its arse, which was charming and there were apparently clashes outside between our train escort and the heavy-handed riot police on the long march back to the train station, a foot slog of bloody miles. We ourselves boarded our coach and had an unmemorable trip back to London.

Oldham Athletic, 25/11/2000, won 1-0. I missed the games at Wigan and Bristol Rovers, the latter being a win, which I had never seen us manage at any of Rovers' grounds, bloody typical.

My next away game was another coach trip with Simon and Ted to Oldham, my third visit. As we neared Greater Manchester, we passed dilapidated dark satanic mills and commented that if these were in London, they would be luxury loft-style apartments before you could say shafted by the estate agents. When we got into Oldham itself, we reached the limit of the coach driver's knowledge, so he decided to drive around and around a roundabout until the police rescued us before we all got too dizzy. We eventually got off the coach and went into Boundary Park.

I did my customary pre-match loo trip and thought my luck had changed when I found an *FHM 100 Sexiest Women* magazine, seemingly sitting all on its lonesome on a washbasin. I thought 'Come To Papa!' and picked it up only for a Northern voice behind me to say 'That's mine!' as he emerged from the WC trap just as I was about to walk out with it. Pardon me but I thought that this was the type of magazine that you took into the toilet, not left outside!

I took up my seat behind the goal with the others, in a stadium that was a throwback to football's golden age; in particular, The Lookers stand to our right was a real Trades Descriptions job in terms of design and occupants. It's fine having a stand called 'Lookers' as long as the occupants don't look like Iain Dowie's less attractive relatives. The pitch was one of the worst that I'd ever seen; their groundsman appeared to have taken some sort of threshing machine to it, probably to stop Millwall's silky football.

THE CONTINUING DIARY OF A MASOCHIST

Oldham's Muppet was called Chaddy The Owl, which again very kindly showed us its arse. I may have imagined this; I often have fantasies about owls, who doesn't? The atmosphere was so bad that one bloke sitting behind me said 'This is the best attended funeral I've ever been to!'. The only noise came from some young boys barracking us from the Lookers Stand. We replied with a few chants to highlight their piss poor opposition status - 'Back To School on Monday'/'Does Your Mother Know You're Here?' and 'Little Boys!', not forgetting the classic 'How Much Does Your Mother Charge?'.

The 500-plus of us saw a referee reverting to type and doing his utmost to stop us from winning, sadly he failed and we won 1 - 0. Cheerfully we left the ground, got outside and the fact that Boundary Park is one of the highest grounds in the league became apparent; it was high up and bloody freezing, thermals and breathing apparatus were the order of the day. Mind you, to a southern softie like me anywhere up north is cold. It was now dark, which enabled us to take in the breathtaking panoramic views of Oldham which, piss taking aside, were actually quite impressive, at night anyway. The coach trip back was uneventful save for a service station visit when a bloke got back on board with a glass coffee container he'd taken from the cafeteria. As everyone on the coach did mock tutting to him, he said 'I thought it was a takeaway' to which one bloke replied 'Watch it mate, you'll give Millwall a bad name!'. This prompted howls of ironic laughter all around.

Wycombe Wanderers, Tuesday 19/12/2000, FA Cup 2nd round replay, lost 2-1. Unfortunately, I missed Rotherham away, so my next game was the FA Cup replay at Wycombe following a draw at the New Den. Dave drove Simon, Ted and I the short distance to Buckinghamshire. We arrived at 6pm and decided to go to the pub but this was a big mistake, the bar had two staff, one of whom then left to change a barrel, thereby dropping a bit of a financial bollock as the pub was packed to the rafters with thirsty Lions. Dave tried for 20 minutes to get a drink, gave up and we left along with many dry others.

We drove to the ground and parked in the industrial area surrounding Adams Park. The gates were late opening and Ted went completely off on one at a steward about the delay, who said to him 'Calm down sir!'. I pointed out that unfortunately this was calm. Eventually they opened up and we went straight to the refreshment stall. Standing in the queue was Alvin Martin. Simon decided that it was his civic duty to have a pop at the ex-Hammer, so he did.

Wycombe is a nice compact/smallish ground that has no atmosphere, save for a brass band, in my opinion the desperate act of a scoundrel. We sat with various Lions mates in the Roger Vere Stand among 861 Millwall. Our spirits collectively sank when we saw that as per the home game the referee was Uriah Rennie, a real Millwall favourite (sic), nothing to do with his colour, just his ineptitude. His performance consisted of allowing dodgy goals, disallowing good goals, turning down blatant penalties, booking Christophe Kinet for letting himself get kicked up in the air and generally making a pig's breakfast of the whole night's proceedings. Big black-belt bloke he might be, but then he needs to have a high level of martial arts to defend his decisions. He got plenty of stick including 'The Referee's A Racist!'/'You're Not Fit To Referee!'/'You're Not Fit For Sunday League!' and 2-1 To The Referee!'. Someone in our section shouted out this play on words - 'Oi! Rennie You Give Me Guts Ache!'. Wycombe, as Rennie found out and Martin Taylor knows very well, is one of the worst grounds if you're trying to avoid our attention. Taylor got his usual Derby play-off abuse including 'He's Behind You!' and 'His Name Is Martin Taylor And He Likes To Run, He Do Run, Run, Run, He Do Run, Run!'.

The night was topped off nicely with an after-match toilet visit. Inside it was ankle deep in an unidentified liquid, precisely the time that you realise that your shoes leak. The flood was caused by some bright spark putting toilet rolls and a cistern lid into one of the toilet bowls. This was one of those nights - Uriah Rennie, an FA Cup exit and piss-filled shoes, marvellous! The only good things were that we could now concentrate on the League and we got home early.

Bournemouth, 23/12/2000, won 2-1. Dave drove Simon, Pat, Nathan, Dave Murray, Ted and I to this pre-Christmas weekend match in his minibus with Millwall top of the League. It was a typically bleak winter's day with the roadside fields shrouded in thick fog. As Bournemouth's ground is located in the middle of a park, we wondered if the match would actually be on but ploughed on regardless,

We arranged to meet Colin and Paul in the ground. Colin was making his way from Bridport and Paul was in Southampton visiting his girlfriend Helen. As I was navigating, I have to say that the internet map was wrong when we took the wrong junction. Still, the country lane that we found ourselves in enabled us to 'water' the roadside grass as it were. We picked up the correct road and arrived in Bournemouth a short while later. We headed straight to a chip shop/restaurant, sat down and watched a farce unfold before our eyes.

It was like Rorkes Drift with the Millwall throng playing the part of the Zulus. We watched the Chinese couple who ran the shop having a nervous breakdown, whilst taking orders that they had no chance of filling and battling against a tide of Londoners. After about 45 minutes, we were served, ate our meal, left and warned anybody else thinking of going in not to. We drove to the ground, parked up and found that although it was murky the match was on; we met up with the others and went inside.

Dean Court is another rough ground but with no hint of threat from the locals. We had around 1500 fans split between our open terrace behind the goal and a ramshackle side stand to our left. This game was played after Theo's BBC2 *Back To The Floor* documentary on which Neil Harris complained about having to pay for his toast at the training ground, hence the 'I'll Pay For Your Toast Bomber' banner and the toast bombardment that he got before the game. Pre-match, Bournemouth's stewards and Muppet gave out little plastic rattles, what a good idea I thought, I know where they will end up. Surprisingly they were used to pelt the overly officious police and stewards trying to quell our minor pitch incursions following our goals - told you so.

We won 2-1, left the ground and headed for our minibus parked in the stadium car park. This area was like a mad house with horns hooting, flags waving and 'Cheer Up Mark McGhee!' filling the air. As we queued to get out on to the main road, the racket continued unabated. It was bedlam with a continuous Lions cacophony; the locals must have thought that we were all mad. Happy Christmas! A win, top of the league and new socks from my aunts. Ah, bliss!

Reading, 6/1/2001, won 4-3. Reading isn't hostile but for some reason visits are always action-packed. This was to be yet another eventful day in Berkshire. It was Mark McGhee's first game at Reading since his less than amicable departure and Millwall were still top of the league. Dave drove me, Ted, Paul, Nathan, Simon and his brother Kevin, a Man U fan who was there because Pat was ill, to the game in his minibus. We went via Earl's Court, passing some Chelsea on their way to Stamford Bridge. As we got close Dave slowed down, opened his side window and greeted them with a damn good wankering. It had to be done.

The excellent Madejski Stadium is located close to the motorway; we arrived early, parked in the club car park and wandered around Madejskiville. We got something to eat and went to Tempo's as Ted was thinking of buying a new television. He didn't buy one in the end because he didn't fancy leaving it in the minibus. We then went into a huge JJB Sports, where we found that you could buy golf clubs, cricket bats and baseball bats, in fact everything that the dedicated Hoolie could wish for, a sort of 'Do 'Em All's'. We finally set off to the ground, en route I noticed that the swish hotel complex appeared to have the chairman's name spelt wrong in bloody great letters outside; to me it looked like it said Millennium Madejski Hotel, a bit of a cock-up on the megalomania front there. I also noticed that Reading appeared to be sponsored by LA Gangsta rappers as they had 'Westcoast' on their shirtfronts. We eventually went inside and on to the non-smoking South Stand; this modern phenomenon must strike terror in to the heart of any ardent puffers.

Today was a good day for spotting Gloryhunters and 'Don't Usually Go Away' fans. The tell tale signs - they walk up the stairs looking at their tickets trying to locate their correct seat, as opposed to the away veteran who has a quick look to decide if the allocated seat is any good and if not simply sits in the best available seats.

The casual 'good-time' away fan doesn't have the haunted post-traumatic stressed look of a come rain or shine veteran that we all carry as the mental scars of seasons of horrors etched on our face. 'The Floaters' also invariably laugh at a chant/comment like they have never heard it before, when they have been prevalent for weeks. These are just a few indicators to identify these 'Johnny-come-lately' newly-acquired away fans.

We did our customary glance at our real seats before deciding to sit in better ones. We met Dave Murray and his mate Martin, who had come over from Cavan in Ireland. He appeared to have taken a drink and he sang and abused the opposition all afternoon, bravo! There was a pre-match penalty shootout between Zampa and home Muppet Kingsley, another Lion, consisting of them flashing their arses and making mock 'offering out' gestures to each other and the crowd, which was good for a laugh.

Reading's manager Alan Pardew had slagged McGhee off in the local press. With the heat already on, this raised the temperature even further, Millwall's turnout of 3112 reflected this. Reading's crowd is always very lippy in the ground but conspicuous by their absence outside, which I always find odd. Today they were especially agitated with McGhee considered a Judas. Club announcer Jonathan Richards didn't help when he went into an anti-McGhee tirade; we sat there looking at each other thinking - what's this bloke on? He was strongly disciplined for this, nothing wrong with a bit of Miss Whiplash. Reading later apologised and he resigned in a bit of a strop. I must say that I had never heard anything like it before or since, it's just as well that we're such well behaved fans otherwise there might have been trouble. All the rant managed to do was wind us up, it was like a personal affront to us all.

Before the match Richards put on *Daydream Believer*, a big mistake as we belted out the 'Cheer Up Mark McGhee' version so loudly that Denzil looked up startled at the racket emanating from behind his goal during the pre-match warm-up. It also backfired on the pitch when Millwall put in one of the best away performances that I've ever seen, going into a 3-0 half-time lead including two Neil Harris goals and a totally against the norm own goal by former player Ricky Newman. Neil Harris completed his hat trick early in the second half to make it 4-0. Reading staged a comeback leaving the final score 4-3 with the last goal at the death. The scoreline flattered them enormously; if we had tried a bit harder, we could have declared at half-time. This game had everything, a great Lions performance, a mighty Lions roar and all the extra fun that went with it. For example, on top of what I have already mentioned, after Millwall scored the first goal Ted went to the toilet only to then go AWOL. After some time had elapsed, I called him on his mobile to see if he'd gone back to Tempo's. I eventually got him and asked 'Where are you?'. He said 'I'm outside, I didn't do anything and they chucked me out!'. It later transpired that he had intervened when some home stewards were trying to eject some Millwall fans in the forecourt and in his public-spirited way, whilst trying to help fellow Lions, he employed his less than diplomatic approach, abusing stewards and police. Subsequently he himself was ejected. They eventually allowed him back in with a quarter of an hour to go. He saw only one Millwall goal, but was in time to see two of Reading's comeback goals.

After the game the police tried to get every Millwall fan parked in the car park to go on a totally pointless walk, up to a roundabout along the road, around it and back to the car park. I can only assume that this was a Thames Valley police get-fit campaign. Nobody took them up on their kind offer and we stood there questioning them, less than politely, as to what this ridiculous policy was all about. After an ample time had elapsed for the police to show their authority, they eventually let us back to the cars. On the way towards the motorway we took a wrong turn and had to do a U-turn across a pedestrian footpath with Dave doing a good impression of a getaway driver.

This was a real day for adventure and a fitting first return for Mark McGhee. The team and fans had responded magnificently to this big, grudge match, for me this was one the great away days.

Colchester United, Tuesday 6/2/2001, won 1-0. Simon's son Pat and Clive joined the usual East End contingent for the trip to Colchester. We picked Clive up en route and were then stuck in a massive traffic jam near Brentwood; it eventually took us three hours to do the 50-mile trip.

We arrived at the ground at 7pm, parked in a side street a distance from the ground, then hurried to the match. As we walked the heavens opened with a mixture of torrential rain and hailstones, set against the theatrical backdrop of thunder and lightning. Naturally, we got thoroughly drenched arriving at the ground like drowned rats. The programme sellers said that there had already been two pitch inspections with the game touch-and-go even before this new deluge. Luckily, the game was on. Amazingly, I have never been at a postponed or abandoned away match. The pitch was deemed fit although it was more suitable for scuba diving than flowing football. In a moment of great irony, the referee's name was T. Leake,

At the best of times Layer Road is a monstrosity; however, with a flooded pitch, it was like being at an outdoor swimming gala. Most of Millwall's 1400 turnout were on the tiny Layer Road End terrace, with no facilities or means of easy exit. We gave a great impression of a tin of sardines when the home announcer asked if we could move along to make more room, I think not. As always it was a great viewing experience, with the few steps on the terrace behind the goal meaning that the highest you could get was barely above the crossbar's height and subsequently you had no perception of on-pitch distances. Bizarrely the away seats are at the other end of the ground. To highlight what we thought of the ground we chanted 'Shit Hole!'. One of few highlights was when Mr Leake was summoned by a call of 'Oi Ref!'. As he looked up the caller shouted 'You're A Sex Case!', which he laughed at. A rarity - a referee, who was wet, had a daft name and a sense of humour. As expected the game was a total farce, with water lying all over the swamp of a pitch, though we got out of jail with a 1-0 win and managed to come away still on top of the league.

As we hadn't managed to get anything to eat before the game, we stopped at a Chinese chip shop that we passed on the way out of Colchester. Like Bournemouth, it was full of Millwall supporters; naturally, they had no food ready so we had to wait, for half an hour as it turned out. This gave me an opportunity to look around at what they had on offer; my eyes rested on a delicacy that I hadn't seen before even up North - 'Mushy Pea Fritters!'. Mmmm! Lovely! They also sold reconstituted Mushy Peas (?). There was a poster on the wall for Pukka Pies featuring a loving couple in their car gazing gooey-eyed at each other tucking in to a romantic meal of Pukka Pie and chips, spread out on paper between them with the slogan 'Get Close with Pukka Pies'.

Only a gypsy violinist and red roses could have conjured up a more romantic scene. I said to Clive 'Here's a night out for you and the wife, Valentine's Night is coming up, why not suggest it to her'. Apart from the fact that she'd divorce you, obviously. We got our food, went back to the bus and drove home.

Swansea City, Sunday 11/2/2001 1pm, drew 0-0. Nathan picked Ted and me up to get a 7.30am club coach. It was so early that Nathan hadn't gone to bed at all, preferring to kip on the coach. Luckily he can sleep like a log on a clothesline. We again arranged to meet Paul in the ground, as he was staying with Helen in Cardiff where she was at University.

There were seven coaches in all. Unfortunately, ours had three blokes on board, who were about 12 sheets to the wind. They were sitting directly in front of us and immediately began drinking out of spiked Coke/Lemonade bottles; consequently, their behaviour degenerated until they had reached F...ing nuisance status. When we stopped at services, they got off and began fighting each other, getting covered in mud in the process. Everyone on board was thoroughly fed up with them, one bloke said 'Why don't we wait until they go to the khazi and padlock the door!'. This was greeted with cheers all round and sadly, they stayed with us all the way there. Grandad's posse also sang most of the way up, as they had for the Friday night Cup debacle years before; the land of song and unintelligible road signs must inspire them.

We crossed the Severn Bridge into South Wales and bandit country. The weather was once again bloody horrible; the sloped hills that we passed were full of sheep standing on the inclines at an angle. This led me to wonder if they had been genetically modified to have a short leg on one side to enable them to stand on a slope, although this might make a Welshman's welly-wearing 'Animal Farm' antics a bit awkward, I'd imagine. We picked up our police escort and headed into Swansea, which looked just like our own dear Southend. This seaside façade does not give you a real feel for what to expect inside a ground full of rabid Anti-

Englishness. On arrival, we disembarked and took up our position on the West Terrace behind the goal, in yet another old-fashioned football ground.

The PA announced that the game would be delayed for 15 minutes to allow Millwall's train contingent, which Paul was among, to get to the ground. We charted their progress by the police helicopter in the sky edging closer to the ground. The train 'Firm' arrived amid the usual plethora of riot police, prompting the best comedy moment - two columns of police marching from either side of the ground managed to career in to each other on the cinder track right in front of us, much to the delight of the 1400 away contingent. Pointing out the blindingly obvious, we sang 'You Don't Know What You're Doing!'. As I stood there I noticed that the 'Stretchout Stand' at the other end was sponsored by a stretch limo company; ironically, it didn't 'Stretch Out' because it only covered about two thirds of the stand. Our terrace was a covered shed with 80s-style perimeter fencing, necessary because the natives are none too friendly. My only other visit a Friday night FA Cup game had been one of the most hostile home crowds that I've ever been in, only surpassed by a night match at Leicester's Filbert Street.

Swansea came out to the very apt *White Riot* by the Clash, their fans bounced up and down, threw coins at Paul Ifill, made 'on the pitch' motions and racially abused our black players and us. Other than that, they were nowhere near as hostile as before, too early I imagine. Millwall also threw missiles and motioned to invade the pitch, there was the normal hooligan boasting and exchange of the usual regional pleasantries.

We sang 'Engerland!/Sweet Chariot/Third World Country!/I'm A Swansea City Fan And I'm A Sheep Shagger!' and 'Stick Your F...ing Dragon Up Your Arse - Sideways!' chants accompanied by tossing an inflatable sheep, bleating noises and shepherding gestures. Unfortunately, nobody could make a dragon noise although plenty had had a puff, if you catch my drift.

They sang 'England Is Full Of Shit!'/'Argentina!' and 'Stick The F...ing Queen Up Your A...!'. So there you have it, a sample of the usual glut of anti-English/Royal/Welsh/sheep molesting stuff.

I WAS BORN UNDER THE COLD BLOW LANE

The match was low-key, despite Millwall being denied two penalty shouts, one for handball and one for shirt-pulling; reffing business as usual then. The main highlight was an altercation between Zampa and Cyril the Swan resulting in Cyril decapitating Zampa and throwing her head like a trophy into the home crowd. In response to this we sang 'Kill The Swan!'.

After the game Paul made his way back to the station under police escort and Ted, Nathan and I got back on to the coach. Two of the coach drunks were still there; however, one had gone missing, they assumed he'd gone on the train so they got off to join him, hoorah! Our coaches then sat in the side streets near the ground surrounded by riot police until about 3.20pm. We then set off in convoy with police vans and motorcycles for company. The usual escort policy is to get the away coaches out of town and onto the motorway, peel away and then leave us to our own devices. In this instance they stayed with us until we were across the Severn Bridge and well into England. Every motorway bridge we passed had police on; apparently, there was intelligence that Cardiff were planning to attack us on the motorway, hence this unprecedented action. We saw no Cardiff so who knows if it was true? We saw the team coach, though, prompting much waving, etc. About 70 miles from London, the police insisted that our coaches stop at services for their legal break. We had two drivers who could have switched over without a long break but the police insisted so we had to have a three quarter of an hour stop. They didn't come into the services in any numbers so as the convoy entered en masse there were hundreds of us and it was lawless, many sandwiches, etc went walkies. The more romantically-inclined among us half-inched flowers from the Valentine's Day display to take back to their loved ones, who said romance was dead? It'll be Barbara Cartland books on the coaches next. It was also like a big kid's playground as grown men rode the kiddie rides, with Postman Pat a particular favourite. The police sat outside to make sure we didn't do a moonlight flit so the journey home was taking on epic proportions and we eventually arrived back in London after a six-hour return trek. It was a bloody long day.

THE CONTINUING DIARY OF A MASOCHIST

The following week the *Evening Standard* ran an article saying 'Cup Final Fears As Police Seize Soccer Weapons'. It said that police had instigated an operation as a dry run for the first Millennium Stadium Final. They allegedly intercepted a Millwall coach and confiscated an assortment of weapons. It said 22 people were arrested for disorder and weapons possession on the day and that 100 Swansea fans throwing missiles, including a flare, had ambushed 400 Millwall fans at Swansea station. I'm not saying there was no trouble but the police didn't stop any of the coaches in our convoy and Paul was in the police train escort and he said that he hadn't seen any Swansea, let alone any trouble, so draw your own conclusions about the police's statement. That said, Swansea is a trouble spot, the police presence was large and mostly of a riot variety and they had unusually ridden shotgun back into England with us so who knows.

Northampton Town, Tuesday 20/2/2001, drew 3-3. Dave drove Ted, Paul, Nathan and I to Northampton in his minibus. Simon and Pat were due to go but Simon was ill. Dave was himself suffering from flu and looked about to conk out at any moment, a bit worrying as he was driving on a motorway at the time; fortunately he didn't. We left at 3.30pm but due to congestion and a motorway oil spill, we didn't arrive until 7pm. Dave asked the home stewards if we could park in the main car park. Excited by his first visit Ted shouted out 'Let's Park Here You C...s!' prompting Paul and Nathan to jump on him to shut him up. I don't think they heard him but they pointed us to the visitor's car park anyway. We parked up and took up our seats in the South Stand behind the goal, with 1200 other Lions.

Sixfields is a nice compact new ground with its own Jews' Hill directly opposite the away end and like Reading it's surrounded by shops and restaurants. Northampton, 'The Cobblers', a great club to take the piss out of - their radio station is 'Radio Cobblers'; I thought they all were? There's also 'Talk Cobblers', which I usually do, a 24/7 mobile info service. Moving away from gonads, their Muppet was called Clarence The Dragon, a big green thing. Some may remember Clarence the Cross-Eyed Lion but Clarence the Drug Flashback Dragon? Mind you, how would you depict 'Cobblers'?

I WAS BORN UNDER THE COLD BLOW LANE

The game was pulsating and played on a superb pitch; unusually the atmosphere was also very good. We went 2-0 up sadly they came back to make it 3-2 aided by the ex-player phenomenon in the guise of Dave Savage, who scored two penalties, The game finished on a relative high when we scored a late goal to make it 3-3, gaining a point when we had initially been cruising. For each home goal they played Tina Turner's *Simply The Best* and more worryingly the *Can-Can*. Thankfully it didn't prompt a frilly knicker gusset-flashing high-kicking dance from the home 'boys'. Bizarrely the home fans sang a song about hating Peterborough, apparently it's held together with superglue (?). I think they had been sniffing superglue to come up with such a chant. More sensibly, they sang 'You're Top And We Don't Know How?'. As we silently stared in disbelief at our disappearing lead, they sang 'Two Nil And You F... It Up!' and 'Can You Hear The Lions Roar? No, No!'.

In the second half as the home side took hold of the game many of us stood up and the police surveillance box in the corner of the away stand suddenly burst into life, presumably trying to see why we were standing. The PA told us to sit down, naturally, everyone then stood up and we sang 'Stand Up If You Love Millwall!' prompting the home fans to sing 'Sit Down And Shut Your Mouth!'

Northampton's fans were another group full of bravado in the ground who then vanished into the night, outside, as I said it mystifies me why fans are like this. In truth, we didn't sing much on the night I think we were all in shock. Never mind, it was a good game and we were thankfully still top.

Oxford United, 24/2/2001, won 2-0. Dave was now better and once again drove myself, Paul, Ted, Nathan and a foreign female friend of Nathan's the short distance to Oxford. Simon and Pat were now both ill so didn't come with us. The Foot-and-Mouth epidemic came to prominence this weekend and during our drive we noticed that unusually the passing fields had no livestock in them.

We arrived early in Headington and Nathan's friend decided that spending the afternoon shopping and sightseeing in Oxford was preferable to watching Millwall at the Manor Ground's palatial splendour - women eh! We parked up and told her to get a bus into town because it was a walk and a half to Oxford from here. We ourselves headed to the chip shop and ate our food whilst standing outside their club shop. The shop's windows were filled with merchandise for celebrating the final game at the Manor Ground, unfortunately Oxford were practically relegated by this time and there didn't seem to be much enthusiasm for celebrating. We then headed to the ground and Dave tried to get in with his Northampton ticket, much to the bemusement of the turnstile man. Luckily, he also had the correct ticket on him and soon joined us on the terrace behind the goal.

We stood at the back of the Cuckoo Lane End behind the goal with my old mate Micky Fisher and his brood. Millwall's 2000 fans were split between this terrace and a small corner stand to our left. The Manor Ground's mismatched stands, perimeter fences, primitive facilities and open end with a bloody great CCTV camera on a large metal arm aimed directly at us, made me think 'My God I hope we get out of this Division.'. Ex-Millwall staff David 'Hoofball 'Kemp and Alan McCleary were Oxford's management team for this game. Macca got a mixed reception; he was never as popular as Rhino in their Millwall pairing.

It was a top against bottom clash and the atmosphere was relaxed, it was an afternoon for taking the points and the piss. In the warm up, we sang the sarcastic (I think?) 'There's Only One David Tuttle!'. I assume this was in the same vein as the old 'Ooh Ah! Phil Barber!' chant. As we sang the Tuttle chant, one cruel wag behind me said 'Thank F... For That!'.

Willy was in goal with Denzil as sub and we realised that of our two goalkeepers, one had an alleged Big Willie and one was called Willy. Strangely, this was the first time that we had noticed this. Referee Mr M J North was a cross between Adolf Hitler, Fawlty Towers' Manuel and a member of the Freddie Mercury appreciation society. He got 'Get Your Book Out Adolf!'/'Who Do You Think You Are Kidding Mr Hitler?'/'Oi! Manuel Book Him!' and 'The Referee's A Rent Boy!'.

The game was like a practice match as Oxford looked every inch the relegated side. Naturally, we pointed this out and to their credit, with gallows humour the home fans sang 'We'll Never Play

You Again!' and 'We'll Meet Again, Don't Know Where, Don't Know When!'. In the second half, Willy was up our end, as it were, and we sang 'Willy, Willy What's The Score?' to which he did the worst imitation of Ted Rogers finger juggling on *3-2-1* that I've ever seen.

We eventually won 2-0, although if we had put ourselves out it could have been 12-0. We were beginning to open up a large gap at the top with games in hand, a very nice place to be. We met up with our foreign shopper and drove home.

Bury, Tuesday 6/3/2001, lost 2-1. Paul, Nathan, Ted and I went to the New Den to pick up our 1pm coach and on arrival we found that it had been overbooked and we were on an overspill minibus. Nonetheless we still managed to have Larry as our steward. I had arranged to meet Colin and his son Chris in Bury as they were up North for Chris's interviews at Universities in Liverpool and Salford. It meant that Colin had the opportunity to see Millwall and Chris, my godson, had the dubious pleasure of being at his first ever Millwall away match.

Following an uneventful trip up we arrived and were greeted by signs that said 'Lion's Den'. I thought 'That's strange', until I realised that it was 'Swinton Lions', who share the ground. There was also a glut of 'Save Our Shakers' posters on the walls. To aid their fight they'd organised various fund raising days, one of which was a do at Old Trafford featuring the Neville brothers fabulously named dad Neville Neville and Scotland's manager Craig Brown; they must have been banging down the doors to get a ticket. Tonight Bury had a 'juniors for a quid night', a bit odd for a skint club. From experience, what often happens for cheapo games is that the youngsters, rather than being so enamoured with the club that they will willingly pay full price next time, usually just turn up for the next cheap game. All a skint club really needs is for the people who come out of the woodwork for fundraisers etc, to go to the home games and the club wouldn't be in such a financial mess in the first place,

We met up with Colin and Chris in the covered stand behind the goal along with 600-plus other hardy souls. This was only my second trip to Gigg Lane, my only other visit had been an end of season match when they had clinched promotion from Division 2 and the home fans applauded us fans after the game. Since then it had changed radically, it was now all-seater and none too shabby. This was a good night for some interesting incidents and sights. For example, the pitch looked like an undulating corrugated fence and vied with Oldham for the worse pitch that I had ever seen. The groundsman appeared to have adopted the Barnes Wallis Bouncing Bomb School of groundskeeping. It was certainly not helped by the fact that it was also lashing down with rain as well.

Their Muppet was a bizarre entity called Robbie The Bobby; dressed in an Olde Worlde hat and tailcoat outfit, it was one of the oddest *It's A Knockout* type of characters I've ever seen. On this planet the man inside is a 15 stone builder who was apparently not averse to a bout of Muppet fisticuffs, mind you I'd be in a fighting mood if I had to cavort about in this get-up as well.

There was a glass-fronted restaurant overlooking the pitch inside the ground in the left-hand corner of our end. Humorously they shut the curtains just as the match started, which said a lot about the home side I thought. The ground has the cheerfully named Cemetery End. There was a conservatory around the players' tunnel, presumably sold to them by the world's great salesman - 'Yes that's the perfect spot for a conservatory Sir!'.

Willy was again in goal and in homage we sang 'We've Got The Biggest Willy In The League!'. Willy was in and out of the team prior to this extended run and Simon gave this explanation as to why: 'Willy can't play if it's too cold, because he shrivels up!'. You know it's true, men.

The toilet in our stand was like a paddling pond, caused by our fans in retaliation for Bury fans wrecking our toilets and moaning about the pies and beer on *Back to the Floor*. It prompted our chant 'If You're Gonna Smash The Toilets Do It Now!'. On the mass murderer spotting front Bury had a steward with glasses, a bushy grey beard, jumper and an anorak who got 'There's Only One Harold Shipman!'. There was a bloke sitting behind us moaning like stink about Millwall from start to finish. I know it's a free country, but why waste your money and time only to then slag a manager and team off who were top of the League?

I WAS BORN UNDER THE COLD BLOW LANE

Bury's PA man was a real Lancashire tosspot who ran the gamut of celebratory music and hyperbole. He played *2001 A Space Odyssey* as they came out and *Celebration* and *Another One Bites The Dust* for their goals. He also referred to the pot-less club and smattering of fans as 'The Mighty Shakers'. The game that prompted all this nonsense saw Millwall have a goal disallowed and the home side scored their winner with practically the last kick of the match. Following this gutting defeat Colin and Chris left to drown their sorrows in their hotel. Paul, Nathan, Ted and I had no such luxury; we climbed back on our little coach and suffered a miserable trip arriving in London at 2am; never mind, we were still top.

Bristol City, Friday 16/3/2001, lost 2-1. Nathan drove Ted, Simon and me to Bristol. The game was switched to Friday night in an attempt to stop us travelling, which didn't work because 1100-plus Millwall fans travelled to the West Country on the night. A trip to Bristol City is always very interesting; with a long-standing history of trouble between the two clubs, this particular trip was a nightmare from start to finish. We left at about 3pm and decided not to get to the M4 via Earl's Court as the Ideal Home Exhibition was on. Instead, we went via King's Cross, a big mistake as the area's one-way system was gridlocked due to roadworks. Eventually, it took us over two hours to get to Hanger Lane.

On the M4, our nightmare continued because major bridge repairs caused extremely bad tailbacks due to huge cranes blocking our way. I'm sure the police knew of this when they rearranged the game. To add to the fun Simon had declared himself fit when he wasn't and due to his stomach problems our car was getting rather rank. We were continually stuck in traffic so had no chance of a real toilet stop, all we could manage were impromptu roadside stops and pissing in a bottle and lobbing it out the window. Perhaps we should've bought the flowers; they were selling on the roadside, after all. We ploughed on regardless, nearing Bristol whilst listening to the local radio's match countdown. Miraculously we arrived at Ashton Gate just a few minutes late and managed to park right outside the ground in a company's forecourt. We wondered if it would still be there after the match, it's certainly not normally this easy.

THE CONTINUING DIARY OF A MASOCHIST

By now the game had started and I managed to lead our party to the home Atyeo Stand, which wouldn't have been a good idea. As we turned and headed towards the away end, there was an almighty roar and James Brown's *I Got You (I Feel Good)* reverberated around. The home side had scored in the first five minutes. As we arrived at the gates of the Blackthorn Wedlock Stand so did Millwall's 'Firm' who were trying to push their way past the heavy riot police and police horse barriers in their way. We became caught up in this but eventually managed to get through to the turnstiles and into the ground forecourt. Ted and Nathan then negotiated the police horse blockade before getting into the tunnel between the home fans and the away stand behind the goal, where they ran into a hail of missiles from the home stand to the left of this tunnel. Simon and I went to the toilet and we too then had to battle our way into the same tunnel, no missiles for us though. There were now 10 minutes gone, which throws me for the whole match. What security genius decided that leading away fans via a tunnel that runs alongside the less than friendly locals was a good idea? Why not put entrances behind the away section? Inside we were encircled by riot police and stewards. I have been to Ashton Gate numerous times and the atmosphere is always hostile and loud, which I prefer myself. The stadium has improved radically over the years, now all-seater unlike my early visits when the away end was on an open terrace at the opposite end of the ground, now the Atyeo Stand. We were now located in what used to be a home stand at the other end.

Simon and I had lost track of Ted and Nathan and because the night's mood was its usual highly-charged self it was too noisy to hear anything on our mobiles, so we decided to stay put and look for each other at half-time. We didn't have much choice of seats and found ourselves in the corner of the covered away end. Our £15 tickets said 'restricted view' and true enough we had posts in our way holding up the stand roof. We took up the best position that we could and spent the first half trying to get a good angle to watch the match, to compound it further the seats had no backs. Mind you, seats weren't especially important because we stood up all night on a war footing. Simon's stomach problem meant that he soon had to go to the toilet again. When he returned he said that there were a dozen Millwall taking Charlie in there. Driving 125 miles to destroy their nasal passages, which they could do in Bermondsey, struck me as odd. Obviously there would be no City fans to fight in South London though.

Naturally, 'I Can't Read...' was our chosen favourite on the night although we also gave full reign to our Foot-and-Mouth chants. Bristol's female physio got the full gamut of sexist abuse - 'We Can Smell Your C... From Here!'/'Get Your Tits Out For The Lads!'/ 'Do You Take It Up The A...?' /'Show Us Your Beaver!'/'Beaver!' and 'Dodgy Beaver!'. I felt sorry for her, it had been no better at the New Den. As an aside there's a dry-cleaning company in the East End called 'Beaver Cleaners', a strange name for a feminine hygiene company but what a great logo.

Returning to the game, we pulled a goal back and dominated proceedings in the first half but couldn't get a second goal. At half-time we joined the others and were entertained by a Wurzels Megamix of *Drink Up Your Cider*,' *I'm A Cider Drinker* and *Brand New Combine Harvester*! etc. I wasn't sure if the locals liked this stuff or whether the DJ was just taking the piss. We don't play *My Old Man's A Dustman*, *Maybe It's Because I'm A Londoner* or *Gercha!*, do we? Perhaps we should, together with Honky Tonk piano, spoon solos and half-time Pearly King and Queen knees-ups, then again perhaps not. I've no idea what Bristol came out to before the game as we were listening to local Radio Bumpkin at the time, but in the second half they came out to *Star Wars* which I didn't think was very rustic.

During the second half, the crowd hostility went up a notch when the referee lost the plot completely. Both teams had men sent off, including our forward line of Harris and Moody (somehow). Their goalkeeper got injured so he added eight minutes' injury-time and we conceded a 90 minutes-plus penalty thanks to a linesman's frantic flag waving, they scored and we lost 2-1, bloody marvellous! At the end of the game, Millwall's Boys surged towards the home stand throwing missiles, including seats, at the home fans and the riot police positioned between them and us. The police responded by driving the front line back with batons. Several Millwall retreated, streaming with bloody head wounds.

This was certainly not the first time that I had seen trouble at Bristol City, there has been violence at every single game that I've been to there. Footage of tonight was apparently shown on London news programmes that evening. In the days that followed it got further airings, Bristol's papers went to town and the *Evening Standard* put its two pennyworth in by printing a rogue's gallery of Millwall supporters involved in the trouble on the night. It was this match that prompted a future upgrade of the club's photographic fan database.

When the problems subsided we were allowed out and edged our way through the local meatheads and police trying to disperse them. Outside the stadium gates, there was the usual Hoolie shouting and running about, you know the sort of thing. To be honest we were more interested to know if the car was still there, which miraculously it was. We got aboard just as Bristol fans appeared to be running from the Millwall fans in the train escort. I said to Nathan that we should just head out-of-town until we found a motorway, we did and came upon the M5, unfortunately heading towards Weston-super-Mare. Luckily there was very little traffic on this road so we drove on until we picked up signs to turn onto the London-bound M4. By this time, it was pouring down like the motel scene in *Psycho* and our windscreen wipers were going 19 to the dozen. Unfortunately, our main companions on the motorway were huge lorries who tailgated us on full beam at high-speed, dangerous bastards! In the midst of the trucks, it meant that we had the added hazard of spray from their wheels. At one point it was as if someone had thrown several buckets of water at us at the same time. From my front seat I couldn't see anything, quite how Nathan drove I have no idea. We passed the bridge repairs and stopped at a garage to get some refreshments. Inside, I queued up behind ex-Millwall manager Billy Bonds, whom I believe had covered us on Capital Gold. We then passed Millwall's team coach, quick hoot and wave; you know the form by now.

It had been an eventful trip that's for sure - 12 hours-plus, a defeat, sendings-off, piss poor refereeing, a load of aggro and a tedious, not to say perilous, journey there and back, a proper night out! We had also slipped down to second place.

Wycombe Wanderers, Tuesday 27/3/2001, drew 0-0. There couldn't be a bigger contrast from a trip to Bristol than Wycombe, which is certainly not a hotbed ground by any stretch of the imagination. We paid our second visit of the season with Clive driving Dave's minibus containing the usual East End group, including Simon and Pat. We arrived around 6pm and this time went straight to a chip shop. Clive and I were served first so we waited outside. A car pulled up alongside us with a dog in the back that had two different coloured eyes, Clive said 'Look it's David Bowie!'. I told the driver that I was a Korean and asked if I could have his dog to go with my chips; deeming us mad, he chose to ignore us. Everyone soon emerged and we headed to the ground.

Pre-match we stood at the front of the away stand because Patrick, a seasoned autograph hunter with a stack of unintelligibly inscribed home and away programmes, was on an autograph hunt. Pat once did a classic at Bournemouth a couple of years previously. During the pre-match kick-in he pestered Nigel Spink for an autograph. Nigel asked him to hang on for a minute, Pat continued until he relented and walked towards him whilst taking his gloves off, as he went to sign the programme Pat said 'No, I don't want yours! Can you get me Paul Moody's autograph?'. Specifically, tonight he wanted Tony Cottee's, who was making his debut, having been brought in as cover for Harris and Moody. Pat said to Willy Gueret in his Cockney accent 'Can You Get Cottee?' Willy gave a Gallic shrug and said 'Vot Is Zis Cottee?'. Adopting the usual Englishman speaking to a foreigner routine, we all shouted at him and pointed in Tony Cottee's general direction. Cottee came over, signed the autograph, and was greeted in equal measure with 'There's Only One Tony Cottee!' and 'We Hate West Ham, Etc!' which he seemed to find amusing.

We sat down along with 1350 Millwall fans and looked out on the 4500 home fans, knowing full well that their number would quadruple at least come their FA Cup semi-final against Liverpool; who are we to talk after our Wembley glory hunting turnout? The air was once again rife with the smells of dope, more disturbingly though there was the unmistakable aroma of roast lamb, which Pat first noticed and said to me 'Can you smell burning Bal?'. We all agreed we could smell lamb cooking, presumably from the burning of sheep on a foot-and-mouth bonfire.

This game had originally been scheduled for New Year's Day and was called off at the last minute so for this game Wycombe sold us both programmes for the price of one, which was damned decent of them. In homage to Lawrie Sanchez, the home DJ played *Me and Mr Sanchez*, a Latin hit from the 1980s and the teams came out onto a pitch in amazing condition for the time of year. For some reason Millwall kicked towards our end in the first half. Consequently, Taylor got his customary abuse and missile bombardment out of the way early. Naturally, he responded by playing a blinder and largely due to him the drab game finished goal-less. Two points dropped. From a historical perspective, when Tony Cottee came on with 15 minutes to go he became the first player ever to play in all four Divisions in one season, having played for Leicester, Norwich, Millwall and Barnet. We left after another quick paddle in the toilet with Millwall remaining in second place.

Walsall, 31/3/2001, drew 0-0. The following Saturday the Wycombe eight also went to Walsall. We left early and Clive again did most of the motorway driving in Dave's minibus. As we headed on to the M1 Dave suddenly announced that the brakes were playing up, which isn't exactly what you want to hear as you set off for a 250 mile round trip, but luckily we had no problems on the way up. As was now usual there was very little livestock in the fields. We did see an ominous plume of smoke though, presumably another sheep funeral pyre, particularly as there were signs everywhere saying 'This Is a Foot and Mouth Infected Area'.

Walsall is one of the easier away trips with the ground right next to the motorway, so we arrived in just over two hours and parked up outside the newish if prefabricated Bescot stadium for my second visit. It still looks like a B&Q Superstore from the outside. We had another wander around including visiting Pat's second home, McDonald's. We then went to another JJB Sports as Simon was looking for a football pump for Pat. We found that, like

Reading, it too had everything that the dedicated yobbo could wish for. This store sold golf clubs, cricket bats, hockey sticks, pucks, pool cues and balls. More humorously, they sold assistant referees' flags that you could use to create mayhem if you sat in the front of a side stand. We then headed to the ground and into Walsall's programme shop, where strangely they sold programmes and fanzines from all over Britain and Portuguese flags. Eventually we entered the ground, taking up a position on the far left of the away William Sharp Stand behind the goal.

This game was a table-topper. Officially we had 1878 fans, but as an outside gate had been forced open pre-match, there were people without seats standing in the aisles. Skirmishes broke out at the opposite end of our stand between Millwall fans and the police/stewards. As we stood watching the shenanigans, Ted decided to abuse anyone in the stand to our left with his usual aplomb and industrial language, leaving the kid sitting next to Ted to look up at him warily. The Mad One was living up to another of his nicknames, lambasting people he thought were home fans. We pointed out that it was an overspill from the away section and they were our fans so he stopped his rant and turned back to us as if nothing happened. Although not a trouble game, we stood up for the whole match, only sitting down at half-time, as is now the norm. The home atmosphere was poor, strangely, though when they sang they seemed to have pinched all their chants from other teams. They sang their own versions of Pompey's *Chimes*, Manchester United's *Pride Of All Europe* song, adapted to include a hatred for the Brummies - nothing wrong with that - and, more bizarrely, they sang *The Blaydon Races*. Next time we visit they will probably be singing *EIO*, *Let 'Em Come* and *No One Likes Us* as if they were their own.

Kasey Keller's old adversary Don Goodman played for Walsall with a hairdo like a 'They Don't Like It Up 'Em!' fuzzy wuzzy. He got 'There's Only One Bob Marley!' and 'He's Got A Pineapple On His Head!'. A hairy pineapple, lovely, how would you know which was the rough end? He responded by patting his arse like an Asda advertisement, presumably implying that we could call him what we wanted as he had a large wedge of wages in his back pocket.

THE CONTINUING DIARY OF A MASOCHIST

Like many games of this nature, it was far too tense for any good football. The only excitement was a second half mass scramble in the goalmouth at our end, accompanied by a plastic bottle barrage from our fans as the only other crowd incident of note, and the game finished goalless. I had now been to this ground twice and their old ground once and had yet to see us win at Walsall. After the match, we reboarded the minibus and set-off, brakes willing, back to London. On the way to the motorway, Dave announced that he was dying for a slash and utilised one of my empty Pepsi Max bottles for the purpose. He did this with a rare precision, masterfully filling the bottle to its regulation liquid capacity, screwing the cap on and throwing it out of the window on to a nearby street. If anyone found a full bottle of what looked like Irn Bru in a Pepsi Max bottle that tasted a bit funny now you know! When we arrived in London we drove through Earl's Court, passing a drunken woman with the look of a working girl, as we passed Dave shouted out of his window 'Are you working love? Fiver?'. Mind you, he shouted this to a drunken bloke that we passed as well. We arrived back home safely, thankful that the brakes hadn't malfunctioned.

The game at Walsall was the last away match before a series of four home matches so it would at least give my arse and wallet a break from going on a tour of Britain's motorway network for a while.

Rotherham United (home) 7/4/2001, won 4-0. This was the second game in the run of four and we had gone back to the top courtesy of a 2-0 win over Stoke City. Rotherham arrived late for this table-topping clash, then received a less than friendly greeting as we booed and taunted them.

The game, in front of 14,600 Londoners and 1400 northerners, had an Old Den atmosphere and their players adopted the old policy of 'The sooner we're off this pitch the better!'. As a result we comfortably won a game that even included a bout of 'Ole's' as we did a keep-ball performance like 70s Leeds United. To confirm that we'd frightened them their manager Ronnie Moore later said 'We've not had this at other grounds; their crowd was abusive, boisterous and hostile' really? After the game we stood near the ticket offices and one of their players came out to get on their coach whilst being offered some friendly Millwall-style encouragement. In response he told us all to 'F... off!'. Nothing like a good loser, I always say.

Typically, rather than major on our win or the fact that the game was a Kick Racism Out day, with the focus on Millwall's' black players, the Sundays chose to link the match with a 2.30pm march in Bermondsey by the BNP/Anti-Nazi League following Damilola Taylor's murder. What happened at the march I have no idea, I was at Millwall at the time, nevertheless, they implied that every Lion in the crowd was at the march and we were all hood wearing members of the Ku Klux Klan. Yet again the BNP's by-election victory in Millwall, E14 was linked to Millwall, SE16. Having vanquished our main rivals our fate was in our own hands.

Cambridge United, Tuesday 17/4/2001, won 5-1. The Wycombe/Walsall 8 again drove to Cambridge, a game moved from Easter Monday to Tuesday night, presumably to stop our heathen hordes from ruining the religious Bank Holiday. We arrived early and made our customary chip shop stop, try saying that when you're pissed. En route we passed a newsagents with local newspapers carrying 'They're coming!' headlines and saying that due to the expected trouble every Cambridgeshire pub would be shut. Obviously, it wasn't possible to bring your own booze or get lagered-up at Liverpool Street station.

We went to the ground at 6.30pm, which wasn't yet open so we joined the long queue running alongside the shrubbery and stream outside the turnstiles. Eventually they opened and we went in. I went straight to the toilet, where I saw one of the funniest things that I had ever seen at a match. Standing just inside the loo was a very embarrassed looking PC, a first for me.

A few options sprang to mind -

1) Had he heard that Millwall took the piss?

2) Was he on helmet watch?

3) Did they think that we would wreck the toilet?

At Cambridge, you'd have to renovate it before you could wreck it. I felt sorry for the hapless Plod, fancy being designated Pc Bobby Bogwatch. One bloke near to me said to him 'Blimey, you must really have pissed someone off to get this duty!'. Another said 'It's the first time I have had the Old Bill looking at my old bill!'. Once we stopped laughing, we took up a central position behind the goal, on the half a dozen steps that constitute a terrace at The Abbey Stadium. Cambridge is a lovely place but their ground is a tip. On the South Terrace behind the goal, we met the Essex contingent and Dave Murray with another long-suffering Lion, Trevor, confirming the newspaper's prohibition claim they had travelled by train, then had to get a cab to and from the outskirts of town to find an open pub. The 2000 official Millwall fans were spread among the open terrace and a covered seated stand to our left, although there were more Millwall dotted around the ground. John Beck had returned so it would be a football purist night due to his customary Route 1 bombardment and *Land of the Giants* forward line.

Once again, Uriah Rennie was the referee (sic). The conspiracy theorists started talking about the league's plot to stop us getting promotion by using Rennie to stop us. Prior to the game, there was an impeccable silence for the referee North, the Oxford ref (?) who died at Southend United shortly before. Rennie then blew his whistle to start the normal mass outpouring of cheers that follows any silence and I said that would be his first and last correct action of the night. In the end it was Cambridge fans who chanted 'Can We Have a Referee?'. They also sang 'You're Scum And You Know You Are!'. Welcome to you as well!

The game was a cruise, with a Paul Ifill hat trick that I had only seen the likes of when Alex Rae scored three blinding goals at Notts County in the 1990s. As far as I can recall this was the most emphatic away win that I had ever seen. It prompted 'Now You're Gonna Believe Us, We're Gonna Win The League!' and '5-1 To The Champions!'. This was unusual because a Millwall fan's mentality usually will not allow any celebration until it's impossible for us to f... it up. Neil Harris came on late as substitute for the recently acquired Steve Claridge and immediately gave a defender a '5-1' fingers signal. 5-1 down and the Golden Boot contender comes on. At the end of the game, Christophe Kinet tried to join the celebrating fans in the side stand chanting his name. The security tried to stop him; presumably because he hadn't played they thought he shouldn't be on the pitch, despite the fact that everyone in the side stand were singing 'Ole, Ole, Ole Kinet!'. Eventually he persuaded them that he was 'Ole' Kinet and joined the singing throng.

There were a couple of other humorous incidents; anything is funny when you've just won heavily on the way to promotion. At half-time, Cambridge paraded several kit options for the following season in the wrong colours, sort of 'Yes, we know they're pink and orange but just imagine that they're yellow and black!'. As we left the ground there was a female police dog handler with an Alsatian, who was serenaded with 'Who Let The Dogs Out?' I'll leave you to decide who we were singing about.

Wrexham, 28/4/2001, drew 1-1 - A Big Flag Day. For me Wrexham was on a par with the Hull City championship game and the Chesterfield great escape game. Ted, Dave, Nathan, Paul and I went via club coach in a convoy. Our coach driver was a man who 'entertained' us with his Max Bygraves 'live' tapes on one trip, very much appreciated as you can imagine. As we headed up the M1, it became apparent that our coach was the runt of the litter because milk floats and cyclists were almost passing us, we were going 40mph at best. Ted lambasted the driver and I was getting feelings of deja-vu, a nightmare trip, on this of all days. Eventually the driver admitted there was a fault and said he'd stop at Toddington to sort it out. In the end we limped up the motorway eventually pulling into services near Coventry.

Fortunately, a mechanic met us, quickly fixed the problem and off we went again now at a more sensible speed. The only other time that I had been to Wrexham, we went via Shrewsbury where the countryside didn't fit my image of Wales at all. However, today it was like an advert for the Welsh Tourist Board; hills, valleys, rivers, forests, peculiar road signs and the return of flocks of sheep. Sadly, no male voice choirs in coal-mining outfits, but then you can't have everything.

We took in the breathtaking views when unfortunately we passed a muck spreader with our skylight open but luckily it was shut quick sharp. To add to the rustic feel we had to stop to let a pheasant cross the road. Our coach was full of Millwall/St George flags and inflatable St George 'thumbs up' which were waved about in jocular England family fan fashion; the mood on the coach was certainly a happy one. As we neared the Wrexham junction our driver, with maps spread out on his lap, of where I do not know, ignored a sign saying 'Wrexham' and headed in the direction that said South Wales. Everyone noticed his gaffe and yelled at him, not for the only time as it was to turn out. He then did a three-point turn on a narrow road and we headed in the right direction.

Despite all the traumas, we arrived in good time and took up our position in the now all-seater Marston Stand behind the goal, along with an official away following of 3300. The Racecourse ground had been renovated since my other visit, when the area to the right of the away stand consisted of a derelict pub and ramshackle stand; this was now the Pryce Griffiths Stand, which, although an odd shape, was a vast improvement on its predecessor. There was now only one terraced area left. an Old Den-style shed behind the goal at the opposite end of the ground.

Prior to the kick-off ex-Villa, Bayern and Bonnie Scotland forward Alan McInally, now a Sky pundit, walked in front of our end and was warmly greeted with chants of 'Who The F...ing Hell Are You?' and 'You Scotch C...!' which he acknowledged cheerfully. Strangely, the goals were pushed to the side of the pitch, which I had never seen before. Two blokes from our end ran on, put down a jumper and a trainer in the traditional 'Jumpers For Goalposts' manner and pretended to have a kickabout until stopped by the spoilsport Jobsworths. Obviously the real goals were moved into position prior to the kick-off. We adopted the customary Millwall policy of sitting where we liked; the stewards had done nothing to ensure that we sat in the correct seats.

From where we sat our stand appeared to be oversold; it was becoming increasingly difficult for anyone to find a seat so the PA announced that there were about 50-60 empty seats in the left-hand corner and people should head there. Just before kick-off around 30 Millwall emerged from the upper part of a Wrexham stand to our left, and moved to the lower tier to be closer to us.

The match kicked off with more latecomers now arriving to our right. A couple of hundred fans then spilt on to the cinder track from our overcrowded stand, prompting the referee to take the players off with 6 minutes of the match gone. Latecomers were then allowed onto the Pryce Griffiths Stand where some moved the police segregation nets and walked towards the home fans who fled. Wrexham, unlike its South Wales cousins, isn't hostile at all. McGhee and Paphitis came out to plead for calm and the PA announcer made dire threats of abandonment. Eventually the police decided to relocate all the extra Lions fans into the stand to our left's lower portion and all was calm. Wrexham appeared to have no contingency for any extra Millwall fans turning up. Anyone who has been to a big Millwall away game knew that this sort of thing was likely. Theo was lauded for his placating on-pitch announcements and the fans causing the delay were gestured at and serenaded with 'You're Just A Bunch of Wankers!'. Some took umbrage, but the home fans applauded the PA announcements that the vast majority of Millwall fans didn't want them causing trouble. In truth it was more disorganisation than any malicious intention from what I could see.

When order was restored, the teams returned to the pitch and naturally Wrexham scored. Thankfully, in the second half, Tim Cahill equalised leading to wild celebrations. Placatingly we sang 'Back, Back, Back!'/'Sit Down If You Love Millwall!' and 'Sit Down Millwall - Sit Down!'. Naturally, some fans still spilt onto the pitch; assuming they were the vanguard of another 'invasion' the referee took the players off again, and the PA reiterated that if the problems continued the match would be abandoned. I'm sure all North Wales police wanted was 3000+ pissed-off Millwall fans on their patch.

In total, the hold-ups had lasted 20 minutes and we heard on the jungle drums that Reading had lost at Colchester United; perversely we hoped that we didn't score again, as a second goal might prompt another celebratory invasion and the match would actually be abandoned. With 20 minutes left Theo's voice came over the PA saying 'We're Up - Stay Where You Are And The Players Will Come To You!'. This led to the party starting for real and we ran through our entire repertoire, including 'Grandad's Going Up!'/'Stick The Second Division Up Your Arse - Sideways!'

and 'Que Sera, Etc, Were Going To Barnsley (Man City)!'. The most popular chant involved a double-header of our promotion and Palace's relegation with 'Millwall Up And Palace Down, Do Dah, Do Dah, Millwall Up And Palace Down Do Dah, Do Dah Day!'.

The end of the match came amid joyous celebration. Broken-legged Joe Dolan danced on the pitch whilst waving his crutch in the air and flashing his shiny dome prompting the 'Baldy Joe' chants. Denzil was asked if he'd give us a celebratory flash - 'Denzil, Denzil Show Us Your Cock!'. Steady, you'll embarrass the police horses! Willy got the French national anthem and a conga line broke out on the pitch. The PA announced that train travellers should cease partying or they would miss their train, which had amazingly been delayed just in case.

Outside it was like a madhouse with mass outbreaks of singing 'Knees Up Mother Brown' being a favourite, There was flag-waving and car hooting and cars driving up the road with people standing through sunroofs waving Millwall flags. On the way back six of our coaches pulled into a service station where there were some West Ham fans and the enclosed area reverberated with 'Who The F...ing Hell Are You?'. Due to our elated state, nothing violent happened as far as I could see and we continued on our London-bound trip. Our coach came off onto the M25 and merrily sailed past the M11 turn-off amid hoots of derision. We took another junction further up, went around a roundabout and come back on ourselves in the opposite direction to pick up the correct junction. All was well until we went through Blackwall Tunnel when we again took a wrong turning near the Millennium Dome, and ended up outside a water treatment plant. Once again, the coach had to turn on a sixpence in order to head towards the New Den. It eventually took us over one and a half hours to get from the M1/M25 junction to the ground.

We arrived back at 10.45pm, amid much sarcastic cheering and a standing ovation. My first inclination had been to get home and have a celebratory light ale or 10; sadly, by the time I got back to where I live the local pubs were shut. I assume my liver was grateful but I bloody wasn't. A very tense but eventually happy day 'Going Up, Going Up, Going Up!'.

I WAS BORN UNDER THE COLD BLOW LANE

Obviously, in the days that followed the press largely chose to ignore the fact that we had been promoted and scoured their thesaurus for another word for 'Riot'. Strangely, our pitch encroachment was referred to as an invasion whilst similar pitch incursions by celebrating home fans at Rotherham and Palace at Stockport were reported in the media as joyous celebrations. The Sunday tabloids in particular perfectly highlighted that we're not on a level playing field when it comes to reporting - compare the coverage of Wrexham with incidents at Oldham's home game against Stoke City at the same time. For those who don't know, the problems at Oldham involved large-scale clashes before and after the game between hundreds of Stoke/Oldham fans and the local Asians, trouble that included rioting and petrol bombs being thrown. The events were triggered by a vicious Asian gang attack on a 76-year-old white war veteran in an alleged No-Go area for whites.

The Wrexham tabloid headlines that I saw included 'Chaos'/'Lions Joy On Day Of Drama'/'20 Minutes Of Madness' and 'Lions Promoted Amid Fan Chaos'. They all mentioned our 'trouble', most with shock horror colour photos of riot police and tearful young girls. Of the papers that I saw *The News Of The World*, *Sports First* and *The Sunday Mirror* didn't mention the Oldham trouble at all, whilst *The People* had a footnote of around five lines about petrol bombs being thrown and a dozen or so arrests at Oldham. On Monday *The Sun* had a six-inch deep by one-column-wide article with the headline 'Petrol Bomb Terror' about the Oldham v Stoke problems. In all the scant Oldham reports that I saw there wasn't a picture in sight. When you compare the way that the two events were reported, there certainly seems to be some sort of hidden agenda. I know that I was reading the London editions of the newspapers, but news is news.

How can disorganisation at a promotion game and minor pitch encroachments be more newsworthy than what amounts to large-scale racially motivated violence? You tell me because I don't know. Wrexham was merely overcrowding and bad planning, not malicious; it was very minor, high-spirited and foolish, maybe, and badly organised by the stewards and police, definitely. To put the crowd trouble into perspective there were apparently 10 arrests in the ground or if you prefer around 0.3 per cent of the official away figure.

Oldham Athletic (Home), 5/5/2001, won 5-0. Promotion made up for our Auto Windscreen and Division Two play-off semi-final disappointments and showed just how far we had come back from the brink thanks to Rhino/Macca and McGhee. Today we could add the icing and clinch the title. With a sell-out crowd of 18,500, it was obviously going to be a 'They'll Be Coming out the Woodwork When They Come' affair. Why do people only turn up for Bertie Big Bollocks games? Don't get me started!

The whole ground was opened to home fans. The North Stand was full for once, with Oldham's fans positioned beneath the police box in the West upper. Pre-match, Mick Brown went through the footie rabble-rousing repertoire of *Vindaloo, Daydream Believer, Let 'Em Come, Sailing, We Will Rock You, Rockin All Over The World*, etc at a volume like a Led Zeppelin gig, leaving my battered old rock and roll years whistling for the first 15 minutes of the game, cheers! The whole day had the feel of Blackburn/Wembley about it - there was tickertape, flags, silly wigs, banners, balloons, etc. Naturally, the huge St George flag was unfurled and passed along the stand and as the goals flew in we sang our repertoire of 'Champions' chants.

Despite numerous announcements about staying off the pitch during the game a bloke came on from the CBL lower, ran about for a bit with his ears stinging in condemnation, then headed towards the Junior Enclosure where he was met by a fellow Millwall fan who punched him in the mouth and bundled him down the stairwell to much cheering - only at Millwall! When the match ended, they began to bring on £10,000s worth of Nationwide podium. Requests not too invade the pitch post-match were obeyed, at least initially. After the podium was mounted, the trophy awarded and laps of honour completed, some invaded the pitch ending proceedings. The podium was then unceremoniously dismantled and carried piecemeal through the club gates, much to the chagrin of the sponsors who demanded it back - Champions!!

I WAS BORN UNDER THE COLD BLOW LANE

All the usual crew were at the game and after the match we went onto the pitch where we met the Fisher clan. We stood facing the West stand, singing, taking photos and continuing our celebrations. Surprisingly, Mad Ted suddenly appeared among the players and officials in the upper tier. He'd been to every home and away game, including LDV Trophy matches, no mean feat, and he too deserved applause in my opinion.

Eventually we left the ground and reconvened in The Barnaby where we met numerous other mates and my cousins. I also saw a man with the biggest cigar I've ever seen in the flesh, the full Malcolm Allison as it were, a real fire hazard. We got stuck into the lagers and had a bloody good singsong inside the pub. As we got more 'relaxed' the celebrations took to the street and everyone was dancing and singing in the road with the 'Millwall Up And Palace Down' chant being very popular, if sadly inaccurate. Some cars hooted in support, some waved and Sean Dyche pulled up outside the pub, leant across his female passenger, and waved his fist towards us with a 'Yesss!'. As our fan blockade started to get larger, some cars tried to drive through including a limousine that got a roof battering, another driver got his car booted and glasses were thrown as it sped away.

By this time, cars and buses were turning around rather than trying to get through; naturally, the Old Bill arrived to stop our fun, so some of us decided to go to an Old Den haunt, The Albany. As we walked there, we bumped into Lottery Larry et al, with his legendary accuracy he told us that they had just burnt 'The Barnaby' down! Wrong. We arrived at The Albany and continued to give the lagers a good seeing-to before heading eastwards at closing time to await the next day's thumping hangover. It was all worth it.

6.

From Knees-Up
To Punch-Up

Celebrate Good Times - 7/7/2001 After our old Division 2 championship in 1988, there had been no 'official' parade as the police wouldn't sanction it. However, for this Division 2 championship there was a South East London parade, culminating in a dinner at the House of Commons organised by local MP Simon Hughes. About as welcome as Guy Fawkes' visit I'd imagine.

Simon, Patrick, Paul, Nathan and I had decided to go at the last minute so only had a vague idea of route/timings, etc, and after driving aimlessly around various Millwall haunts we decided to go to the New Den. There were numerous people milling about, with many others heading by foot or car towards the Blue, decked out with flags, etc. We knew then we hadn't missed it. We parked up near Surrey Canal Road and then waited under a bus shelter on Ilderton Road in the pissing Wimbledon-fortnight rain. Having waited 20 minutes, we decided to head off on foot towards the Blue. Naturally, as soon as we moved Millwall's open-topped bus sailed past with a hooting and flag-waving convoy trailing in its wake, we gave them a cursory wave and they were gone.

We dashed back to Nathan's car and tried to pick up the parade; unfortunately; we had lost too much time and had lost the scent. We decided to drive to Parliament where we found hundreds of fellow Lions. We parked in an NCP car park and joined everyone else, including Dave Murray, near Big Ben and waited for the bus to appear. With Millwall colours well to the fore, numerous bemused tourists gawped at us. I'm sure that a large gathering of England's most notorious fans was probably not in their guidebook as a 'Must See'. When the Lions convoy eventually came into view, many fans took to the bridge and Millwall songs filled the air, only adding to the foreigner's confusion.

The bus stopped outside Parliament where the singing reached a crescendo. People threw various items of clothing on to the upper deck attempting to get autographs. The players, etc, duly obliged. The players, Paphitis, McGhee and Gritt, etc then disembarked through our chanting and backslapping crowd and made their way to the opposite side of the road for a photo-call by a statue. Everyone re-boarded the bus for a final pass, before disembarking and going into Parliament with their wives and girlfriends, etc through an impromptu fan corridor of honour.

Neil Harris was hoisted onto someone's shoulders, not ideal I wouldn't have thought. His testicular cancer revelation had brought us all down to earth. My thoughts ranged between 'Poor bastard, I wouldn't wish that on any man' and 'Typical Millwall luck, we go up, largely due to his goals then this happens', reflecting how a football fan's mind works - well mine anyway. Obviously, Millwall's problems were of little consequence, he could have died for God's sake.

Once everyone had gone inside, we went to pay the ransom on Nathan's car before driving past a large contingent of fans still waiting outside; we hooted in recognition and went to the pub. The parade had been surreal and unique as far as I know; after all, The House of Commons isn't exactly a local town hall and Millwall and Parliament are usually only combined in a sentence when questions are raised regarding football hooliganism, Millwall related or not. Talking of which -

Rhino's Testimonial Millwall v Spurs, New Den, 4/8/2001. I don't usually go to friendlies, considering them glorified kickabouts; I made an exception today, as I wanted to pay a long overdue homage to Keith Stevens. As it was a friendly, we had arranged for Spurs fans and one Gooner to come with us. We decided to pick up our guests individually and reconvene in the ground.

I had organised a first trip to Millwall for Spurs fan Paul Hawkins, one of my oldest mates. I met up with he and Clive early and we went for a drink in a quiet pub behind Surrey Quays shopping centre. Paul said that on the way over from Kent he'd passed pubs surrounded by riot police. Clive said that he'd heard rumours that Spurs were planning to attack various pubs in South-East London. Paul wasn't used to this sort of thing; he's Welsh and really more interested in Rugby with its on-pitch violence than football. After a few drinks, we drove to the ground to meet the other Paul, Nathan, Dave, Simon and Patrick in the CBL. The only home absentee was Ted, who had gone to watch Middlesex CCC.

Some of the Spurs fans and the Gooner, Dave's brother-in-law Timmy, sat with us with instructions to ignore any Tottenham goals. Others opted for the apparent safety of the away end. Just before kick-off Spurs 'Firm' arrived in the North Stand upper tier, bearing all the standard hallmarks: late arriving, mob-handed and flanked by riot police, lord knows I know the signs. Clive again mentioned the pub aggro rumours which Simon and Dave had also heard.

Pre-match, Grandad did a presentation on the pitch to Rhino with Hurlock, Kitch and Teddy. Rumour had been that Teddy would be playing for both sides; sadly, he was injured and didn't. The atmosphere was volatile but not overly so, in fact I thought it was quite civilised for us. The days of gas hissing have largely gone, nonetheless, there was still plenty of anti-Semitic abuse, largely about Spurs fans being gay and having no foreskins. Paul H said 'It's a nice ground but the atmosphere's not quite Twickers, is it?'. Well erm, no! The game went off without much incident and we lost 2-1.

After the match, most of us headed to Dave's minibus in Oldfield Grove and Paul H went back to his car, more of whom later. Nathan got a call from one of his and Paul's mates, who had chosen the 'safety' of the away end. He said that Millwall had attacked Spurs from all angles outside the ground, by the railway arches, near South Bermondsey station and in the surrounding streets before and after the game, forcing the two brother's mates to seek refuge in some bushes. Luckily, they weren't wearing colours so Nathan said that they should be okay. He told them to wait where they were and we arranged to pick them up outside South Bermondsey station. We set off and soon passed numerous police vans heading rapidly towards Surrey Quays station.

I WAS BORN UNDER THE COLD BLOW LANE

Outside The Golden Lion a large Millwall contingent met any passing vans with a hail of glasses and bottles, some preferred a personal touch and ran out into the road to punch, kick or hurl bottles from close range. Luckily we were on the other side of the road so we managed to get past without being hit. We turned into Ilderton Road, which was strewn with broken glass and bricks. The bottle banks at the top of the road had been overturned and emptied out to provide ammunition. What genius thought this was the best place for a bottle bank?

We found Nathan/Paul's friends unharmed and they gratefully got aboard. We then gave them the bad news that we needed to go back in the direction that the police vans had been speeding to. We edged slowly along Rotherhithe New Road amidst hundreds of Millwall, a large contingent emerged from Southwark Park, carrying various gardening tools, including a pair of shears! I was leaning out of an open window with a Millwall shirt on, surveying the police lines further up the road, when a bloke walking alongside us said to me 'Are You Old Bill?'.

I said laughing 'No mate!'

He said 'Well you look like Old Bill!'

I pointed out to him that if I were I'd want to be dressed in a crash helmet with a riot shield for protection. He walked on, presumably convinced and we sat waiting for the customary Millwall v riot police battle, like spectators at a medieval joust. Timmy, sitting next to me in the front, thought the Spurs rout and this pursuit was hilarious. The situation obviously worsened - Millwall threw missiles and the police baton charged. Ted would have loved it, he was born for days like this.

Dave somehow managed to edge up the side of the police lines and turn onto Lower Road by The Caulkers pub, despite riot police bashing our vehicle with their shields and truncheons trying to stop us. Here we saw the full magnitude of the police operation. There were a couple of dozen police vans lined up opposite Surrey Quays tube, stretching back to The China Hall pub opposite Southwark Park. The vans had more officers on board in reserve. There appeared to be Spurs fans standing behind this wall of police vehicles. I heard later though that Spurs Boys came back afterwards for a bit of pub smashing. We eventually reached the Tunnel and headed east. On the way one of the Spurs fans confessed that this had been his first away match - what a way to lose your cherry! We said that not all away matches were like this, I am not sure that he believed us at this point.

Returning to Paul H, he'd inadvertently walked into Tottenham's Boys, some in colours, who asked who he supported and he said 'Spurs'. They asked why he was coming from Millwall's end and he said he'd been with a Millwall mate and they let him pass. Unbeknownst to him Millwall were behind him and suddenly launched an attack on the Yid Army after smashing up a brick wall for ammunition. Paul said Millwall were diving across cars to get at the Spurs fans. Fortunately he managed to get to his own car and drive off, unfortunately towards The Golden Lion where he too ran into another fracas. Fortunately he got home unscathed. He later said to me 'Why all the trouble if it was only a friendly?'. Ah! The naivety of a non-football goer, I had to explain that a 'Friendly' didn't mean it had to be friendly.

7.

Happy Days Are Here Again!

Season 2001/2002 Division One

Birmingham City, Sunday 19/8/2001 (noon), lost 4-0.
I missed the New Den demolition of Norwich so Birmingham away was my first match of the season. It had been designated a Sunday noon kick-off due to aggro concerns.

On Saturday night I didn't get home until 4am, so I decided to stay awake despite being shagged out as I had to meet Dave, Paul and Nathan at 6.30am to get a 7.30am club coach. There were eight coaches and I managed to lead us onto the wrong one. We sat down and then had to get off whilst I admitted that due to sleep deprivation I was a twat. We got on the right coach and my heart sank when I realised that our driver was the Wrexham one. Despite this, we had an easy trip up and I slept on and off on the coach which is very rare for me, I prefer to stay bolt upright and wide-awake especially for trouble games.

We soon neared the land of the Yim Yams, with its sea of tower blocks, Fort Dunlop, electricity pylons, electronic paraphernalia and a bloody great gasholder. The only attractive things that you pass are the megaflash complexes The Fort and Star City, especially lovely at night, very romantic. Most football clubs seem to adopt 'Area 51' style anonymity; unusually for an old ground, St Andrews was well signposted, signs normally appear as you're just about to pull up outside. As we entered enemy country, our sit down comedian driver told us that the police said that we had to take down any Millwall flags, etc; oddly, though, we had no police escort until we arrived at the ground itself for my fourth visit.

HAPPY DAYS ARE HERE AGAIN!

Because of the previous aggro they had built a coach-holding pen outside the Railway Stand, with a dividing wall to stop a repeat of the Zulu attacks. Next time perhaps we should put on redcoats and white pith helmets... sorry, I came over all Michael Caine for a minute.

Strangely for such a volatile game you could pay on the day, which seemed to negate the logic in making the game all-ticket for us. We went into the ground, which, save for a side stand, was a vast improvement on my last visit, in 1998, when they had been building the stand we were in today. Our seats were to the right of the lower tier behind the goal, where all the trouble had been in the mid--1990s. I had missed this game although obviously I heard how bad it had been from mates. As per that game, the segregation wasn't what it might be. The Brummies were behind a narrow 'no man's land' to the right of us, in the seats above us and behind stewards/police lines to the left of us. It could easily go off. The kick-off was delayed until 12.15pm to allow the train contingent in, i.e. Millwall's 'Firm'. On arrival, they positioned themselves next to the Brummies to our right. We had around 1500 fans there, not a bad turnout for an early Sunday kick-off.

Pre-match they paraded a 'celebrity' from *Big Brother* who they presented with a shirt in the middle of the pitch, he said that it was good to be back amongst people who understood him, pardon? Birmingham's keeper Nico Vaesen sported the vilest kit I'd seen since the acid flashback era of the Nineties. He wore a grey shirt, lime-green shorts and black socks, eek! Millwall wore all green, how did that happen? Neil Harris and Joe Dolan sat in the away section, leading to 'Super Neil!' and 'Baldy Joe!' chants.

The teams came out and Birmingham's fans stood and clapped their way through *Can You Feel It?*, which they did again before the second half. They also sang *Keep Right On To The End Of The Road* very loudly.

The atmosphere at Birmingham was odd though, especially for such a one-sided game. It veered between ear-splitting and a deathly hush; mockingly we often mimicked a librarian's SSSHHH!'. Although we ourselves weren't overly vocal naturally we sang Karren Brady's usual sexual favourites; 'Karren Brady Is

A Slapper!' and 'Brady Takes It Up The A...!'. We sang pro-Villa chants which didn't go down too well and there were the normal Hoolie chants the best of which was 'Where's Your Famous Zulu Firm?'. This led to a funny incident just after it was sung; with perfect comic timing two black Brummies came down the stairs, prompting finger pointing and shouts of 'There they are!'.

Amid the usual posturing and banter, one Brummie made himself a target, in this case he taunted us whilst dressed like a 70s medallion man in a pink shirt. He got 'Who's The Wanker In The Pink?, which he seemed to revel in.

Birmingham had a vast array of chants; I've listed just the ones I hadn't heard at the time. To the tune of 'No One Likes Us' they sang 'You're All Cockneys, You're All Cockneys, You're All Cockneys Yes You Are, You're All Wankers, You're All Wankers, You're All Wankers, Yes You Are!'. They sang the hilarious 'You All Talk Funny Over There!', a bit rich coming from people with the worst accent in the entire realm. They also sang 'Time To Go, Etc La, La, Time To Go Etc - F... Off!'/'We're Only Taking The Piss!' and 'No Noise From The Cockney Boys!'. One I had heard before was 'Shit On The Cockneys 'Cos They're All Shite!'. This reminded me of a delightful video that I saw in Amsterdam *Cack Sisters*; it wasn't a video charting the works of the Nolans, so I'll leave it to your imagination to guess the contents. Moving on...

We were 4-0 down by half-time and it got worse when Richard Sadlier missed a second half penalty. Birmingham is a Bok ground for me; with this game, I had seen one draw and three defeats and we hadn't scored a single goal. There was no trouble inside the ground; the fact that they slaughtered us probably helped.

However, apart from the fan banter there were no bright spots for us. I wished I had gone to bed and I could then have assumed it was merely a bad dream. After the game, our coaches were held in the car park for an hour whilst the Old Bill dispersed the locals. At least we were now in what I consider our rightful Division, which was not much consolation today.

Crystal Palace, 8/9/2001, won 3-1. I missed Crewe away but this would more than make up for that. Due to family commitments I missed the FA Cup win in the 1980s and the Uwe Fuchs inspired

2-1 win on our last visit. The only game I can remember seeing us win there was a pre-season 3-1 friendly win if memory serves, when Trevor Aylott did his Rab C Nesbitt impression. The East End and Essex contingents went to today's game by train from London Bridge, along with hundreds of other Millwall. As we waited for our train, we saw a strange sight - there was an elderly man wandering around the concourse in a black micro-mini skirt, a real treat on the eyes it was too. We got our train and for the first time ever, we got off at Selhurst station, instead of Norwood Junction. The outnumbered Palace fans there were laughed at and randomly abused as Millwall songs filled the air. Ted tried to punch one Palace fan in the head but fortunately, or otherwise, he missed. He continued to abuse any poor home fan that happened to cross his path all the way to the ground. The Millwall throng heading towards the ground smashed several car windows and the sound of car alarms filled the air - the unopposed invasion had begun as per usual.

Unlike Birmingham, the lack of home threat is very noticeable. Mind you, as my cousin Gavin, who was with us, rightly said Millwall's invading army can be a menacing sight, as many appear to be on a day out from debtor's prison or extras in *Thriller*! We reached the home end and had to climb the very steep Holmesdale Hill to the away section we wondered if any Palace fans would come rolling down this hill later on. Thankfully, this game was tickets in advance so we didn't have the queuing palaver that used to happen at Selhurst years ago, a policy that resulted in chaos outside the ground. We went into the ground, met several Lions mates and joined our 6072 'official' turnout on the Arthur Wait Stand, with Millwall also dotted all around the ground. Who the bloody hell is Arthur Wait anyway? Sadly, it appeared that their Disney sponsorship had fallen through, as Pete the Eagle etc were still there. Shame, that.

Prior to kick-off there was a minute's silence for Brian Moore, someone let off a smoke bomb close to the Holmesdale and recriminations flew between the home and away sections. The *Palace TV* video screen behind the goal peculiarly screened the game live in colours resembling a colour-blind test but didn't show any of Millwall's goals. The atmosphere from our section had been ear-splitting all afternoon, in total contrast to the silent home fans. If it hadn't been for us, there would have been no atmosphere at all. Mind you, for them Millwall's visits must be like having a mad neighbour around for tea. The game was marvellous and we won 3-1, prompting wild celebrations all-round.

At the end of the game we rubbed our victory in and a few seats were thrown forcing riot police to move in to our section next to the Holmesdale. Outside we found that everything was tighter than a duck's arse and police Hoolievans/Robocops blocked the Selhurst station route. One of the riot coppers we saw also wore an ambulance paramedic badge, I thought 'Blimey that's handy, he can hit you over the head and then put a plaster on it for you!'.

We went home via Norwood Junction, grinning like Cheshire cats at our great win against the loathed local rivals.

Wimbledon, Tuesday 25/9/2001, drew 2-2. September became fair-weather Charlie month as I missed Gillingham and Preston away. Therefore my next game was another trip to Selhurst Park, this time to see Wimbledon. Most of our usual contingent made the London Bridge trip; sadly, though, our mini-skirted OAP wasn't around - presumably a Palace fan. This time we disembarked at Norwood Junction and went into the chippy where Dave bought a saveloy, which he waved in front of him like a big red willie. If Palace is non-threatening then Wimbledon is even less hostile.

As we strolled through the suburban sprawl towards Selhurst, we didn't see a single Womble. Even so, there was still a large riot police presence, naturally all for our benefit. Police on horseback flanked us and Pat asked them if he could have a ride. We pointed out that they weren't a local horse riding club but the omnipresent police cavalry. We entered the stadium and where walking up the steps towards the away stand when Pat shouted 'Bal, there's a load of gypos on the pitch!'. He learns it all from us I'm afraid, God help him. On the pitch were numerous Korean dancers and drummers promoting the 2002 World Cup as they also did at half time. Their 'bongo fever Morris men on speed' performances were certainly different. Simon said 'I wonder if we've sent our Morris dancers to

Korea?'. Nathan said 'What are Tim Cahill and his relatives doing on the pitch?' Ethnic stereotypes eh!

Officially, 2337 Millwall were there but again, many more were scattered all around the ground. If there's a less intimidating crowd than Wimbledon, I cannot think of them. Tonight, rather than get behind their side, they were more intent on badmouthing their chairman Koppel's Milton Keynes proposals. They sang 'Koppel Out'/'Koppel Is Full Of Shit!'/'Milton Keynes Is Full Of Shit!'/'You Can Stick Milton Keynes Up Your A...'/'We're Not Leaving Here!' and 'Show Me The Way To Plough Lane'. To their credit they also sang 'Stand Up If You Hate Palace!' which went down rather well all around.

For our part we sang the following - 'Que Sera, Etc, You're Going To Milton Keynes!'/'You Dirty Northern Bastards!'/'No Ground - No Fans!'/'Shit Team - No Home!' and 'You're Just A Bunch of Squatters!'. We also sang 'You Can Stick Your F...ing Wombles Up Your A... - Sideways!'. Particularly Uncle Bulgaria!

Wimbledon's *Blue-And-Yellow* fanzine had a special version tonight that they were trying to get everyone to buy rather than the club programme. In a show of solidarity, we bought the club programme, which contained a couple of oddities. For example, it said that they weren't running any coaches to Crystal Palace! Whilst many programmes show away fan figures, Wimbledon had a note about the weather. Who cares if it was snowing at Grimsby when they played there?

Wimbledon's Muppet was called Wandle! I don't remember him from the telly. Pre-match the line-ups were displayed on the renamed *Dons TV* compiled by a dyslexic - Steve Claridge was called 'Steve Cladridge'. More humourously, Richard Sadlier was referred to as Dick Sadler. Some sort of sexual equipment-maker I think.

The highlight of the match was a Steven Reid free kick prompting a wild 'Reidy!' finger-pointing celebration as he ran towards us. Although we lost a 2-1 lead and it finished 2-2 it was an excellent game, one of the best of the season in my opinion. On the way back to the station, police horses again flanked us, with the riders now sporting lights on their boots and stirrups, which I'd not seen before. Presumably they were a police disco horse-riding display team.

Walsall 29/9/2001, drew 0-0. Nathan drove Paul, Ted, and I to Walsall in a Bristol City-style deluge with tailgating lorries again spraying our windscreen all the way there, he doesn't have a lot of luck when it comes to weather. We stopped in Walsall near the shopping area, as Paul wanted to get some cash. He and I, dressed in Millwall shirts, wandered fruitlessly around looking for a cashpoint for 30 minutes, not something I'd recommend in many Midlands towns. Some locals advised us that we wouldn't get in any pub in colours, we told them we were actually looking for a cashpoint; their eyes glazed over, leaving us to assume they have no need for cash here. We eventually found a machine, headed back to Nathan's car and found a cashpoint near to where we had parked, bloody typical. We got aboard and shortly afterwards parked in a side street near the Bescot.

We went inside joining 850 Lions in the stand behind the goal as before. Apart from their soulless nature, smallish prefabricated grounds have a couple of problems. The low stand roof means that pre-match kickabouts can be a real adventure as any wayward balls are able to ricochet back off the roof or the back wall and hit you full in the head if you're unlucky enough to be in its path. Because the side stands are low, it also enables any agricultural defenders to boot the ball clean out of the ground, which they did four times in this game, if memory serves - 'New Balls Please!' as the man hit in the nuts with a rake might say.

The atmosphere was again low key and although Walsall sang their magpie repertoire, they hadn't stolen any Millwall songs yet. There was a kid sitting in a side stand in an Aston Villa shirt, its Hammers-like colours obviously attracted plenty of attention. Never mind support your local team at least have the decency not to wear a rivals shirt at another team's home match.

There was one real entertaining incident; prior to kick-off a fat 'pie' girl had the misfortune of walking past the cinder track at our end, trailing behind her was a male colleague carrying a tray of uneaten pies; assuming this was her lunch one bloke in our section shouted out 'You're supposed to sell the pies, love, not eat them all!'.

HAPPY DAYS ARE HERE AGAIN!

The game was another unmemorable 0-0 draw and I have still yet to see us win at Walsall. Even though the game was nothing special Ted was very hyper on the way home - on a scale of one to bonkers he was all the way to Upney i.e. one stop past Barking. Luckily we had the tranquilliser gun handy.

West Bromwich Albion, Thursday 11/10/2001, won 2-0. At last, a Thursday away match courtesy of ITV Sport. I had now been to an away game on every day of the week. We could have watched the game on this elite television channel but instead Ted and I decided to go in the flesh. There was only one club coach, due to depart 2.30pm though eventually it left at 3pm.

Initially, the coach was late. Then, having gotten only a couple of hundred yards, steward John realised that he'd left a bag of videos on the floor in the car park. He dashed back to the ground as we sat waiting and after 10 minutes he arrived back sweating and out of breath to ironic cheers. In a 'without further ado' fashion he grabbed the mike and gave the coach steward's equivalent of a pilot's speech, saying something like 'Welcome aboard the good ship Millwall, we will be going all around the motorway network to West Brom. On arrival you may find Birmingham a culture shock and the locals will talk in a peculiar accent - do not be alarmed!'. You know the type of thing, he also said 'I'll be coming around with raffle tickets and scratch cards shortly'. He did all this in an out of breath manner, prompting one bloke to shout out 'What's the prize, an asthma pump?'. This was greeted by much laughter. The only video that he put on I had seen, so for me he may as well have left them in the car park.

Having left late the journey was a motorway enthusiast's idea of heaven as we went M11, M25, M1, M6 and M5 on the way up and M5, M40, M4 on the way back - you can't beat variety. Grandad, etc, sang all the way up, accompanied by banging the seats and windows. John, having regained his breath, pleaded for quiet but to no avail. Tonight this straightforward journey took on nightmare characteristics. There was a massive traffic jam in the Midlands, due to cones being laid out for maintenance starting the following weekend. We also passed a serious accident; a lorry had overturned and spilt its chemical contents all over the road, requiring environmental health officials. Naturally, everyone slowed to black their nose, meaning the journey up took over 4 hours non-stop. The smokers among us must have been crawling up the windows at this point. Why doesn't the club sell Nicorettes gum/patches on the coaches? They could customise them with a club badge; they'd make a killing. Luckily, smoking isn't one of my vices, eating and drinking yes, smoking no. This is because my dad smoked 60-80 fags daily and his early morning coughing fits persuaded me that it wasn't for me.

We eventually met our police escort close to the ground and pulled up outside the impressive Hawthorns, apparently the highest ground in the League. On the way in Ted had his customary civil rights argument with a steward about his right to search him and went unmolested. We sat with the Essex Boys in the ground to the right of the Smethwick End, behind the goal in a vastly improved stadium. West Brom fans were to the left of us behind segregation netting. We had 378 fans there; I didn't think this was too bad considering that it was on TV and a Thursday night, an odd night for football, it just does not feel right. As per usual, we were videoed and pointed at all night, don't these people know they are stealing my soul each time they photograph me?

At most away grounds, Grandad's antics draw quizzical looks from the security, especially when he performs his stand up, raise his baseball cap and waving it around routine. Tonight he appeared to be on the verge of a manhandling. We discussed what would happen if they touched our spiritual leader and decided that it would spark a Grandad Jihad. He appeared to have sung too much on the coach and began his first chant croakily so we scrabbled in our pockets for Strepsils to assist him and discussed carrying a throat spray on the coach with us should any such problems occur in future. Fortunately, he recovered his voice.

Before we got in to our vocal stride, West Brom sang 'Shall We Sing A Song For You?', my first experience of the chant. Despite our number, we then made a good racket. Alex Rae sat among us away fans; with his Wolves connections Albion is probably not the best place for him nowadays and we greeted him warmly. As an aside, I flicked on to The Fantasy Channel, by mistake obviously, and they were showing a film called *Midas Touch* in which one of its stars was called Alex Rae! This is a true story. Why do they never show Harry Munk films on coaches? Don't answer that.

This game was a great all-round Millwall performance. Two first-half goals by Richard Sadlier in front of the home end and a second half display of 'They Shall Not Pass' proportions on Darren Ward's debut sealed 2-0 victory, largely silencing the usually passionate 'Boing, Boing Baggies'; what's all that about, are they mad? Cheerfully we headed towards the exit when a head steward, with a capital Dick, in a luminous jacket and a 'Look at me, I've got a head set/mouthpiece!' importance started having a go at Ted for no reason. Several of us told the officious twat to f... off and he slipped away into the night. I hate these self-deluded little Hitler types, don't get me started.

The coach drove away from the ground and a policeman gave us a thumbs up and a '2-0' hand sign, not a Baggie then? The motorcycle escort led us back towards the motorway and one of the riders kicked his way through the traffic cones to make a path, lucky sod! This has always been one of my ambitions. Ted was again in hyperactive mode, it must be something in the Midlands water; he sat behind me on the coach continually moaning about the strange route we were taking.

When we reached Perivale, he decided that he was getting off to get a bus, convinced that they must run all night from here to Bethnal Green. I spent the rest of the journey talking him out of this; everyone must have thought that we were both mad to listen to us; we eventually got off at the Elephant & Castle and splashed the cash on a cab.

Wolverhampton Wanderers, Wednesday 31/10/2001, lost 1-0. I missed the Stockport demolition, so my next trip was also to the Midlands for this Hallowe'en night game at Wolves, a lively enough place without the added horrors of ghoulies and ghosties. Dave wanted to go on the coach, as he feared for our car if we drove there. Unfortunately, they had sold out so Paul drove Ted, Nathan, Dave and I in a car with no speedometer. If stopped and asked 'Do you know what speed you were doing sir?' he'd have to reply 'No, surprise me!'. Dave hadn't been to Molineux for 30-odd years but came armed with a bottle and Stanley knife nonetheless; glad to see the Boy Scout training hadn't gone amiss. Ted suggested that we should carry cricket/baseball bats for these type of matches. I suggested that as it was Hallowe'en we should carry sharpened stumps in case we encountered any vampires, sorry, I have watched too many old Hammer films. If you wanted something sporting for protection, golf clubs would be the best bet, especially if you wore plus-fours and Pringle jumpers to persuade the police of your sporting intentions.

I was in my Fat Blokes Privilege front seat position, navigating, and the trip up was easy until I missed the turn off for the M6, the navigator's cardinal sin. Consequently, we couldn't stop at services and found ourselves in Birmingham's rush hour desperate for the loo. Sod's Law being what it is, the traffic wouldn't allow us to pull up to any roadside bushes or the hard shoulder, so we had to wait. When we got to the outskirts of Wolverhampton a short distance past a probation centre (always a mark of a town's quality), we could wait no longer and pulled up near a derelict house and did our best *Who's Next?* album cover re-enactment, it was blissful. I have an idea - side-street match-day 'piss zones'. They could put in urinals, washbasins, hot air blowers, Durex machines, well you never know, and have a bloke offering towels and aftershave as they do in the West End. What do you think? To continue…

It was the first time that any of us had driven to Wolverhampton and we were unsure of our directions. I knew Molineux was near Wolverhampton station but that was about it. Luckily, a local girl driver we asked said that she was going past the ground so we should follow her, which we did, arriving at 6pm. We tried to park outside the away stand but a steward who spoke like an uneducated Noddy Holder told us that we couldn't do this. As it was early we were able to park in a company's car park opposite, next to a pub, more of which later. We had over an hour to kill, so had a walk around the outside of Molineux. Paul and Nath hadn't had the pleasure before so I pointed out the usual post-match trouble spot, the underpass behind the home South Bank.

Highlighting former glories, we passed a statue of Billy Wright by a home stand. Nathan said 'I wonder what would happen if we had a slash up the statue?' Nothing we would have enjoyed, that's for sure. We went into their club shop where they sold videos of Mark McGhee's Wolves reign. We then stood outside the John Ireland stand with Andy and Mark of the Essex contingent waiting for it to open; when it did, we went inside and sat beneath the executive boxes near the back. During my numerous visits, Molineux has blossomed from a ramshackle old ground to today's impressive, if yellow, Premiership-quality stadium. It's a ground that moves its away sections about; in addition to tonight's stand I have also stood and sat on the South Bank home end on previous visits.

There were 1100 Millwall in the ground including quite a few 'Boys'. We heard stories on the night of pub attacks, two Stanley knife stabbings and trouble in the town centre before the match. There was also trouble outside with the riot police just before the kick-off. Wolves had two Muppets, Wolfie the infamous Bristol City brawler and Wendy Wolf. You may wonder why I normally mention the Muppets; the main reason is that when I was very young, two elderly female lodgers lived on the middle floor of our house. One day I passed their landing and one of them emerged wearing a Mickey Mouse mask, which scared me shitless! After all, what I saw was a five-foot mouse. You can imagine the effect that all these drug fantasies have had on me since. I personally think that those inside the costumes should be named and shamed. However, if you to have to have them you may as well have one who likes a row, I say.

Wolves came out to *Liquidator* and *Hi-Ho Silver Lining* with 'Wolverhampton' replacing 'silver lining'. They also sang 'I Love To Go A-Wandering', have they no shame? Wolves is volatile and hostile at the best of times, however tonight it was up a notch due to the return of McGhee and Claridge, who the home fans abused. We responded by singing our paedophile chants to Dave Jones as I listed previously.

The game was predominantly a rearguard action and we deserved a point for determination if nothing else. Naturally, in the 90th minute ex-Lion Alex Rae scored, the PA played *Song 2* and they announced 'Wolves 1 Millwall 0' just in case we hadn't noticed. This left us all with that horrible sinking feeling that follows a last minute goal as the home fans erupt all around you. Late in the game, they had announced that the London train would be leaving at 9.50pm, or very soon if you prefer. This was an attempt to jolly us out and away; unfortunately, it didn't legislate for the usual underpass fracas with Wolves' Subway Army.

Outside the ground the police had sensibly blocked off the stairwell to our right, effectively forcing us on a collision with the home 'Boys' from the South Bank. As we spilled into the car park, I saw the most stupid thing I'd ever seen at a match, which is saying something. Bearing in mind that there were hundreds of pissed off Millwall facing him, one rogue Wolves nutter decided it was an ideal opportunity to barge into as many of us as he could. After a couple of shoulder barges, one Millwall bloke said 'Who are you barging, you c...?' then punched him in the mouth quickly followed by other Lions raining kicks and punches on him until riot police intervened. If it was an effort to provoke something it certainly worked. The weirdness was to continue. We lost contact with Dave so Paul decided to go to the car park to see if he'd gone there.

Nathan, Ted and I wore colours, trouble ground or not, and took up a conspicuous position on a grass verge close to the pub opposite the ground in case Dave reappeared. We had a panoramic view of the inevitable subway melee and police were charging about everywhere. Several bizarre individuals then passed us looking like extras in *The Rocky Horror Picture Show*, Hallowe'eners presumably. Their route/timing could have been better; all hell was now breaking loose. As we stood on the verge there was a Wolves meathead, with a small child, looking at us. He looked remarkably like cricketer Merv Hughes, kept staring at us and mumbling in a bizarre, Black Country dialect. We were well aware of him but ignored him largely because we couldn't understand a word he said. He became animated when I wandered off briefly to see if I could find Dave; presumably, because I was the biggest of the three of us.

Shortly after I returned Dave and Paul emerged from the car park. We got in the car when the meathead decided to pick up a breezeblock and try to throw through it through our windscreen.

HAPPY DAYS ARE HERE AGAIN!

Our options were to get out and give him a good hiding/buckle up and quickly drive off or run him over. Sadly, we were stuck in traffic so only the first option was a goer, but before we could act riot police came charging towards us subway-bound and our attacker reverted back to his father of the year posture. The traffic then cleared and we drove off, it was all very bizarre.

Heading out of town, we saw a lady of easy virtue in a side street wearing an archetypal prossie outfit. She wore a very, very tight pair of skimpy denim shorts, white stockings and suspenders. Ted had to be physically restrained from giving her some business. She may have been another Hallowe'ener, more trick than treat, though. I'd now been to Wolves seven times and never seen us win, nevertheless the night was incident-filled, I'm sure you'll agree.

Sheffield Wednesday, 8/12/2001, drew 1-1. I missed Grimsby and Bradford. I was especially annoyed as I love the smell of fish and curry and Bradford would have been another new ground, so my next away trip was to Wednesday.

We were going by train and I had to negotiate a building site obstacle course outside St Pancras before meeting Nathan, Paul, Ted, Dave Murray and his mate Simon inside. Unfortunately we learnt that the 10.25am train, on which Millwall had two coaches, was suffering from a points failure and would be delayed. Suddenly memories of a previous trip to Wednesday in February 1990 swept over me. This had consisted of replaced engines, snowstorms, no heaters, no buffet, piss-taking Chesterfield platform policemen, a 4.30pm arrival at Wadsley Bridge followed by a trip around Sheffield to return to London without seeing a ball kicked.

To add to today's fun on the concourse a prat drove a provisions cart through us and the police came among us with sniffer dogs looking for drugs. I rather wished that I'd had a curry the night before, if you get my flatulent drift. The police's attention was focused solely on us even though due to the delays there were also Gillingham, Leicester, Bolton, Southampton and Southend fans there. As there was no news, we began to wander sheep-like from platform to platform as each train came in, accompanied by Millwall chants, which must have been very welcoming for the general train punters disembarking. Eventually, our train left at 11.45am on what turned out to be an uneventful journey. We occupied far more of the train than we were supposed to due to the delay. En route, we passed Pride Park, Derby, a new ground we had yet to visit, prompting the usual dash-to-the-window ground identification game. In typical Millwall style, there were video cameras aplenty along with police on Leicester, Derby and Chesterfield station platforms merely because our train briefly stopped there.

On every previous trip to Wednesday I had been on club specials to Wadsley Bridge, then been route marched to Hillsborough through an area alarmingly like in *Last of the Summer Wine*. Today we alighted at Sheffield station, where the massed police herded us onto the Supertram to the ground, via the much nicer town centre route. We then had the customary gawping session with any locals we passed before arriving at our Leppings Lane stop. Dave and Simon went their separate way and we remaining four went into the ground at 2.30pm, where we met up with the Essex contingent.

Hillsborough is an old-fashioned but still impressive stadium and although there were 1352 of us in the upper portion of the infamous stand, now simply the West Stand, we rattled about but generate quite a racket with the help of a roof.

We don't need a bloody brass band and a big drum to get us going. To highlight this we sang 'You Can Stick Your F...ing Drum Up Your A... - Sideways!' and 'Who's The Wanker With The Drum?'. To indicate the low-key nature of the home fans we sang 'Nice Ground - Shit Fans!'. Naturally, we also sang the usual plethora of regional abuse - 'Factory/Ferret/Pigeon Loft, Etc.'

My dad was a foreman in an East End scrap-metal firm and before I was born he had the opportunity to run their Sheffield yard, which he declined. Shame, I could have talked like Geoff Boycott and been the fat bloke in *The Full Monty* displaying my wares, not that I'm paranoid about my weight but when our crowd sing 'You Fat C...!' or 'Belly's Gonna Get Ya!'. I often think they mean me, although at Sheffield it referred to their topless Tango man, I think? It's not easy staying fat but having a season ticket to the chip shop helps. What frightened me was that Wednesday didn't have meat and potato pies! How can a northern side not have meat and potato pies? I can take or leave pies myself, as CCTV cameras nationwide will confirm. If I'm honest I get them on prescription and if I don't get a fix it makes me twitchy.

Wednesday, like Wolves, came out to *Hi-Ho Silver Lining*, the theme tune to any shit wedding reception in my experience. In the game the first half was low-key with the only high point being Denzil's penalty save at our end. There was also a funny incident - Grandad, sitting a few rows in front of us, stood up with a huge inflatable phone pressed to his ear and said 'Hello? Hello?' followed by 'We Are The Millwall Boys!', a true classic. In the second half, we went 1-0 down but salvaged a point thanks to a very persistent Sadlier goal. Wednesday is another ground where I have never seen Millwall win; in fact, today's 1-1 draw was the best result that I'd seen there. As we left the ground, I heard one Yorkshiremen say to t'other 'I tell you what, they don't half make a bloody racket don't they!' High praise indeed.

The Supertram to Sheffield station was now a mixed home and away affair; it was packed and very unwelcoming to a claustrophobic like me. I fought my way on board, and then off again, before relocating to a less packed part of the sardine tin. In the process, I lost the others. I knew they were on board, so I called them and we arranged to get off a few stops before the station. I cannot think why but it was a big mistake, we were miles from anywhere. We had to hike across tram tracks, through subways, and across walkways toward Sheffield station, with only a rudimentary idea of where we were going, not to be recommended at some grounds. We located the station by following the glint in the night sky from the massed riot police helmets and the blue spinning lights, as good an indicator as any.

The station was full of riot police and as we waited for our train there was a loud shattering of glass, which the police blocking the stairwells caused - you can't take them anywhere. We met Dave and Simon on the platform. For our amusement, they had laid on a female announcer who appeared to be on helium, which gave her the perfect unintelligible train-announcing voice. Our designated train, already occupied by 'normal' people, arrived 10 minutes late and we bundled aboard in the usual scrum-like fashion trying to find an empty seat. I noticed that the first class carriage had tables laid out for dinner. I hope that no one had booked a romantic candlelit meal on this particular trip. Our party were scattered around the train, I myself had a table with an empty seat opposite. We pulled into Chesterfield, it was full of riot police and there were also a few Southend supporters there for an FA Cup game. One Southend fan got on, sat opposite me and we got talking. He said 'Who are you lot?' I said 'Millwall.' He said 'Do you know that all the riot police were waiting just in case any of you lot got off?' I told him that this was far from unusual but he couldn't believe how we were normally treated.

We are so impervious to the Millwall police state that we almost don't notice it any more. We spoke of our away experiences and he told me that Southend had encountered trouble at clubs whose fans wouldn't dare approach us. For example, he said that Orient fans had bricked their open-topped bus! I eventually stopped laughing. He said being aboard a Millwall train was no different to being with anyone else's fans, but that's reputation for you.

We arrived at St Pancras at 9pm and disembarked with our singing bouncing off the walls of the ancient station nicely. Paul, Nathan and Ted went home and I went for a sherbet with Dave and Simon in the station bar. At closing time, we decided to find somewhere for a late one. We found ourselves in a nearby pub resembling Sodom and Gomorrah but beggars cannot be choosers so we carried on drinking there until 1.30am.

I then walked home in the classic comic drunk fashion, one step forward two steps sideways, arriving home several hours later. That'll teach me.

Crystal Palace (Home), Boxing Day 2001 noon, won 3-0. Pre-Christmas I was in an Islington pub, with mates Lee and Lal for an after work drink. For some reason, there was also a large contingent of Palace fans there who had obviously had a sniff of the barmaid apron, because their main song was 'We All Follow The Palace, Over Land And Sea!'. Although not to Millwall obviously - Millwall at Palace 6000-plus, Palace at Millwall just over 1600. Piss and poor spring to mind.

HAPPY DAYS ARE HERE AGAIN!

The New Den was very hyped today helped by our win at Selhurst. Pre-match, Mick Brown played Smokie's classic *Living Next Door To Alice* and turned the volume down when the chorus came around, the enormous noise that emerged from the Millwall sections when we sang 'Palace? Palace? Who The F… Are Palace?'. Must have frightened the life out of the few Palace who had braved South Bermondsey, bloody marvellous it was too. Slightly different from Palace fans at Selhurst, that's for sure.

Palace chairman Simon Jordan had made Theo sit on a toilet seat at Selhurst, which backfired badly when we won. In a chairman's agreement, as we had won Jordan was supposed to dress as Zampa at Millwall, who'd know? He declined but generously matched the day's collection for Neil Harris's *Everyman* appeal; obviously, we still took the piss out of him with 'Jordan, Jordan, Show Us Your Tits!'. I think we had the wrong Jordan.

Today was a piss-take par excellence. Following our win at Palace, Steve Coppell left (again) so we sang 'We Got Coppell Out!'. When we began to romp home, we sang of their new manager Trevor Francis 'We Want Francis Out!'. To the 1600 suburbanite fans we sang 'Is That All You Take Away?' to which they had the cheek to reply 'Is That All You Have At Home?'. Good one! We then sang 'Where Were You At Selhurst Park?', not forgetting the charming chant 'Shit On The Palace Today!'. Mind you, this may just have been an anti-royalist chant?

In a festive mood we sang 'You're Just a Bunch of Turkeys!' and 'Jingle Bells, Jingle All The Way, Oh What Fun It Is To See Millwall Win Again!'. We also 'Ole'd' each time that Palace managed to get the ball and booed whenever Millwall had it, superb stuff.

Our 3-0 win was sweet and surprisingly easy. Neil Harris had only recently returned and had he been fully fit this would have been a chuck in the towel job. So easy was it that the Palace sang 'You're Not Fit To Wear The Shirt!'. Certainly true today. This first double for 42 years made up slightly for Palace's lack of relegation in 2000/01.

Watford, New Year's Day 2002, noon, won 4-1. I missed Burnley away so, Watford was my next away match. Dave drove Ted, Simon, Pat, Nathan and I there in the minibus. Paul went to a party in Hertfordshire the night before and arranged to meet us at the ground. I very sensibly had a relatively quiet New Year's Eve myself so I was okayish and everybody else appeared to also be relatively unscathed, except for Nathan that was. He went to a school uniform party at the London Arena, got home at 6.30am and we set off three and a half hours later; consequently, he was like the walking dead.

The journey was a doddle due to the post-party paralysis syndrome. I have been to Vicarage Road so many times I cannot actually recall the number, it was the venue of my first real away trip in 1970 and is another ground that moves the away areas about. Today the away end was the Vicarage Road End, the opposite end from our recent visits, so we no longer had to yomp around the allotments. I have now been in every section apart from the run-down side stand. We parked near the Rookery and headed to our stand and en route we passed Reg Burr getting out of his chauffeur-driven car looking a bit too close to Homer Simpson's boss Mr. Burns for comfort. We tugged our forelocks and carried on our way. There isn't a hint of threat at Watford and we continued unmolested; how unlike our own dear Den.

This match was initially all ticket but then changed to pay-on-the-day. At many similar matches Nathan has got in as a junior, he looks five or six years younger than his 20 odd years, especially if he wears a baseball cap. Nathan was unsure if he'd make the game, didn't have a ticket so had to pay at the turnstile. I said 'If I were you I'd pay full price today', which he did. He might look 14, but if breathalysed he'd be charged with under-age drinking and he'd forgotten his cap anyway.

Watford has one of the league's narrowest turnstiles, certainly not ideal for someone with a fuller figure like Fat Reg, or me especially not after Christmas. To get through I practically had to grease myself up and get my mates to pull my ample carcass through from the inside; sadly, this is only slightly embellished. Once inside we met many of the usual away cronies and after a round of 'Happy New Years' we went on to our stand behind the goal. Nathan appeared shortly after having somehow negotiated the entrance. Paul arrived a few minutes later.

146

HAPPY DAYS ARE HERE AGAIN!

Bizarrely Millwall's 3289 fans were split into two groups by black meshing that ran from the TV gantry at the back of our covered stand to the front, protected by a heavy police presence, the most peculiar segregation policy I'd ever seen. Whom they were trying to protect I don't know but it made for some good banter between the sections - 'Is That All You Take Away?'/'Who Are Ya?'/'You'll Run And You Know You Will!'/'Can You Hear The Left Side (Right Side) Sing?' and 'It's All Gone Quiet Over There!'. As per usual Sir Elton had to endure the customary gay chants listed earlier, as did Vialli.

The home side had reinvented themselves as the Golden Boys; today Golden Shower was more like it. The home atmosphere (sic) consisted of a few half-hearted 'Vialli Army' chants accompanied by a big drum. We acknowledged this with the customary 'SSSHH!' and 'We Laugh At the Golden Boys!'. It always amazes me how a home team can play in front of such bloody awful atmospheres.

We strolled to a 3-0 lead. Watford then scored a consolation goal and their DJ put on their goal music so we sarcastically stood up and 'EIO'd' their goal to take the piss, very unlike us. Late on Watford brought on the fabulously named Nordin Wooter, with a hairdo like a besom broom. He was greeted by cooeing, limp wristed waving and wolf whistling, topped off with the first ever rendition of 'There's Only One Whoopi Goldberg!'. At 3-1 Neil Harris scored after running from inside Millwall's half before unleashing a superb 25-yard curling shot. We went berserk; I had tears in my eyes, as did most Millwall if we're honest, due to the significance of this first comeback goal since his return game against Barnsley in September. It was the icing on the cake of a great away performance. Every man in the team mobbed him, including Denzil who sprinted the length of the pitch. Bomber was then carried shoulder-high to the Hornet TV video screen in the right hand corner of the away stand where the whole team viewed the goal again, against a crescendo of 'Super Neil Harris!'. He bowed towards us, presumably to thank us for the support he'd received.

I WAS BORN UNDER THE COLD BLOW LANE

The goal, and what followed, was the most poignant thing that I have ever seen at a football match, or anywhere else for that matter, in my 30-plus years of following Millwall. It put football into perspective and will live in the memory of everybody who was there on the day forever more I'm sure.

Norwich City, Sunday 20/1/2002, drew 0-0. Nathan drove Ted, Paul and I to Norwich for a TV-arranged 2.15pm Sunday game, my fourth visit. At Liverpool Street, I found there were no trains to our meet in Walthamstow or to Norwich, only replacement buses - it's a conspiracy I tell you! So I got the tube, changing a couple of times before eventually meeting the others.

Nathan's car was written off shortly before this match. Fortunately, the company he works for loaned him a jeep with a petrol allowance, so we had a free ride to the country. It was uneventful save for passing the replacement buses and Millwall's team coach en route. Near Norwich, there were signposts for both Norwich City and Ipswich Town; generally, you don't get any signs let alone to two different grounds.

On arrival in the land of Bernard Matthews and Alan Partridge (Ah Ha!) we parked in a police station car park and set off to the ground. En route, we passed the new Norwich and Peterborough stand, a brick edifice more like a block of flats than a football stand from outside. I don't like brick stands, don't ask me why. Norwich is a rustic club, nowhere else have I seen such a vast array of friendly ageing farmers and their families walking to the ground. Since my visit in the 1990s Carrow Road had been vastly improved, save for the ramshackle away side section, which from the outside looked like a condemned cowshed. We went through the turnstiles and headed to the refreshment stall that Delia Smith appeared to have taken over. There was a designated matchday pie, which today was chicken and mushroom - doesn't she know I only eat meat and potato pies? Obviously, I bought one anyway.

During the game Delia had to endure 'Delia Takes It Up The A...!'. Not on her TV cookery shows she doesn't, otherwise it would be renamed 'Delia's How To Bugger!'. To highlight our preferred chef we sang 'Oh! Jamie, Jamie, Jamie, Jamie, Jamie, Jamie Oliver!'. We went inside where the stewards unusually led us to our correct seats. We had the right hand end of the South Stand running along one side of the ground. Our tickets said 'Impaired View' and they weren't wrong; metal posts ran along its length and there was also a low roof. We couldn't see the corner flag at the opposite end of our stand so we stood the whole game for a better view. It was also raining and we discovered that the roof leaked as rain dripped on our heads all afternoon. Nevertheless we had still paid top dollar. We had 1690 fans there for a vital clash that would effectively settle our play-off berth at worst.

Family club Norwich had three Muppets:

Captain Canary, a yellow canary, who got the old favourite 'You Can Stick Your Yellow Budgie Up Your A... - Sideways!'.

Kitty Kat, a blue and yellow striped cat thing. I was rather hoping that he'd attack the Canary but unfortunately he didn't. This particular creature had a huge head, so we sang 'You've Got A F...ing Big Head!', just in case, it hadn't noticed.

The trio was completed by a six-foot mobile phone with no name but legs - aren't drugs wonderful? We were too stunned to abuse this thing.

Pre-match there was an immaculate silence for an ex-Norwich player who had recently died. We then traded pleasantries with the locals behind the goal, another set of fans exhibiting 'bravado in the ground/arse for dust outside' policy. They sang two adapted Millwall chants 'No One Likes You 'Cos You're Shit!' and 'No One Likes You 'Cos You're Scum!'. They also sang 'Londoners Wank, Wank, Wank!'. A boy has got to have a hobby.

To remind them of their opening day hiding we replied with '4-Nil Etc!'. We certainly made a racket with the aid of the roof. Naturally we sang rustic chants like 'I Can't Read, Etc, I'm A Norwich City Fan And I'm A F...ing Wanker!'.

The game had very few incidents of note apart from Norwich's Darel Russell being sent off early on for an elbow on Mark Bircham although it was a dubious dismissal; we still screamed blue murder. It didn't help that Russell sported a dreadlocks and black woolly gloves ensemble; he had previously been 'Pineappled' and had his manliness questioned with 'Who's The Pooftah In The Gloves?'. Despite their 10 men we couldn't break them down and it finished goalless. The highlight of the day came when Norwich's announcer said something like 'Mr... Believed To Be In The Norwich And Peterborough Stand, Your Wife Is Giving Birth To A Baby!' This got a huge cheer and laughter from the mostly male crowd - a new baby or football, mmm? Norwich fans sang 'Loyal Supporter!' in what was a classic PA moment.

After the game I went to the gents, which had a split stairwell with 'In' and 'Out' above it. I wondered why it didn't also have 'Shake It All About!'. As we walked back to our Jeep in the drizzle, Ted lambasted every local within earshot, who looked at him in a 'the village idiot's out again' fashion.

Nottingham Forest, 9/2/2002 noon, won 2-1. The next away match should've been Manchester City but sadly we had been denied that particular pleasure, so Nottingham it was. Whilst I've never seen trouble at Forest on any of my four visits, Nottingham is the 4th most violent city in England and *Hooligans - No One Likes Us* had footage of a Forest 'Firm' en route to the New Den in October 2001, promising to 'twat' Millwall, whatever that might mean in English. There had been aggro after the match near South Bermondsey station. As a result, the police made it a noon kick-off and shut numerous city centre pubs on the day.

Paul, Nathan, Dave Murray, Ted and I travelled to this game on the 8.55am train from St Pancras, where there was again a huge police contingent; sniffer dogs walked among us and the same tosser drove his supply wagon through us, and they appeared to be selling drink at the station. We supposedly only had three coaches and some reduced First Class seats, although we appeared to have the entire train. It was obviously going to be a big turnout with Millwall now third and with the added possibility of trouble swelling the numbers.

Once we were aboard the train we hadn't gone far when we noticed that Ted was in an agitated state. He appeared to be rehearsing his arrival in Nottingham by repeating the mantra 'Come on you Forest C...s!'. Ted is very much of the method acting school, that's for sure. As per usual police were massed on Bedford and Leicester stations where our train stopped, just in case we got off. The number of police that we had seen so far was nothing compared to what was to face us at Nottingham station when we arrived at 10.40am. Every train trip to Nottingham has invariably meant being held in metal pens outside the station, whilst the police videoed everybody individually. For this match it was business as usual, what police state? Whenever the police have adopted this herding tactic it has prompted bleating noise to mimic our plight, mostly by Simon it has to be said, but it made me wonder why the police don't introduce sheepdogs and dog handlers? They could go through their 'Come By' and whistling routines and easily herd us to the ground.

Paul had broken his foot playing football and had been walking with the aid of crutches. However, he decided that they would be too awkward getting on and off trains and the police would probably confiscate them as weapons, so he chose instead to wear a special shoe over his plaster. Even at St Pancras, he was struggling and on the outbound train, we discussed getting a taxi to Forest. I said I'd ask the police if we could go out to the cab ranks.

As I walked out into the holding pens a PC and WPC were standing at the foot of a stairwell. Just ahead of me were a father and son and these police asked them if they wanted to go upstairs to avoid the crowd, which they declined. I naturally assumed that they would let us go out this way, once I told them of Paul's predicament. I explained our plight, politely asking if we could get a taxi. The WPC, who had a face like a bulldog chewing a wasp, said 'No!'. I restated our situation and she again said 'No, you'll have to walk to the ground with everyone else'. We replied with a sarcastic 'Thank you!' that really meant 'Well F... You Then!'.

We set off inside a huge police escort, surrounded by enough surveillance equipment to film *Titanic*. In all we had big furry mikes, video, TV and stills cameras, barking Alsatians and police spotters all around us. There was even a bloke on a raised platform getting a dandruff's eye view of the top of our heads, near the river crossing turn off to Meadow Lane. All that was missing was a director in jodhpurs with a riding crop shouting 'Action!' through a megaphone. If they were trying to get abusive footage, they were in luck. How did they think we would react to this totally unwarranted intrusion? As a seasoned veteran of CCTV footage nationwide I've never seen the like. As we walked past Meadow

Lane, several people relieved themselves against the outside walls, something spicy for the cameras I suppose.

It's only a short walk from Nottingham station to either of the city's grounds, not today though because we were on an epic trek including crossing a couple of bridges. On one of the bridges a bloke decided to have a slash into the river and we noticed that there was a police boat parked in midstream; were they expecting a river assault by Millwall's SBS Division? One good thing was that we passed a girls' hockey match full of lightly perspiring short-skirted young girls - it was a real 'tasche-twiddling/cravat-wearing, come over all alike moment and it took the sting out of our 45-minute walk, now taking us completely around the City Ground. I'd never had this police detour before and all it managed to do was anger people. We eventually arrived at the City Ground and queued up to get in to the Bridgford Lower behind the goal, as the locals looked down through glass windows from the upper tier. We greeted each other in the customary manner.

The game had been designated all-ticket but again we found that you could also pay on the day, which I found both annoying and strange, especially when you consider the match was category C and the security had been extremely tight getting to the ground. It also negated any membership scheme that Millwall had in place. We went inside and sat in the corner of the lower tier, among nearly 2500 Lions, including a large 'Firm'. Home fans were above and to the side of us. We wondered why the players had black armbands on and found out when we were asked to stand for Princess Margaret, who had died that day. This silence was followed by that peculiar trait of a huge crowd roar the instant the whistle blew. It's as if it's essential to shout out as soon as possible, to make sure that you hadn't lost your voice. Ted's train rehearsal paid off when he began haranguing any Forest fans within earshot; he was going into one to such an extent that the bloke sitting in front of him turned around and shook him warmly by the hand for his spirited performance.

Morning kick-offs can have a lethargic atmosphere; however, we had already had a 2-hour-plus train journey and a bracing walk in the Nottinghamshire air so we were wide awake and well up for it. The home fans, though, seemed to be metaphorically still in bed. It didn't help that this once great club didn't have a financial pot to piss in, having recently sold their forward line, so the home atmosphere had a whipped dog quality to it. To highlight this we sang 'Upstairs Give Us A Song!'/ 'Shall We Sing A Song For You?' and the Millwall copyrighted 'Your Support Is F...ing Shit!'. We highlighted their financial situation by singing 'Where's Your First Team Gone?'/'Sell, Sell, Sell!'/'Where've Your Strikers Gone?'/'Let's All Have A Whip-Round!' and 'You Don't Know Who You're Selling!'.

The best moment though was when they announced that the inappropriately named Brian Cash was coming on as a substitute, at which point we sang the classic 'He's The Only F...ing Cash That You've Got!'. Naturally, the day couldn't pass without 'Robin Hood' being played and in response to this we sang 'Robin Hood, Robin Hood Riding Through The Glen, Queer As A C..., Takes It Up The Bum, Etc!'. How we could sing this about a man who wore fetching green tights and lived together with umpteen similarly dressed men in a forest, I don't know.

The game was another good performance and, whilst Forest huffed and puffed, it was only a highly dodgy penalty award that got them a goal in the second half and we came away with a thoroughly deserved 2-1 win. Forest is a lucky ground; in fact, Nottingham in general is, I've only seen one defeat at either ground amid a sea of wins.

After the match we were let out of the ground into a car park filled with smoke, a fire or smoke bomb I don't know, but either way the police made us stand in it. Why they did this I don't know, sadism springs to mind. We then set off on our march back to the station with Paul again struggling badly. He'd shown true devotion to the Millwall cause today, that's for sure.

We got back to St Pancras before the afternoon's games had finished, which was an odd feeling after our full away day.

Barnsley, 2/3/2002, drew 1-1. Originally, we were going by train until Millwall withdrew their ticket offer due to engineering works. Rather than drive, Paul, Ted and I decided to get a club coach. Paul was now free of plaster. Three coaches including the

I WAS BORN UNDER THE COLD BLOW LANE

Junior Lions left the New Den at 9am. Steward Larry as per usual did the raffle almost immediately we left the ground. Unfortunately, one of our two coach drivers won the prize of a coach ticket to Portsmouth, which he'd probably drive to anyway. He was offered an alternative prize of naked photos of Larry draped seductively on his parka, but naturally he declined.

On the motorway, Theo bombed past us at Mach 1 hooting in recognition and another car 'wankered' us after hooting to gain our attention. Our driver said this reminded him of a Spurs trip he'd done to Man United in the days when coaches were like a Jolly Boys boozy outing. Unfortunately, coaches didn't have toilets in those days, just a piss bucket positioned near the driver.

Spurs' coach came from an Enfield coach company and his chosen route took them through Altrincham, coincidentally playing Enfield that day. Twenty locals saw what they thought was an Enfield fan coach so abused and 'gestured' them. One Spurs bloke sitting at the front asked the driver to stop and open the coach door, which he did. This bloke picked up the piss bucket and threw it all over the Altrincham fans. They then hastily drove off, leaving the locals smelly and sodden, thinking that Enfield had done it. Charming, eh!

Today's first moody video presentation was Vinnie Jones' *Mean Machine* months before it officially came out. We also had hours of *Only Fools and Horses* as per Larry's usual custom. After a brief services stop, we continued northwards and picked up our police escort at the Catcliffe roundabout. We were then held for ages due to earlier trouble in the town centre. Eventually we continued into Barnsley through an area now even more schizophrenic than my last visit. The numerous huge chimneys and industrial plants pumping out poisonous pillars of smoke, silhouetted against the backdrop of the rolling hills and closed coalpits, now rubbed shoulders with a brand new shopping mall and Barnsley Metrodome. Despite the modernizations you were still in no doubt that you were Oop North.

Unusually the ground was again signposted as was Barnsley General Hospital, just in case anyone really did lose his bottle in Barnsley. We arrived at the ground, parked on a muddy grass verge near the away end, disembarked and headed inside. The ground had been vastly improved since my last trip, a night match, when Dave Mitchell scored to give us a 1-0 win. The away section had then been an open terrace and only the main side grandstand had been built.

Oakwell was now all-seater with three new stands including the vast covered away end. Only the old stand to our right was original, although this now had seats on the lower portion where terraces had once been. I sat in this old stand for my first visit and we had been personally ushered to our seats as per the Norwich trip. In the ground, we met the Essex contingent and sat together high up on the right hand side of the North Stand behind the goal with 745 Lions. The home fans were nowhere near us but even so we had segregation netting to our left and a large police box to our right. From our position, we had a panoramic view of the car park and pre-match we saw the arrival of Millwall's 'Firm'. They had presumably come by train somehow and were walking towards our end surrounded by police cavalry, meat wagons, with a police chopper hovering above and a copper each.

When the 'Firm' shepherding was over, I made my customary pilgrimage to the pie stall to buy an excellent meat and potato pie - 5 stars on the Balstars Pieometer - pastry heaven! I then visited the loo and found myself alone with an oldish bloke happily dancing away to Bon Jovi's *Living on a Prayer*, playing on the PA at the time, it seemed a shame to have disturbed him. Barnsley's DJ appeared to be auditioning for the job of wandering England DJ and played a massively loud Megamix, of Jive Bunnyesque crap, and bloody annoying it was too. Stewards/police were again eyeing Grandad suspiciously, particularly when he did a 'Raise The Roof' dance to the DJ's half-time dance selection.

The ref was supposed to be everyone's favourite schoolmarm David Elleray. However, supposed Premiership referee Mike Riley, from nearby Rotherham, replaced him. Presumably he'd been at home filling out his application for a traffic warden job or molesting his ferret when he got the call. He was one of the worst whistle-happy homer referees of the season. He totally lost control of the game when a Barnsley penalty hit the underside of the bar, Geoff Hurst-style. He received no guidance from the lino and it ended in total confusion. Matt Lawrence was sent off shortly after the debacle for very little - 'Professional Referees, My Arse!' When Barnsley 'scored' the DJ played Showaddywaddy's *Hey Rock 'n' Roll*!. Aye, it takes you back to when music were shit!

The match had had one of the better home atmospheres that I'd witnessed there, although watching Barnsley was certainly not like watching Brazil now. The game ended 1-1, more two points lost than gained, but you cannot beat the man in black. I've still yet to see Millwall lose at Barnsley in half a dozen visits, somehow I have always missed the games we've lost.

We boarded our coach and set off. In a side road outside the car park there was aggro involving station-bound Millwall home fans and truncheon-wielding police. I tend to equate aggro with passion and Oakwell is certainly not passionate in an Old Den sense. That said. my first visit in the 1990s had been like a morgue but after the game the police warned us to pull the train blinds down because missile attacks were a Barnsley speciality. Fortunately nothing happened. On the motorway we passed two Palace coaches returning from a 5-2 coshing at Grimsby. Safely aboard a coach some 'wankered' us while others looked at us in abject terror so we greeted them in time-honoured fashion. We were half an hour from Millwall when Larry decided to put on an exceptionally moody video of George Clooney's *Ocean's Eleven* only just out at the pictures. Sadly he didn't realise that a two hour film doesn't go into a half hour journey.

Portsmouth, 9/3/2002 noon, lost 3-0. Pompey/Millwall games are always fun, hence the early kick-off. Today was certainly a memorable trip for all the wrong reasons.

Humorously, on the road to Portsmouth you pass some particularly apt place names for a hostile trip e.g. Cosham and Hurtmore, not forgetting that great *Carry On* name Burpham. Nathan wasn't sure if he wanted to drive and as I didn't fancy the train I bought a coach ticket just in case. He eventually rang me on Friday to say that he would drive and I arranged to meet him and Ted at 9am, foregoing my coach trip.

HAPPY DAYS ARE HERE AGAIN!

My mate Ian Glasby, who lives in Australia, was in England for his mum's funeral. He was shortly due to go back to Oz so we arranged a mobhanded farewell piss-up on Friday night. It started at 5.00pm and ended at 2.30am, comprising of a pub-crawl, karaoke and a trip to see naughty naked ladies at a pole dancing club - a pukka night out. Ian stayed at my place and as soon as we got in I took a Resolve, drank as much water as I could and went to bed hoping for the best.

At 8 am I awoke in a 'what hit me?' style, had another Resolve and left Ian to sleep it off in the spare room. Nathan picked me up and we set off to Pompey with only a rudimentary idea of where the motorway was. Unfortunately, I was in no state to navigate so we took a wrong turn at the Elephant & Castle, then hit every set of traffic lights, numerous jams and somehow found ourselves in Herne Hill. We stopped at a garage where fortunately a helpful Rasta told us the way to the South Circular/A3. Although now heading the right way, our traffic problems continued; it had now taken two hours to get this far and would be a miracle if we arrived on time.

Paul was in Southampton visiting Helen who comes from there, and had arranged to meet us there. He called around 11am to say he was almost there. Despite his doubts that we'd make it we hared up the motorway at 100mph, tailgating and hooting whilst Nathan and his friends exchanged texts. We had Capital Gold's match build up on the radio and shortly before kick-off we sailed past the huge 'Sail of the South' sculpture on Pompey's outskirts. There were no signs for Portsmouth FC so I told Nathan to head for Fratton train station, as I knew it was near there. We reached Fratton with the game now in progress. Pompey's chairman had threatened to withhold his player's wages shortly before this game because they were crap. The threat worked, as we soon heard that Millwall were two down. Nevertheless, we were here now and parked in Lidl's car park near Fratton and headed to the ground. We had colours on and as we walked past Fratton's Tudor cottage, a smiling Pompey fan said 'Is it worth you going in?' to which we cheerfully replied 'F... Off!'. We reached the turnstiles at 12.15pm just as they were about to shut but fortunately we got in. Nathan went to find Paul whilst

I WAS BORN UNDER THE COLD BLOW LANE

Ted and I went into the toilet and decided to meet up with Paul and Nathan later on.

Fratton Park is still largely an old style ground, although since my last trip it's now mostly all-seater. The away Milton End behind the goal now had seats on the old terraces, but still had no roof. When Ted and I got in all the seats were full, so we stood on the small piece of remaining terracing in the left-hand corner as a gale blew around us. The opposite end of the ground had a new stand, 'KJC', with some bloke's head depicted in the seats who I didn't know from Adam. Renovated ground or not, the toilets and refreshment facilities were awful. As we arrived late, I don't know if they still had their 'Hello Sailor!' man, but they did have a drug fantasy blue frog Muppet, named Frogmore after the outside road. As per usual, riot police surrounded our section, though the police dogs were muzzled, which was nice of them.

There's a tradition that every Portsmouth game has a continual backdrop of them chiming 'Play Up Pompey!' and us responding 'F... Off Pompey!'; so it was today and bloody monotonous it is too. Pompey Looney John Portsmouth football Club Westwood accompanies their chimes with his bell and bugle and the KJC stand now housed this twat. He seemed to have given up on the bell today perhaps someone had sensibly stolen his clapper. He majored on the bugle with all the skill of a nursery kid on a recorder so it was no less annoying. Nonetheless, Pompey managed to sing along with him, God knows how.

It was still 2-0 at half-time and Pompey's PA treated us to a sailor's hornpipe medley. We should fight back with a Cockney medley next time they play at the New Den, that'll teach 'em! It became 3-0 early in the second half. We were then awarded a penalty at our end, which Pompey fan, ex-player and ex-manager Steve Claridge took and naturally missed. It was one of those games. Pompey sarcastically sang 'There's Only One Steve Claridge!' and 'You'll Be Back Again Next Year!'.

We had 2300 fans there, by far the largest turnout I'd seen at Pompey, but we made little noise. The open end didn't help, nor did the score, the weather or the fact that we continued to play crap. Nevertheless we abused Peter Crouch and Graham Rix as listed previously and both sets of fans traded the usual Hoolie boasts. Millwall sang of a Waterloo station victory in December with 'You Got Run At Waterloo!'. Pompey sarcastically sang 'Let's All Run From Millwall'. By midway through the second half many Millwall had already left the ground, offering out the home fans on the way out. The KJC then sang 'Let Them In, Let Them In, Let Them In!'. It became obvious that the match was lost so Ted and I spent our time looking down on to the street where the massed Millwall were in a Mexican stand-off with the riot police. Though nothing much happened it was still more interesting than watching our woeful on-pitch performance. The game ended 3-0. Unlike Barnsley, Pompey is a Bok ground for me. I've seen only one Millwall win among numerous defeats, including the 6-1 'Rioch Out!' game.

Straight after the whistle I went to the toilet where someone had sensibly stuck a mustard dispenser from the refreshment stall in a urinal and wrecked a pipe on one of the cisterns, leaving the floor like a piss paddling pond, cheers. I then joined Ted outside the ground to wait for Paul and Nathan. Apparently there had been numerous Pompey arrested on Friday night and we heard that there was trouble at the station prior to the match. Even so, in addition to letting people out whilst the match was on, they let everybody out straight after the match together, thus allowing Pompey fans to come through our ranks and vice-versa, though I saw no trouble close to the ground.

Despite a history of Millwall/Pompey trouble, the only incident I'd seen at Pompey was when Simon once had a cup of hot coffee thrown over him in the ground. I'd seen plenty of aggro at the Old Den but not at Fratton. Until today, that was… The brothers emerged and Paul set off to his car, parked on the home side of the ground, through the massed Pompey ranks. We wished him luck and we three joined the back of a large Millwall contingent heading towards Fratton station, roughly in the direction of Nathan's jeep. An army marches on its stomach, well I do anyway and due to my delicate condition and our mad dash, I'd had nothing to eat, so I stopped at a burger stall in the street and bought a sausage/burger, consisting of a pound of sausages and three quarter pounders, with onions and ketchup in a king-size bap. I thought to myself - if the home fans don't kill me, the cholesterol in this will. I then rejoined the very slow moving throng whilst eating this culinary monster. The police stopped us some distance from Fratton station to avoid clashes with the Pompey massed there. We were then allowed to edge forward again only for missiles, including glass bottles, to start flying over our heads. The familiar sounds of altercation filled the air from further up the road and we stopped again. Millwall sang 'Where's Your Famous Pompey Firm?', in front of us, I think. There were numerous residents looking out of upstairs windows relaying the gory details on their mobiles and Pompey were being forced up side streets by riot police ahead, more of which later.

Gradually we got near enough to try to get back to our jeep. The police had shut Lidl's and a nearby garage and we had to persuade them that we really were parked there before they allowed us through; we got aboard and set off. Instead of heading towards the station, we drove up a side street listening to the local radio relay tales of the 'disgraceful' scenes near Fratton station. We turned into another street and found ourselves amid a dozen or so brick-carrying Pompey. Fortunately our coats were zipped up, hiding our allegiance, because they walked all around our jeep, which was blocked in by cars on all sides. Ted stayed quiet, he's mad not daft and I was grateful that my mobile 'Let 'Em Come' ring tone hadn't rung. We really would have been in serious trouble if they realised we were Millwall. It was worse than Wolves because we didn't even have enough room to get out of the jeep, let alone run them over or drive off. It would have been like shooting fish in a barrel.

Never mind Ted's Wolves' ideas, bulletproof glass looked appealing at this point. Luckily, we went unrecognised and managed to edge slowly to the end of the road unimpeded as the sound of police sirens filled the air and the locals scattered. We found the motorway and thankfully headed home whilst discussing how fortunate we had been, Paul also got home safely.

Sheffield United, Tuesday 19/3/2002, lost 3-2. Or Sheffield Tuesday if you prefer. My 13th away match, which on reflection explained a lot. Ted and I travelled to Sheffield United for only my second visit in a club coach convoy consisting of three coaches, including the Junior Lions, which left at 2pm. The game was originally scheduled for 22nd February and some tickets had been returned so our coach was half-empty. Ted and I sat in separate seats both up and back. Omnipresent steward Larry put on a very moody Mel Gibson video, *We Were Soldiers*, two hours of shootin' and shoutin' that had only been on at the cinema for two weeks.

Scenes of death and destruction certainly lightened the mood of our play-off jitters, with the team at the time in results freefall. At 4.45pm we pulled into Donington Park services, about 50 miles from Sheffield. The driver conveniently parked so close to the coach next to us that you either had to be a limbo dancer or very skinny to get off. Sadly I'm neither but somehow managed it and I headed for my obligatory extortionate sandwiches and Coke so I'd have even more problems getting back onto the coach. Thankfully I managed to squeeze back on board at 5.15pm. As we sat down the coach driver hared past, heading for the coach toilet, armed with a tin of air freshener because someone had transgressed the unwritten law and had a sly fag in there. Satisfied that the loo once again smelt of mountain freshness, we set off. A while later Ted, a diabetic, had to inject himself and headed into the fresh smelling toilet to do it, somehow without lights and with the coach's wheels bouncing about like Billy-O he managed to complete the feat. It had been too early to do it at Donington in case you wondered. We met our police escort at Catcliffe again before setting off. Oddly the lead police motorcyclist was a gentleman of the road and refused to go through red lights. I thought this was a perk of the job?

Like Barnsley, the sign for the ground was a combined notice with the hospital - were they trying to tell us something? We arrived at Bramall Lane at 6.45pm and the instant the coach doors opened United's over-eager programme sellers practically boarded our coach. Presumably they were on commission. We went into the Bramall Lane stand where we met some of the Essex Boys. Previously I had sat on the alarmingly steep upper tier of this stand; tonight though we were on its lower section, which unlike the upper tier had plastic seats. Naturally we still had the normal OTT security and there were segregation fences either side of us. Last time the ground also only had three stands with an empty space along one side but it was now an impressive all-seater stadium with four sides and all the modern pre-requisites. Except that the PA didn't work too well, seemingly only fully audible in the home stands, rather like 70s Orient where the PA only worked properly in the toilets.

It was an incident-packed pisstaking night. On the cinder track female catering staff walked past us and got the usual 'Get Your Tits Out For The Lads!'. We would be bloody shocked if they did. The goal net was tied to two side poles ideally positioned for pole dancing - now that would be proper pre-match entertainment!! One of the catering staff, wearing a black dress, was of the big-boned variety and she walked past in an arrogant 'my shit doesn't stink' manner; unfortunately, her huge rear end prompted one bloke to cruelly shout 'Yes love, your arse does look big in that dress!'. That certainly brought her down a peg, if not a dress size or two.

United's Paul Peschisolido got the usual 'You're Shit And Your Wife's A Slag!', which unsurprisingly he didn't like and made gestures at us.

Four days before this game United were involved in the scandalous 'Battle of Bramall Lane' against West Brom, so we booed them and implied that they were feigning injury any time a home player went down during the match. One of those sent off in the, WBA game was goalkeeper Simon Tracey. Unusually both teams kicked towards their own fans in the first half, so when he took up position in front of us he obviously got 'Off, Off, Off!' and 'Cheat!'. Due to his name, he got 'Where's Sharon?' and 'Tracey Takes It Up The A...!' accompanied with wolf whistling and cooeing. He also got one the best abusive chants ever, the classic 'Wow! Tracey, Wowo! Wow! Tracey, Wowo! She Comes From Dagenham And Takes It Up The Bum!'. I bet he couldn't wait for half-time and safety.

Although there were only 600 or so of us, we got behind the team whereas the home atmosphere was like Birmingham - morgue like one minute, deafening the next. The home 'Boys' in the Arnold Laver Stand to the right of us were verbal all night though. They chanted 'Sit Down - Shut Up!' and 'You're Just a Bunch of Wankers!'. They also sang a golden oldie that I hadn't heard for donkey's years - 'You're Gonna Get Your F...ing Heads Kicked In!'

HAPPY DAYS ARE HERE AGAIN!

This was met with ironic cheers, laughter and the usual 'come hither' gestures from our section but nothing happened in the ground. Continuing the vintage chanting they sang 'United!', we sang 'Shit!'.

We appeared to be in control of the match. It was 1-0, 2-1 and then 2-2 until we succumbed 2-3, conceding two goals in the last two minutes following a Mark McGhee substitution highlighting tactical genius at its best. The match programme said 'Time to tweak the Lion's tail'. It should've said 'Time to kick the Lion in the Bollocks!' Their third goal left us staring in disbelief and to ease us through the trauma the home fans sang 'Worst Support We've Ever Seen!'. The game finished with tensions rising high and the home fans again struck up 'Heads Kicked In!'. Irrespective of this aggro clue, everyone was let out together at the end of the match.

Outside there were only a few 'normal' police milling about, seemingly unaware of the local 'Boys' rapidly heading down the hill towards us. We saw them and decided to make a stand by our coaches parked behind the away end. Eventually the local Plod twigged it as well and a riot copper charged through our ranks from behind, whacking anyone in range with his truncheon clearing a path for the cavalry galloping behind him. Trouble was averted, just. Once the streets were clear we got back on our coach, which was like summertime in Malaya during the game the drivers must have been cultivating tropical fruit on board.

Thankfully, the journey back was practically non-stop due to our two drivers. The modern way to wile away a return journey is to text the absent with reports of the night's fun. Another modern phenomenon is widespread - 'No One Likes Us' or 'Let 'Em Come' ringtones, prompting the ridiculous sight of everyone scrabbling to find their mobile whenever one rings. I put mine on vibrate and keep it in my jeans front pocket, I might as well enjoy myself while I'm at it. The old regional 'Got The Time Mate?' quiz is unnecessary nowadays; a hooligan merely has to wait for the mobile to chirp up and bingo.

The result of this game looked like the play-off situation was out of our hands and with Birmingham rapidly closing in I was beginning to come over all 1971/72. I even heard somebody say

'Every game is a Cup Final from now on'. I didn't know people actually said this in the real world. Fortunately, our coach returned via the East End, good news for Ted and me as we didn't have to get back from the New Den, one of the main problems at night matches without a lift. This match coincided with a baby being left in a phone-box close to the ground. As far as I know no Millwall fan found the baby so surprisingly the press headlines weren't 'Millwall Thugs Ignore Abandoned Baby!'.

Gillingham, Sunday 24/3/2002, lost 1-0. LWT's *Soccer Sunday* live match and another 2.15pm kick-off. I hate the word soccer - it's football, not bloody soccer!

Nathan drove Paul, Ted and I to Kent in the buckshee jeep. We left at 11am in case we had any traffic problems. There were none and we arrived two and a quarter hours before kick-off. On the motorway we had passed a sign for Thong. We should've wasted some time by having a rummage in Thong, that would have been fun! We drove past Priestfield and decided to turn around to face the right way for a quick getaway. Knowing Gillingham like the back of our heads, we drove up a side street and a car coming towards us pulled over sharpish, revealing two police dog handling vans behind it.

We sat there in colours waiting for the police to pass, bemoaning the fact that no one was getting out of the way. The first police vehicle pulled alongside us and the driver leant across and said 'Where are you from?' Ted very helpfully said 'Scotland' to which the police officer sarcastically said 'Okay sir, don't they have one-way streets up there? Because you're the only ones going the wrong way up one, sir!' We sheepishly reversed back, turned around and eventually parked in the street behind the away end. We then wandered around the empty and mostly closed shopping area before deciding to risk our lives in a decidedly greasy, greasy spoon. I went straight to the loo, which was exactly like those at primitive away grounds. I survived and rejoined the others to read the Sundays strewn about the tables.

Nathan ordered the full English with baked beans for added wind. Unfortunately he was served tomatoes so told the waitress that he wanted beans not tomatoes. Helpfully she shoved the tomatoes over and poured beans on the same plate. I said 'Put ketchup and tomato puree on there and you'd have the full tomato set!' Oh how we laughed. A fat woman then came in to the café wearing a luminous yellow top straining to contain a pair of breasts resembling two overly inflated Zeppelins. Luckily, we managed to get to Ted before he launched into any tit references. Mind you, this woman's breasts were truly what an old mate once called 'Great floppy whackers!'. If she got a nipple erection she'd have your eye out! We left the café and set off to the ground, passing a smattering of Gills fans en route.

The hostility on the street was of a Wimbledon level and surprisingly some pubs were open; usually they board up and lock themselves in the cellar when we come to town. Outside the train station, we saw another example of the burgeoning police state. Three officers made a young Millwall fan take off his trainers so that they could have a dig about in them, presumably looking for drugs; let's hope he'd forgotten his odour eaters, that would teach them. We continued towards the ground whilst being videoed by the police. I am waiting for one of them to say 'That wasn't quite right; could you walk up the road again but with more attitude?' What he did say was 'On the way to the ground lads?' We ignored his silly question. Sarcastically, we should've said 'No, we always go shopping in Millwall shirts and decided to come to Kent today to wander around a closed shopping precinct!'

The weather was warm with several people wearing summer shorts, I myself sweated my cods off in a leather coat in a 'If it gets much warmer I'll have to take my cardie off' style. We then went through the turnstiles for our nostalgic trip back to the days of the terraces. We stood on the left hand side of the Town End terrace behind the goal and I looked upon the new improved Priestfield for the first time, having missed the September 11th League Cup game.

This was something like my eighth trip to Priestfield and I used to snigger to myself years ago when they referred to this ramshackle place as a stadium, but now it was worthy of the name. The ground now had 'The Medway Stand' with executive boxes along the left-hand side of our terrace. Last time this was an empty space, save for a dugout, with kids in the street standing on shed roofs getting a free view and nicking any balls lost through the gap. Our open-air terrace, containing 1320 Lions, was still an unrenovated museum piece though - it had rusty old crush barriers and segregation fencing. We had less than half of the terrace, which was particularly odd as there were numerous empty seats in the home stands. Why didn't they give us the whole end and put the home fans in the seats? They must be awash with money. As an East Ender, I regard Gillingham as on a par with Notts County; however, for our Kent-based fans and the home fans this was a big local derby.

There was a bit of added spice in the ground as we were positioned right next to the home 'Boys' (sic). I thought I'd share the banter with you rather than mention yet another defeat, the fourth in succession and third this season, 1 - 0 in this case. Gillingham are rapidly replacing Wigan as our new nemesis.

From Them To Us: They must have been working on all the chants for weeks. Firstly, a chant brought on by the hallucinogenic properties of hedgehog pie, 'London Is A Shit Hole!'. Mmmm! Let me see London - a major City since Roman times, a leading world financial centre, the finest art galleries, theatres and restaurants to be found anywhere on earth, hundreds of clubs, bars, music venues, cinemas, hotels and several top flight football clubs etc, etc, etc. Gillingham - has the shopping precinct, a bingo hall and is a glorified caravan park. I rest my case. As I once heard someone say, 'If Kent is the garden of England then Gillingham is the shed!'.

Football-wise we got 'Do You Remember 2-1?' and 'We Beat The Scum 2-1 - Twice!'.

Fan-wise we got 'Everywhere We Go, People Want To know Who We Are, Etc We're the Millwall Haters!'/'What Do You Think Of Shit? Millwall! What Do You Think Of Millwall? Shit!/'If You All Hate Millwall Jump Around!'/'We're Not Millwall, Etc, 'Cos They're Scum!'/'You're Millwall And You're Scum!'/'You're The Scum Of London Town!'/'Shadwell Army!' and 'You Can Stick Your F...ing Lion Up Your A...!'. To further highlight a delusion brought on by consuming hedgehogs, they sang 'One Man Went To War, Went To War With Millwall, Etc, One Man And A Baseball

HAPPY DAYS ARE HERE AGAIN!

Bat Went To War With Millwall!'. Pardon, when was this then? To highlight their 'Top Boy' status they sang 'We All Follow The Gillingham Over Land And Sea (And Swindon!)'. Eh! Good old notorious Swindon. We sing 'West Ham', which I think you'll find is a tad more dangerous. In response to our pikey/gypo abuse, they sang 'One Nil To The Pikey Boys!' and 'We Live In A Caravan!'. To highlight inner-city stereotypes they sang 'On The Dole!'/'Tower Blocks, Wank, Wank, Wank!'/'Your Mum Is A Prostitute!' and 'You've All Got The Same Mum!'.

Gills Chairman Paul Scally had only one picture in the programme today, as opposed to his previous megalomaniacs portrait gallery. The locals didn't seem to like him much; whether it's because he supports Millwall or whether he's always loathed, I don't know. He certainly didn't help his cause by coming onto the pitch with Kitch and Theo and waving to us before the game, hence at 1-0 he got 'Scally, Scally What's The Score?'.

Player-wise Steve Claridge got 'Old Man, Etc!' and 'Where's Your Zimmer Frame?'. They then sang to Neil Harris 'Harris Has Got No Balls!'/'You've Only Got One Ball!'/'Where's Your Bollock Gone?' and 'If You've All Got Two Balls Clap Your Hands!'. When the ball came in our section, they sang 'Save The Ball For Harris!'. They said we were scum! We are several rungs up the evolutionary scale from people who think that testicular cancer is fair game and funny.

They weren't the only ones to abuse Harris. Scunthorpe sang similar chants in the FA Cup. I can think of no word other than Cunts! Their chants obviously didn't go down too well with us and Ted was almost thrown out for spitting across the fence at the home fans. Despite the Gills giving it large, the police videos focused solely on us for practically the entire match; even when we pointed out that the Harris chants were extremely offensive to us, they continued to point their cameras at us and us alone.

From Us To Them: Our support had been muted, not helped by the open terrace or the fact that we lose to Gillingham more often than not nowadays. Nonetheless, there was plenty of abuse. Playerwise Marlon King, about to stand trial for various crimes, got 'Nee Naw!'/'You're Nicked And You Know You Are!' and

'Going Down, Etc!'. Gillingham's black goalkeeper Jason Brown got this non-PC medley - 'You Fat C...!'/'Oi Mugger!' and 'Mammy!', the last chant accompanied by Al Jolson-style hand gestures. When the home side scored, they sang 'Jason, Jason What's The Score?'. Very sensibly he put his finger to the lips in a 'SSHH, Not Now!' gesture.

To highlight Gypsy/Kent/Asylum-seeker stereotypes we sang 'Caravan Wheels Go Round And Round, Etc, All Day Long!'/'I Can't Read, I Can't Write, I Can Drive a Trailer, I'm A Gillingham Fan And I'm A F...ing Pikey!'/'You're Just A Bunch Of Pikeys, Smelly, Smelly Pikeys!'/'Gypos Run From Margate!'/'We've Got Central Heating!'/'Have You Ever Met Your Dad?'/'Does Your Mother Know Your Dad?'/'Stop The Interbreeding!'/ 'Inbreds!'/'Who's The Kosovan?'/'What's It Like To Have No Soap?' and 'Have A Wash!'. Also, the bizarre Millwall adapted chant of 'You're Just A Shit Town In Maidstone!'.

Behind fences and rows of police/stewards, their fans' daring knew no bounds; they were very annoying, like a blue bottle behind the curtains that you cannot quite get at. Gillingham's top 'Boy' appeared to be Timmy Mallet, which certainly frightened me! He wore a Gills shirt, shades, baseball cap and had big ears. He had been the main pain in the arse/ears all afternoon and he got the 'He looks hard' suggestion 'Oi! Bruce Willis F... Off!'. He also got 'Dumbo Is Your Leader!' accompanied by a Dambuster's fly-past implying that he could fly with the size of his ears. He clammed up once targeted and silence reigned so we sang 'Can You Hear Old Dumbo Sing? Etc.' and 'Oh, It's All Gone Quiet Over There!'.

Near the end of the match he and some other Gills were ejected by the police, prompting a 'wanker!' deluge from us. Overall, it was a funny day apart from the journey, the game, the result and the earache. We headed back to the jeep as Ted hunted for the brave home fans, now nowhere to be seen. He did manage to have a go at one local before the police intervened and threatened to arrest him. When I arrived home, I found that very sympathetically my video hadn't recorded the game, thank God.

Rotherham United, Easter Monday 1/4/2002 (April Fool's Day), drew 0 - 0. Ee! by heck, a Bank Holiday trip to Rotherham, you can't whack it! I travelled 'Oop North' on my own on the one and only club coach at 9am. The coach had half a dozen empty seats but thankfully it had two drivers, including the Wrexham debacle one. A Junior Lions coach had left the ground much earlier. All I had for company was a fanzine and newspapers to read. The fanzine contained a letter complaining about the amount of minute's silences this season - September 11th, Brian Moore, Princess Margaret, local players, etc. The letter said hopefully the Queen Mother would die in a close season so we didn't have another one. Spookily, she died the day I was reading the letter.

Of all the silences the ones that meant the most to me were September 11 and Brian Moore. I once met him at Spurs as a young boy and he was a very nice bloke, to people of my generation he was very much the voice of football.

The moody videos today were Schwarzenegger's *Collateral Damage* and Jet Li's *Kiss of the Dragon,* American DVD copies of films that hadn't yet arrived in Britain. Due to the Bank Holiday lull, we journeyed North on empty motorways and stopped at Donington for an hour before meeting our police escort at Catcliffe. The police then insisted on holding us until the Junior Lions coach arrived. We explained that their coach left hours before ours and would have already passed; eventually it sank in and we were escorted to the ground.

The police told us that they were going to search our coach while we were at the game; nice of them to tell us, rather like a burglar making an appointment. Even though the 'Boys' don't travel on club coaches I bet the police board every Millwall coach thinking that they are about to encounter a bunch of desperate cut-throats. However, what they find is that the 'normal' hardcore coach community consists of young kids, girls, middle-aged women, old men, some less than combative males and several blokes who look like they may be a handful. There's also a disabled bloke, Kenny, who travels nationwide on the coach in a wheelchair. In other words, the occupants are a cross section of the general population; a real shock to them the first time they board a Millwall coach, I'm sure.

I WAS BORN UNDER THE COLD BLOW LANE

To further blow their preconceptions out of the water at Donington the middle-aged women on board had attacked Thornton's Easter egg collection like a swarm of locusts so by Catcliffe the coach resembled a delivery vehicle for the Easter Bunny as the overhead shelves were crammed with chocolate.

My God, you know you're up North when you drive through Rotherham, it's the epitome of grim. We drove past piles of broken down rusty machinery and old train compartments; it's as though Sheffield had a clearout of its scrap and Rotherham was born. The home fanzine *Rust* is the most honest fanzine title ever. In *TLR*, I read that Rotherham had the highest percentage of under-age pregnancies in Britain; rust must be an aphrodisiac? 'Ee! love, all this rust is getting me going, fancy a shag?' More likely, there's nothing else to do in the land of the Wheel Tappers and Shunters. There was certainly no gentrification here, no sign of any 'Wheel Tapas and Shunters' yet.

We parked up at 1.45pm for only my second visit to Millmoor. On my previous visit, Simon and I had a very graphic conversation with a refreshment stall woman. On arrival I went to see if she was still there, sadly she wasn't. A 'Talk Dirty' phone line probably snapped her up. I then went to the toilet where there was a poster for Blue Square.Com saying 'Whoopee, a visit from Millwall!'. It also pontificated about Millwall's possible promotion; I naturally took this as sarcastic, bloody cheek.

I went into the aptly named Railway End stand behind the goal where I met up with Dave Murray and some of the Essex contingent. Millmoor had been upgraded since my previous visit; the away end was now seated and they had installed executive boxes that looked like Portakabins from building sites, presumably reflecting the working man image of the area. Even though the ground had been renovated to a degree, it was still very much of the old-school variety with the home fans generating a good atmosphere. For the record, Rotherham's Muppet was a peculiar thing with a big round head full of fluffy curly hair and a red cap. What it was supposed to represent in this drug fantasy world God knows.

Millwall wore all green so Rotherham's goalkeeper wore a day-glo orange shirt; he looked like a steward, so 550 of us helpfully pointed this out to him. It was our first visit since pipping Rotherham to the championship so it would also have been rude of us not to sing '4-Nil!' and 'Champione/Ole, Etc!'. So we did. Prior to the match, we had the Queen Mother's tribute. It was also on-loan striker Dion Dublin's away debut. Just before the kick-off Essex Boy Andy said of ref Mr G Laws 'He's the same ref as last year; he's a wanker, he didn't give us anything!' To make him wrong he gave us the first decision. Having got that out of his system, he proceeded to stake his claim for worst referee of the season in the hotly contested 'Home Town Harry' category.

The game was a farce because the pitch had the consistency and contour of corrugated iron. It finished goalless and was certainly not a good advertisement for First Division football. Having completed their task the officials walked off to a standing 'Wankering' from our section. To make sure that they understood our 'waving' wasn't of the Queen Mum variety we walked along the stand to get closer to the tunnel in the corner. In truth the highlight of the day was that the pies were good, which says it all, doesn't it?

My mates and I left the ground and headed South via our separate routes. We stopped at Watford Gap services and Millwall's coach pulled up with Claridge, Reid and Livermore getting off to pick up their cars. Steve Claridge stopped to chat and confirmed that the pitch was a disgrace, as was the referee. We easily got back into London and on to the A12 road towards Blackwall Tunnel; we then hit a massive traffic jam, with the illuminated road signs flashing 'Avoid A12'. Unfortunately, we were already sitting on it, penned in on all sides by traffic, with no way of moving until the traffic allowed. Eventually we got to the flyover near Bow and saw that the police had blocked off the southbound road due to an explosion at a nearby Calor gas factory. Consequently, my coach headed towards Tower Bridge via Mile End, which suited me. I got out at Stepney Green 'I'm alright Jack!' style and walked the short distance home.

Coventry City, Friday 12/4/2002, won 1-0. A Friday night match live on ITV Sport, who by this time were in freefall. Nathan drove Paul, Ted, and I to the Midlands in the freebie jeep. We left at 3.20pm and passed numerous Millwall cars and club coaches on the way up. It was another easy trip and with the aid of an internet map we arrived at 5.40pm. Opposite the away section there was an empty car park that we approached via a side entrance. It had no markings or stewards whatsoever. Nevertheless we parked up anyway, but with reservations - away parking isn't normally like this, it had been just too easy.

It was only in the road facing the ground that we saw signs saying 'Coventry City Members' Car Park, non-permit holders will be clamped. De-clamping fee £50'. A real money-spinner, the dodgy buggers must catch away fans like this all the time. Nathan re-parked the jeep in a nearby road and Ted laid into the stewards about their underhand tactics. Highfield Road wasn't due to open for at least another hour so the gathered Millwall had an early evening constitutional around the ground fruitlessly looking for food or something to do. We found nothing so we made our way back to the away end, by which time the police hi-tech video vans had begun to arrive, as had our club coaches.

We decided to wander around the Aladdin's cave of bad taste that was Coventry's club shop. It had some of the vilest kits known to man on display, with the elephant on a ball club badge. There was a hideous green and black striped shirt, but this paled into comparison with an absolute monstrosity - a brown and beige 1970s kit designed when taste was on holiday. The shop offered a 'made to measure - fat bastard shirt service' for anyone above a 52-inch chest, presumably featuring a fat bloke on a ball? They also sold blue Afro wigs, most probably left over from their 80s Cup Final appearance. We tried to persuade Ted this would set off his baseball cap a treat, sadly he thought otherwise. They were showing Dion Dublin's Coventry goal videos on the TV monitors and they had the local radio on, which reported that tonight's game was a top category match with a higher than usual police presence, adding that they were expecting trouble in the city centre before and after the game. We left the shop and found that a vast array of police vans and 'Smile, you're on Rozzers 'TV' mobile video vans had now assembled near the away stand.

This was only my second visit to Coventry, my only other game being a 3-1 defeat in February 1990, our top-flight relegation season. From the outside it looked a much-improved ground, although the walls were brick. I don't like bricks stands! Having exhausted our timewasting options we waited outside the away entrance in the vain hope that they would open up - they didn't. 45 minutes later there were hundreds of Millwall loitering restlessly outside and someone shouted out 'Open the gates or we'll go up the town centre!'. Taking him at his word, shortly after they opened up and we were funnelled downstairs via a small doorway resembling the entrance to an old style tube station. At the foot of the stairs, we found wooden turnstiles similar to an exhibit in the Imperial War Museum. Stupidly, they had positioned a steward at the bottom who insisted on searching us all. Ted attacked the hapless man verbally for this ridiculous idea and all he said was 'It's the law'. Maybe so but causing a crush by stopping-and-searching everyone at the bottom of a staircase is none too sensible, I'd have thought, but what do I know?

Eventually we got into the ground at 7pm. Ted and I went to the toilets where we had to go upstairs to go downstairs. It seems that a lunatic had designed the North Stand, speaking of which, Ted said 'I reckon the stewards and that think I'm mental!' I said to him 'But you are **Mad** Ted!' Bit of a clue there. We then joined Paul and Nathan who were sitting with Dave Murray and his mate Simon in the seats a short while later. All the fuss about searching everybody was put into perspective when Nathan said that he had two tins of Coke up his coat sleeves that they hadn't found.

Contrary to the rules of Millwall travelling, we sat in our correct seats high up in the stand, on the halfway line, next to the home fans to our left, with only segregation netting between us. This was close to the disabled section that Pompey had apparently stormed when they were there. The inside of the ground was a vast improvement from my other visit, at which time it had an open end behind the goal with a wooden chalet design on the stand opposite. It now had a sky-blue colour scheme throughout the all-seater stadium, with executive boxes and an electronic scoreboard, though no video screen that I could see. 'CCFC' is picked out on the seats; perhaps Millwall should have 'CCTV' picked out on our seats. Naturally, stewards and riot police encircled us and we had banks of police cameras focusing on us all night. Ted was in his element, hurling abuse at any home fans within earshot and making motions to scale the segregation mesh. Unfortunately, we had left his muzzle in the jeep so had to restrain him manually. Eventually the police came up and warned him about his actions. He's mad, have I mentioned that?

For the record Coventry's Muppet, a sky-blue elephant called Sam, was greeted with 'Sammy Is A Sex Case!' and 'Sammy Takes It Up The A...!'. We know how to greet a children's entertainer - if it was possible for an *It's a Knockout* elephant to blush and look embarrassed then Coventry's answer to Joseph Merrick was it.

The two sides came out for this vital game via a voluptuous young girly corridor to The Prodigy's *Firestarter*. The referee was quite good, in the first half anyway, and we led 1-0 at half-time thanks to a Steve Claridge goal. The half-time entertainment consisted of the buxom lovelies doing a 'dance' routine in the centre circle. They may as well have thrown their handbags down and danced around them for all the choreography on display, but they had large breasts though so mustn't grumble. During half-time, Ted disappeared only to reappear in the lower stand among the police. He periodically moved towards the home fans, gave a '1-0 'gesture and some verbal abuse before rejoining the enemy lines.

The performance of the referee radically changed in the second half; paranoia says that the football League put in a call to say 'They're winning, stop them!' which he tried to do by booking every Millwall player within arm's reach. The Coventry crowd had been very quiet; they didn't even bother to slag off ex-player Dion Dublin. I think they assumed that they would win promotion first time to the Premiership and were stunned that they hadn't. They woke up for a bit of banter in the second half but were drowned out by our very loud support, all 2464 of us, and our vocal backing as per usual was fantastic all evening.

A selection of our chants: Coventry's ex-Palace player Richard Shaw, looking like Ruud Gullit's stunt double, got 'Who The F... Are Palace?' and 'He's Got A Birds Nest On His Head!'. Their 'Boys' next to us got 'You're Supposed To Be At Home!'/'You Got Run By Pompey!'/'Your Support Is F...ing Shit!'/'Shall We Sing A

HAPPY DAYS ARE HERE AGAIN!

Song For You?' and 'Shit Ground - No Fans!'. As the game neared its victorious conclusion, we sang 'If You're All Going To Cardiff Clap Your Hands', 'Millwall's Going Up!' and 'Maybe It's Because I'm A Londoner', the last of which got an all too rare airing. We won 1-0 prompting a mass outbreak of air pumping, EIO's and the team celebrating in front of us. This was one of those great Millwall supporting nights with the volume under our covered stand at eleven. It was a real sit-stand sit-stand affair, like a Freemasons' ladies' night.

Once the celebrations had subsided, we headed back to the Jeep, had the obligatory slash in the street and set off home. Getting out of Coventry was a real performance because the police had roadblocks everywhere. After seemingly driving all-round Coventry, we eventually found ourselves in the city centre. This was a real treat on the eyes; it appeared to be 'Dress like an Essex girl 'night, there were young girls walking along scarcely wearing more than Lady Godiva. I'd not seen so many micro-miniskirted, bare-midriffed, naval flashing, pierced belly button and boob-tubed lovelies since I last went to Southend for the night. We drove past crowded streets, bouncered pubs and hordes of riot police as the sound of police sirens filled the air. Whether it all went off I don't know, it certainly had that sort of feel about it. We were too busy trying to get out of the city to worry about it. We eventually managed to find the motorway and head back to London.

Never judge a book by its cover - Nathan seems to be a quiet chap, in truth, he's a karate black belt and bungee jumper, as is Paul. He's also a souped-up version of Ayrton Senna; he did Mach 1 all the way back whilst eating a sandwich, drinking Coke and sending text messages at the same time. He applied the parachute brakes at Watford so as not to overshoot London and I was tucked up in bed well within two G-forced hours.

Grimsby Town, (home) Sunday 21/4/2002 2pm, won 3-0. Shown live on LWT's *Soccer Sunday*. We needed a point to cement our play-off position but this game had all the banana-skin potential you could wish for as Grimsby were demob happy after staving off relegation. Millwall have a habit of blowing these types of situation. There was a pre-match 'Player of the Year' presentation, which always puts a spanner in the works for some reason and we had the pressure of a possible place in the top flight in our sights. Mark McGhee seemed to be feeling the pressure as he was quoting the philosophies of Socrates - the Greek, not the Brazilian - in his programme notes.

As the usual home crew walked to the ground we were nearly run over by some c… driving a motorbike at speed on the footpath, the perfect start! Unsurprisingly the game was sold out with the North Stand open to both Millwall and Grimsby fans. Clive suggested it would be a good day to do a poll to see how many home games people had actually been to. Perhaps Millwall should issue a special 'Woodworkers Convention' season ticket for such matches. We arrived early, sat down and Simon noticed that it said '129' on the foot of the Jumbotron. He said 'That's funny it looks like a cricket bowler's speed gun!' We eventually twigged that it was a clock. D'oh! If it's a real Millwall clock it won't work for too long.

The crowd had an air of celebration. The big flag got an airing and a huge football was being bounced about in the CBL. There were some humorous moments. Birmingham would be our play - off opponents and after initially banning us the delectable Ms. Brady relented and allowed us into St Andrews. Consequently, a blow-up doll was being bounced about in the CBL serenaded with 'Are You Brady In Disguise?'/'Karren Brady Is A Slapper!' and 'Does She Take It Up The A...?'. I don't think a blow-up doll has a lot of say in the matter. I'm not sure if the next chant had anything to do with the blow-up doll but… 'Brady, Brady Here We Come!'. 'Bye for now Les' made a police announcement about a car originally parked in Varney Road, prompting everyone to ask, 'Well where the bloody hell is it now then?' and the CBL broke into 'Where's Your Motor Gone?'. The glory hunters, deemed to be the 'Millwall' in the North Stand, were serenaded with 'North Stand Give Us A Song!' and 'Will You Be Here Again Next Year?'.

As we only needed a point, the game had a strange atmosphere. The first half was good, but as Dublin and Harris set up an easy win the second half was a formality. Simon and I chatted in a relaxed manner; however Clive, based on years of bitter experience, knew that being Millwall we could still lose and he would not be happy until the whistle blew. He told us to shut up and concentrate. For Clive's sake, we quietened down and I vowed to save my voice for Brummie land. I watched the video of the game when I got home and it referred to a party atmosphere, which it was - the first half was the knees-up and the second half the hangover. People watching on TV must have been banging their telly in the latter part of the game thinking that the sound had packed up, as the atmosphere was so poor during the second half.

We needed only a point but easily got three and came 4th in one of our best ever League finishes, surpassing all of our expectations if we were honest, especially as Rotherham and Walsall both struggled. Contrary to normal Millwall custom, there was no chaotic pitch invasion and the team didn't do a lap of honour. After all, it was only a job half done; we had yet to achieve anything concrete - Birmingham here we come.

8.

'Here We Go Again!'

Birmingham City, Play-Off Semi-Final First Leg, Sunday 28/4/2002 noon, Drew 1-1. Having endured the day of the long queue, I mentally prepared myself for another trip to Birmingham. Scanning the media prior to the game there were conflicting messages coming from Millwall. Mark McGhee implored us not to cause trouble whilst Stuart Nethercott spoke of revenge following our 4-0 hammering in August.

After Wolves and Pompey, we didn't fancy driving to Birmingham so Dave, Paul, Nathan, Ted, Simon, Patrick and I caught the 7.30am club coach for the noon kick-off. When we arrived at the New Den, it was chaos. The car park around the ground should've been a coach-only area; however, this hadn't been enforced initially so everyone who had their car parked there had to relocate to the car park behind the North Stand or park on side streets to make room for the coaches. It was like watching a cross between *Wacky Races* and a stock-car meeting. Because of the above, we left about 20 minutes late.

There were about a dozen coaches in our convoy including King's Ferry, one even had tables on! Strangely, some others had Nottingham addresses (?). Due to the obscenely early hour, it was like a flophouse on the coach. I myself sat bolt upright, with visions of April 8th 1972 when we lost 1-0 in front of 43,483 at St Andrews thanks to a highly dubious Birmingham goal and finished third when only the top two sides went up automatically. There were no play-offs then. Following the lifting of Brady's ban, we were given 2800 tickets, approximately 10% of the eventual crowd of 28,282, an allocation that we filled easily.

HERE WE GO AGAIN!

This was only Simon's fourth away match of the season; generally, he is a 15-20 away games a season merchant like the rest of us. However, with the increasingly high prices he cannot always afford to go if Pat also goes, as he obviously wants to do. It's a slippery path, if you start to price out real fans like Simon.

Pat doesn't like travelling on coaches as he's been sick a couple of times so Simon dosed him up with travel sickness tablets to be on the safe side. He's a veteran of coach trips to Manchester City, the Wigan play-off and Cardiff, which probably doesn't help his peace of mind either. When Pat was younger he'd often ask me ad nauseam 'Bal, are we there yet?', usually continuing the questioning about every 10 minutes until our coach pulled up outside the away ground. On one coach trip, he even managed to continue it from inside the coach toilet. He went into the loo and I thought 'I'll have a few minutes' peace, before I get irritable Bal syndrome' until up chirped a little voice with 'Bal are we there yet?'. Just one of the many joys of travelling away.

Near Birmingham, we passed a claret-and-blue gasworks, unpopular with us for its West Ham connotations and with City fans for its Aston Villa connotations I'd imagine. Our police escort picked us up close to St Andrews and a local copper got on board to give us the usual speech: 'Welcome to Birmingham, I'm sure you're all veterans and know the score - no flags, flagpoles, missiles, blah, blah, blah!.' Ted chirped up 'What if they attack us?' Everyone on the coach laughed but the local bobby chose to ignore him, good point though. We again had a police motorcyclist incapable of stopping the traffic, but eventually he overcame his lack of assertiveness and we headed the wrong way up the road to the ground. Our coaches then parked up like sardines in the small segregated car park with ours parked closest to the ground. We got off and headed into the Railway End lower section as per the league game. The bar in the ground was open as was the bookmakers, always a mark of quality. We also met my cousin Gavin and the Essex crew. I had gotten the tickets for them and us and most of us sat together in a long line in the correct seats, near the front. Our 'sit where you like' policy had gone out of the window of late, although Paul, Dave and Nathan did sit higher in the stand in the wrong seats. I was reading the programme pre-match and was delighted to see that it contained a flattering soft focus photograph of Mrs. Peschisolido for us to love and cherish. It also contained some great pearls of wisdom.

1) It had a guide to the New Den that said don't drink in the pubs near Millwall, it was better to drink at the pubs around London Bridge! It is?

2) It said South Bermondsey was well policed, alternatively you could go to New Cross Gate; another good idea, a nice trek and not the least bit fraught.

3) It said that Birmingham's Darren Purse was born in Stepney, as I was, which the programme said was in South London! News to me.

Simon wasn't at the early season fixture but had been there for the aggro game in 1995 and was a bit alarmed that again the home fans were above us. Luckily, no coins, mops, buckets or fire extinguishers were thrown down this time but when it started to drizzle in the second half we both said 'I hope that's rain and not someone having a slash on us from above!' As per the League game, we were next to the mouthy Brummie home section, resulting in the customary exchange of pleasantries. As per usual, the police's cameras were fixed solely on us for most of the match and the 'non-troublesome' Brummies got none of the attention that we did.

To entertain us there were a couple of celebrity look-alike stewards at our end, namely the big baldy bass player from Gillan and a fearsome creature who looked like Fred Emney (ask your dad), precisely the sort of rugged individual needed to stop any Millwall pitch surges. High up in the away section the Grimsby blow-up doll was being bounced about to much laughter, because it now had Karren Brady's face superimposed on it and was wearing a shirt saying 'Brady 69'.

As we waited for the game to start a helicopter hovered *Black Hawk Down* style in the sky above the opposite end of the ground. Simon and I discussed how times had changed over the years - from marbles underneath police horses to hovering choppers; we wondered how you could interfere with such a machine, only a surface to air missile sprang to mind and even we've not tried that yet.

As I've said before I don't like morning kick-offs as the atmosphere is invariably not as good as afternoon or evening games. However, today was better than usual because it was such a vital game. That said the Brummies again ranged from ear splittingly loud one minute to pin drop quiet the next. The nature of this match naturally meant that it was a stand up all day affair, adopting the usual sit down policy at half-time, Pat stood on his seat, as he couldn't see otherwise.

Before the kick off the PA announcer read out Millwall's team in a quick bored monotone voice so swiftly that we had no time to 'Hoorah' the names. He then read out Birmingham's side as if he was announcing Brazil's 1970 World Cup winners. He also played ELO's *Mr Blue Sky*, the sort of music that makes me for one want to fight. Crass isn't the word for it, I assume they were trying to play a Brummie band so why not Black Sabbath? I'd much rather have heard *War Pigs* or *Fairies Wear Boots*!

There was a massive Birmingham flag being passed along the stand at the other end and they played their anthem *Keep Right On To The End Of The Road*, seemingly sung by Kenneth McKellar - once again ask, your Dad. The teams then came out to *What's She Going To Look Like With A Chimney On Her?*. The Brummies stood to a man, clapped, and sang their way through these songs. The match started and Millwall turned in a far better performance than the August League game. Despite the homer referee, who seemed determined to keep the game moving by adopting a tactic that I like to call 'F... the rules, let's go on with it'. He never gave us a single decision. I am a bit biased so this may not be strictly accurate. Although we had the best of the first half, it finished scoreless.

Ted spent half-time hurling abuse at the locals next to us, having finished, he rejoined us. A boy has to have a pastime, and away fan and steward abuse is Ted's. The second half started and it wasn't long before Birmingham scored what looked like a dodgy goal. I was again transported back to 1972, a situation not helped by the fact that Norwich were also in the play-offs and they had been one of the other rivals that season as well.

I WAS BORN UNDER THE COLD BLOW LANE

Ex-Brummie Steve Claridge got a schizophrenic mixture of applause and abuse when he replaced Neil Harris, whose departure prompted the 'Where's Your Bollock Gone?' chant. Cunts! Aston Villa loanee Dion Dublin wasn't very popular with the Brummies, which made his thoroughly deserved equaliser for us 10 minutes before the end even sweeter. It certainly rammed the 'Dion Dublin Is A Wanker!' and 'Shit On The Villa!' chants back down their throats. This goal was the first one that I'd ever seen us score at St Andrews. Obviously, we went berserk mimicking hyperactive maggots in a tin as we leapt about wildly. In truth we should've gained my first ever win in 5 visits, but at least we hadn't lost, which is the usual outcome for us in the play-offs. If nothing else, we had ruined their lap of honour.

I thought I'd list some of the banter exchanged to give you a feel for the day.

From Them To Us The home 'boys' sang 'Zulu Army!'. A bit strange as most of them were white. They sang 'Millwall' in a high-pitched voice, a favourite of theirs. To highlight their love for the capital they sang 'Here They Come, The Cockney Scum!'. They sang 'Sit-Down F... Off!' in a mock London accent to take the piss. When they scored, they sang 'You're Staying Down With The Dingles!'. Presumably Wolves. This time we had a bloke in a pink shirt in our section so they sang 'Who's The Faggot In The Pink?' and 'Do You Take It Up The A...?'. Serves him right for wearing a pink shirt. They also sang a song about doing 'The Cardiff Dance', whatever that might be. I couldn't catch it all due to language differences, there were no subtitles.

From Us To Them We sang the usual glut of anti-Brady chants: 'Hands Up If You Hate Brady'/'If You All Hate Brady Clap Your Hands' and 'Hands Up If You've Had (F...ed) Brady!'. In response to the Brummies anti-capital songs we sang 'Maybe It's Because I'm A Londoner'. To highlight the loud-hush-loud-hush home atmosphere we sang 'It's Just Like Being In Church!' where I'd usually be on a Sunday, obviously. In truth, the only Church I'd like to be in is Charlotte. We sang to the Zulus 'We Laugh At The Birmingham!'/'Will We See You At The Den?'/'Will You Turn Up At The Den?' and 'Where's Your Famous Zulu Firm?'.

HERE WE GO AGAIN!

At the end of the match we stood looking towards the remaining Brummies in the ground whilst waiting to be let out and some people in our section made a few more specific Zulu/black references to the black Brummies, in particular 'Day-O, Day-O, Daylight Come And Me Want Go Home'. Accompanied in some cases with monkey noises, naturally the home black fans didn't like this much, they looked rope-able. Racist, but all part of the game in the banter/abuse stakes, they had a go at us for being Londoners and we had a go at them for their Zulu persona, although we didn't need the monkey noises.

In the home section to our right, a bloke decided that today was the best day to show his Irishness, so he unfurled an Irish tricolour and held it aloft us as he walked down the stairs; we greeted this with 'Engerland!' and 'No Surrender To The IRA!'. A bloke in his own section didn't like this display much either and punched him in the mouth, God knows what the Irish bloke was thinking.

We sang 'Your Support Is F...ing Shit!' and again did a finger to the lips 'SSH!' as we had done previously, this time to highlight the silence that fell on St Andrews when we scored our equalizer. We also sang 'One Nil And You F...ed It Up!'/'You're Staying Down With The Palace!' and 'Can You Do The Cardiff Dance?'.

There were several funny incidents during and after the game. For example, the newspapers had referred to this match as 'Bra Wars' due to Theo's La Senza connection and David Gold's Ann Summers links. This turned out to be very apt as during the game three young girls standing to our right were dancing to our chants, which naturally led to the obligatory 'Get Your Tits Out For The Lads!' which very kindly two of them did by flashing their pert, firm, supple, milky white breasts... sorry, went into one there... by flashing their white bras at us. This got a cheer and 'Are You Brady In Disguise?'. At the end of the game we sang 'Can We See Your Tits Again?'. This prompted one young male Brummie to leap up, damsels in distress style, to defend their honour. Offering us all out for our sexist singing, good idea, he got 'You're Fat And Your Bird's A Slag!'. Eventually he was dragged off by the police.

As Birmingham did their heads-bowed deflated lap of honour, their player Martin Grainger thought it was a good idea to do monkey faces and underarm scratching monkey mimes at us. He was wrong. With our section ringed by stewards and riot police one City woman, dressed in a style more appropriate for a night out at The Savoy, decided it would be safe to get a close look at us, like a visit to the zoo. I don't think her ego was massaged too much as she paraded behind the cordon and we sang 'Who's The Slapper On The Pitch?'. If you want anyone to bring you down to size, we're the boys.

We headed elatedly out of the ground, savouring our best ever play-off result, boarded our coach and were then held in the car park for half an hour. Our coach was now at the back of the convoy next to the team's coach, and we saw Sean Dyche and David Tuttle get on board with the Karren Brady blow-up doll tucked underarm. I suppose that sometimes you have to make your own entertainment. Eventually we set off and close to the ground we saw Steve Claridge and Ray Harford walking up the road seemingly heading for McDonald's. Footballers and their dietary requirements, eh! Our coach had the radio commentary of Norwich City v Wolves on. It kicked off after we had finished and everyone seemed pleased that the other 'big' club Wolves, a comatose giant if there ever was one, were being turned over at Carrow Road. Most people wanted to play Norwich in the final as there would be less aggro, apart from clashes with the Soul Crew obviously. It would also keep the 'big boys' so beloved by the media out of the top flight.

On the coach there was a general sense of job done with the home leg seen as a gimme and most people were discussing their preferred route to Cardiff. This bothered me, I've seen Millwall blow it numerous times before; never mind 'Up the Wall', they have driven me up and over it over the years. To put it crudely Millwall have often been football's equivalent of a prick teaser, tempting us with all manner of delights only to leave us unfulfilled and frustrated. Following Millwall isn't exactly conducive to not getting worry lines and grey hair, that's for sure. They can also turn you to drink, not that I need much turning if truth be told.

The trip home was awful; we left the ground at 2.30pm but didn't get back to London until 6.30pm. Thankfully, Patrick hadn't been sick on the coach and to complete a good day for him at the New Den he found a fiver on the car park floor.

Birmingham City, Play-Off Semi-Final Second Leg, Thursday 2/5/2002, Lost 1-0. When Saturday comes my arse! Yet another Thursday night game and another chance for Karren Brady to visit her favourite ground. This reminds me of the story that a bloke in the play-off ticket queue told me. He said that at the league match on 10th January, she arrived in a limo wearing a fur coat ensemble, big hat no knickers stylee. She managed to avoid any abuse and presumably must have thought that she'd gotten away with it until a small boy walked up to her. He tugged at her coat and as she looked down he gazed up at her and said 'You're a Slapper!'. Out of the mouths of babes.

As this was a Bertie B game, we got to the ground just after 6.00pm where we joined the queue. Not that I'm not used to queuing, but the last time I queued to get in to a home game was following a pre-match floodlight power failure against Blackpool in the 1990s. Who were all these new faces? We were just about to start up a chorus of 'They'll be coming out of the woodwork when they come' when they opened the gates and in we went. We were in the ground so early that it felt like Turkey where they arrive hours before the kick-off. When are they going to sacrifice the cattle anyway?

The overly optimistic air at Birmingham had if anything intensified; the phrase 'Don't count your chickens before they're hatched' sprang to mind. In reality, it was only half--time as they say and it was difficult to see why we were so optimistic with our play-off record prior to this game being P7, L5, D2., not exactly a record to inspire confidence. I usually get everyone's tickets and still had everybody's season tickets in case I had to get play-off Final tickets. Not wishing to tempt fate, I superstitiously gave them all back before the kick-off saying that I'd gladly endure another queue if we got to Cardiff, but would prefer to collect the season tickets after the game.

Mark McGhee was quoted in *The Sun*, Joe Royle-fashion, saying 'We're like caged animals, we will tear into them!' which undoubtedly helped calm the crowd. It was going to be hostile anyway, there was no doubt about that, without a 'rip out their entrails and feed them to the dogs' tubthumping battle cry.

We sat in the CBL upper and noticed that Birmingham hadn't taken up their full allocation, filling only part of the upper tier. We also noticed that in the executive boxes to our right, somebody had a blow-up referee holding a red card. When I saw to my horror that the real referee was the buffoon from Rotherham, the inflatable version seemed the preferable option. If they were trying to stop us, why not bring out Rob Stiles, Uriah Rennie, Andy Hall or Gurnham Singh and be done with it?

On the rabble-rousing front Mick Brown pre-match played *Living Next Door To Alice* to which we sang our anti-Palace version, which must have confused the Brummies no end. I assume that they won the toss as they tried to outpsyche us by making us attack our end in the first half, an odd tactic but it worked. As the teams came out 'Let 'Em Come' filled the air, everyone clapped along and there was a mini Argentina 1978-style blue-and-white ticker-tape display from the CBL.

During the game, Martin Grainger must have realised that mocking Millwall's fans at the first leg at St Andrews wasn't a good idea, particularly as he had to visit us in just four days' time. He looked more than a bit apprehensive when taking throw-ins as he was serenaded with 'Martin Grainger Is A Wanker!' and 'Grainger You're An Ugly C...!'. The atmosphere was very much an Old Den throwback, very hostile and volatile, which can work for or against us, as the crowd baying for blood can get to our own team as much as the opposition.

The match was just too fraught to enjoy, too hostile, too nervy, as highlighted by Ted who stood up in the aisle entrance for the whole of the second half, he was just too tense to sit still. The game seemed destined for extra time when naturally Birmingham scored in front of the CBL at the very death. If Lady Luck is going to kick you in the bollocks, she might as well do it with steel toe-capped boots on, as Confucius might have said - I felt like a fish at Billingsgate.

Irrespective of the result, I felt that Millwall should do a lap of honour so that we could acknowledge what they had achieved during the season. The only problem was that Millwall laps of honour usually result in pitch invasions and chaos, hence the dire warnings made over the PA and the police and stewards encircling the cinder track, with police cavalry and riot police protecting the away fans in the North Stand upper tier. Even so, there were still some prats who came on to spoil the lap of honour, confront Birmingham's players and antagonise their fans. The CBL lower had a full-scale punch up between would-be invaders and those trying to stop them. The on-pitch interlopers were greeted in the customary manner by the bulk of the crowd.

When the night's proceedings were over we left the ground and headed back to our cars in a state of shock. Our cars were parked in Oldfield Grove and when we got there we found that some cars had been broken into, although luckily not ours. A car behind us had had its windows smashed and its CD collection stolen. These smash and grabs were carried out while we were at the game, a nice surprise when you return to your vehicle. The whole season had been marred by such acts; the streets were like a car break-in shopping centre. Where are all the police when this sort of thing is happening?

The flaws in the play-off system were highlighted when the fifth and sixth teams made the Final. Although I wouldn't have complained if we had gone through from that position. At least Norwich had beaten Wolves, which was a very small consolation. To show that some women have got a long way to go footballwise, Colin couldn't get to this game due to work commitments and he couldn't listen to the game on the radio as that's like Chinese water torture, so he settled for scanning Teletext. When he saw the score and started to bang his head on the wall his wife Claire said 'Well, at least your season ticket won't be as expensive as it would have been if they had gone up to the Premiership!' True, but strangely of little comfort to him.

9.

The Strange Case Of
Season 2002/03

I KNOW OUR PLAY-OFF record could most politely be described as shit and I should've expected it but the late Brummie goal had knocked the wind completely out of my sails. My first inclination was to hit my local and get as much mind-numbing Stella down my neck as the remaining opening time would allow. Obviously, other people had alternative stress relief ideas by rioting for a couple of hours. If we're honest every Millwall fan knew it would go off.

I knew where it would go off and roughly how the trouble would pan out, what I didn't know was how large-scale the disturbances would turn out be. The fact that the violence was against the guardians of our society, the police, somehow made it far worse to the media. If it had been between the two clubs hooligan factions I bet that it wouldn't have received half the publicity. The general feel was that if they can do this to the boys in blue what could they do to us? In my opinion it's Millwall's willingness to fight the police that is one of the reasons why our hooligan reputation is what it is. I don't think the result was totally to blame, it seemed far too premeditated and organised for that. Let's face it to some the trouble before or after a game is merely the appetizer/dessert to the match's main course. There had been trouble at home all season as highlighted on *Hooligans - No One Likes Us*.

For riot night, Millwall had sold six tickets per season ticket to home fans as they had for some other games, a bad decision I thought at the time. How right I was. Birmingham were given the same allocation at Millwall as ours at St Andrews. Although they sold only 1800 of their 2800 tickets, it was still nearly 450% up on their league turnout. There were a few possible reasons why they hadn't taken up all their tickets -

1) Fear of attack by home fans.

2) It was midweek.

3) Birmingham didn't start selling their away tickets until Monday 29th April.

They were also sold on merit; those with15+ away stamps first, 10+ second, any away stamps third, remaining tickets would go on general sale.

4) Their play-off record was as bad as ours was so following Dublin's goal they must have thought they had blown it again.

Naturally, after the night's violence the implication was that Birmingham were afraid to come. They didn't seem very scared at St Andrews to me. I don't think the rioters had any idea just how much damage they had caused financially and emotionally to the club and we week in week out fans. Even the pre-season friendly against Steaua Bucharest, a Category Z game, had numerous police and Hoolievans. The police cavalry were even patrolling the recycling plant footpath and there were police spotters armed with mugshot sheets, scanning the small crowd for any Birmingham offenders.

Like the start of 2001/02 when a pre-season German tour had been cancelled due to hooligan fears, the 2002/03 pre-season tour to Bonnie Scotland was also cancelled following the riot. The police didn't want the unholy trinity of Millwall, Cardiff and Birmingham in their area at the same time. The way we're going, our pre-season tour will be Dulwich Hamlet and Fisher Athletic! Rather than dwell on the riot, which has been done to death in the fanzines and media ever since, I thought that I'd try to give a feel for how the club felt the season after. One thing I would say is thank God that we didn't sign Yobo after the World Cup!

Post-riot - the New Den initially had the feel of Jimmy Nicholl's reign, rather than a side that had finished fourth in Division 1. The home crowds dropped sharply, possibly due in some part to the threat of police identification/misidentification, hence the sea of empty seats in the East Upper. The attendances weren't helped by the draconian ticketing policies the club introduced, especially the identity smart card where everyone had to supply photographs and utility bills/passports etc to prove their identity. An attempt to eliminate the bogus element on the database but very unpopular. Many people refused to supply the required information, because having to prove your identity implied by association that we were all criminals who'd all be scanned via this database whenever any trouble arose. In addition, nobody knew what information was actually on the card.

Following the Luton riot, Thatcher decided to bring in a national football identity scheme. An ill-thought-out farce that fell at the first hurdle. That said, since then there have been club membership schemes introduced, at practically every club. That crept up and bit us on the arse, didn't it?

One of the main bugbears with Millwall's scheme was that apart from a couple of games, members could no longer bring friends or relatives on an ad hoc basis as it was strictly members only. There was a simple equation that applied to 95% of Millwall matches in 2002/03 and that was - No guests + No floaters = No cash. The policy was instrumental in the club announcing a debt of £2.5 million to November 2002. ITV Digital's demise played its part but almost halving the home crowd obviously didn't help. Millwall had to do something and in the end they staved off the police's financial and ground certificate threats; however, I assume practically sending the club back into financial administration in the process wasn't part of the intention.

The previous season's reciprocal Man City bans were merely the precursor to numerous bans this season. Initially six sides were banned - Stoke, Burnley, Leicester, Wolves, Forest and Pompey - sides who usually bring a following but who we've had problems with in the past. Despite the lack of away fans there was still a large police presence. Burnley were subsequently allowed up to 500 fans for their visit. The club let in almost 2000 kids free at the Forest, Leicester, Wolves and Stoke games which meant that the North Stand had people in it. Unfortunately, they emitted a high-pitched noise like a schoolgirl's hockey international.

Generally, the home atmosphere was pretty awful - we had lost our roar. The home-only games in particular had surreal atmospheres with the exception of the Leicester game, with its Dennis Wise v Callum Davidson/Leicester's Financial Armageddon/Death Threats edge. Millwall were accused of gaining an advantage by banning away fans, certainly not true. Let's face it, the hostile games are the ones that generate the best atmospheres with the New Den roaring and hostile like the Old Den.

I try to see the humour in adversity and the one shaft of light was the very peculiar police ruling that the 'volatile' games against Reading, Coventry, Palace and Derby, with home and away fans in attendance, had to finish one hour before dark. Truly weird, perhaps we could have aided the police by putting a light meter on the scoreboard like they have at cricket, five lights lit up and it would be police stopped play.

2002/03 Away

Our usual travelling contingent and I have often commented that you only find the 'Boys' in any numbers at the real trouble games, you don't see them at Wednesday night games at the likes of Crewe. Consequently, a blanket away fan ban only really punishes the normal hardcore week in week out fans i.e. the largely innocent fans.

Banning clubs from Millwall punished us when they did a retaliatory ban for the return fixture. The bans were down to the clubs, not police, to decide and we were allowed to go to Portsmouth. However, we were banned from Burnley, Stoke, Forest and Wolves. We were also initially banned from Leicester, then allowed to go, until Wisey's financial claims and death threats upped the crowd trouble stakes and we were eventually banned.

Due to the wonders of technology, Burnley was shown live on Sky and other games were beamed back to the New Den. As with the previous Man City game I couldn't be arsed to watch the beam backs; therein lays madness, shouting and singing at a big television which I can do indoors and, rather worryingly, I have, whilst trying to avoid the neighbours phoning the authorities to get me sectioned. Other than the banned games I only missed Rotherham and Gillingham away, going to 19 away matches in total. Reflecting the low-key nature this season the travelling support was down to hardcore levels, save for the Bertie B and local games. In this chapter I've listed the matches that I went to.

Watford on Tuesday 13/8/2002 was very low-key and perfectly reflected the season. The usual London posse and I drove the short distance to Hertfordshire for the first away match since the riot. It was also the game after the 6-0 Rotherham coshing, consequently there was a very subdued atmosphere among the away fans. The game ended 0-0, nothing else to report, sorry.

Nathan and I went to **Sheffield United on Tuesday 27/8/2002**, his first visit. Due to the hiding sustained by their London colleagues, Sheffield police were determined to give us a show of force. As soon as we arrived they came on to the coach, barged through us as we tried to get off and then rummaged through our personal effects as we stood in the aisle. We queried why we were being treated like terrorists, they ignored us and continued their display. Never mind civil liberty, bloody liberty was more like it.

For this game, we were in the Bramall Lane stand upper tier with its vertigo and splinter problems. It's like a ski slope black-run; if you stumbled as you came down the stairs, you'd take a pearler straight over the front of the stand. They don't so much need stewards up there as mountain rescue! The seats are also wooden and rusty, with the wood worn smooth by years of bums on seats but luckily we survived. Nothing much else to report apart from the fact that the home fans were their customary loud/quiet selves and passed a huge club flag along the home stand at the opposite end before the match, the PA still didn't work properly and as per usual we lost, this time 3-1.

On **Tuesday10/9/2002** Paul, Nathan, Simon, Patrick and I drove to the **Worthington Cup game at lower division Rushden and Diamonds**, Irthlingborough, Northants. None of us had been there before and it brought my personal club tally to 80 and ground tally to 88. Nene Park oozed rural, suburban politeness and the night was a real cornucopia of oddity. During the course of the evening we saw a hot-air balloon, blimp and a hang-glider whizz overhead and their banned items list said 'No masks and no stools'. Bar type or big job, it didn't say. You could buy Dr Martens in the club shop. In the ground, they had the original New Den scoreboard. There were plaster owls on top of the stands to scare away birds from landing on the pitch. The refreshment area was laid out like a seated café. There were Coca-Cola machines inside and outside and they had clean toilets! It was far too civilised for me.

Pre-match, Pat was trying to get autographs at the front of our AirWair stand behind the goal. Rushden's Muppet, Dazzler The Lion, attempted to shake his hand and Pat sent him away with a flea in his ear, leaving one bemused Muppet. When their goalkeeper Billy Turley attempted to get Millwall's Ben May sent off in front of us Pat started the most abusive chant of the night with 'Turley Takes It Up The A...!'. You can look at these two events in one of two ways - either we've schooled him well in the ways of the 'Wall or we've ruined him for life.

We were naturally surrounded by stewards, one of whom was bald-headed with a headset who got 'There's Only One Uncle Fester!' until we spotted another slaphead steward and sang 'There's Only Two Uncle Festers!'. At away matches unwarranted home club steward incursions on to our section are not to be recommended. Tonight a bloke was standing at the very back of the away stand with a young girl. An overly officious steward went up to him and told them to sit down. There was no one behind them and we deemed it an unnecessary infringement. We showed our solidarity when the entire away contingent stood up and loudly sang 'Stand Up If You Love Millwall' until he walked away - people power. To cap an unmemorable night we lost a penalty shootout right in front of us following a goalless game and extra time.

I went on a club coach on my own to **Portsmouth on 14/9/2002**. We outplayed Pompey but, continuing Fratton's Bok status, we lost 1-0. Surprisingly, nothing else happened.

Pat, Simon, Paul, Nathan and I drove to **Coventry City on 28/9/2002**. We found ourselves in a huge jam on the MI near Whipsnade with traffic stretching out motionlessly for miles. We decided that we should get off the motorway and I suggested driving right through Luton, which should bring us out further up the M1. Thankfully it did and we rejoined the motorway past the jams and continued unhampered for the rest of the trip. Time was now ticking on, so we decided to take the first Coventry junction that we came upon.

On the outskirts of Coventry a fellow Lion signalled us and asked us if we knew where we were going. We told him we were following the Coventry-stickered car in front and he replied 'Are they going to the game?' We said that we assumed so, although they could be going to their Aunt Maud's funeral for all we knew. He decided to make sure so we continued our tracking, stopped at traffic lights where he jumped out of his car, ran up to the Coventry car and asked whether they were going to the match. Having confirmed they were he gave us a Jimmy Saville style thumbs up, got back in to his car and we continued to the ground. We parked a distance from Highfield Road and followed some locals to the ground.

There has been trouble at Coventry before but we arrived unmolested and went into the same stand as April 2002. Pre-match, the luscious cleavage-flashing cheerleaders once again did a turn, as it were, this time in very low-cut outfits. I was suitably entertained. I don't get out much. It was Dennis Wise's debut and the home fans roundly booed him. They also sang 'You're Supposed To Be In Jail!' It probably referred to our play-off riot, although it could have been about Wise's Callum Davidson assault so we gave the first airing of 'Dennis Wise, Dennis Wise, Dennis, Dennis Wise, As You Hit The Floor, He'll Break Your Jaw! Dennis, Dennis Wise'. In response to their abuse, we sang the following to Gary McAllister, their ageing, follically-challenged player-manager; 'You're Just A Bald Sweaty Wanker!' Unfortunately, Pat was physically sick in the first half and Simon spent some of the half in the Gents with him. He then fell asleep in the second half and was sick again on the way back to the car, missing one our best away performance of the season, a very enjoyable 3-2 win. For the bloodthirsty, we saw a dead fox in the road on the way back to London.

Paul, Nathan and I drove to **Norwich City on 19/10/2002**. We arrived early and had a lengthy wander around the picturesque City of Norwich, before setting off for the ground through hordes of chatty and friendly locals; such affability is unnatural for a Londoner like me I'm not used to people talking to me. If a stranger speaks to you in the smoke, you think that they are after something. En route, we also passed a samba band marching up and down outside the Norwich and Peterborough stand bashing out an incessant/monotonous rhythm, more of whom a little later.

We were again in the far right corner of the ramshackle South Stand with just over 1000 fellow Lions. Our visit coincided with a 'Let's Kick Racism Out' day and we had a black girl as a mascot. There were anti-racism posters/leaflets on each seat, a yellow and green Norwich version saying 'Canaries Against Racism' and a blue and white Millwall version saying 'Lions Against Racism'. Before kick-off we were asked to hold these cards up to show our support, which many people did.

At half-time, the samba band from outside did a march about on the pitch and we unsuccessfully tried to sing 'Let 'Em Come' to their Latin rhythm. The poor girls in the band carrying the large drums had to wrap their thighs around their drum to be able to walk; this ungainly posture prompted the sympathetic Millwall chant of 'You Walk Like You've Shit Yourself!'. We lost 3-1 on loanee Glen Johnson's debut, and drove home gloomily.

Paul and I went to **Sheffield Wednesday on Wednesday 30/10/2002** on a club coach. For the first time I noticed something truly bizarre on the coach ticket as it said 'Strictly No Jeans, T-Shirts, Trainers Or Shorts'. Bang goes most people's wardrobes, what can you wear then, perhaps a nice summer frock?

Even at this relatively early stage this once great club looked in terminal decline, so to point it out we sarcastic couple of hundred Millwall sang 'You're Going Down With The Brighton!'. It could have been worse, they could have been going down on the Brighton! To accompany the home fans abuse of their manager Terry Yorath we sang 'And Now You're Gonna Believe Us, You're Gonna Get The Sack, Etc!' and 'We Want Yorath Out!'. He resigned the next day, I hope we were of assistance.

The 1966 North Korean conquerors of Italy were presented to the crowd and Steve Claridge scored a corker to secure a 1-0 win, my first ever victory in numerous visits to Hillsborough, sending us Londoners happily back south.

Paul drove Ted, Pat, Simon and I to **Reading at noon on 2/11/2002** with Nathan following in his own car. The game was nothing special apart from the home fans again venting their anti-Mark McGhee spleen with the following medley; 'F... Off Mark McGhee, Etc, Fat Scottish B...... And A Shit football Team!'/ 'Judas, Judas What's The Score?'/'Stand Up If McGhee's A Twat!'/'McGhee Out!'/'He's Fat, He's Round, He's Taking Millwall Down, Mark McGhee!' and 'Sack McGhee!'. We lost 2-0, pleasing the home fans no end. After the game, Ted got involved in a fracas with some home fans in the car park, which I'll not go into to spare his blushes!

Following the excitement, we drove home. I was sitting in the front next to Paul when the windscreen wiper conveniently stopped working on the motorway in the middle of a downpour. Luckily, it was on the passenger side so we could at least limp along the M4, with Paul precariously peering through the driver's side of the windscreen.

The usual East London crew went to **Crystal Palace on 7/12/2002**. As in 2001/02, they charged us a king's ransom to sit in the dilapidated and restricted view Arthur Wait stand. We paid up nonetheless and around 5000 of us took our 1-0 defeat like men. Today the home fans were especially mouthy for some reason; they mostly sang chants about our low home attendances 'You're Banned From Your Own Ground!'/'Will You Turn Up At The Den?' and 'You Only Turn Up For Palace!'. More bravery behind police lines.

Our only original chant on the day came because you couldn't get a beer in the ground and those desperate for a sherbet sang 'Shit Ground - No Beer!'. Although we lost, it was funny that Palace's biggest cheer came not for their win but for the announcement that we would be held in the ground after the game. This reminded me of a Millwall chant at Palace a few years ago. The PA announced that we would be escorted to the station, so we sang 'We Don't Need An Escort!'. After a short while we added 'We've Got Ford Cortinas!'.

As promised, we were held in the ground and then the street accompanied by numerous Old Bill for half an hour. Eventually we were marched mobhanded to Norwood Junction station where everyone tried to get on to the first train. It was chaos, caused 100% by the police's OTT corralling tactics. Outside the station, we had been surrounded by what looked like the entire Metropolitan police force.

On **1/1/2003** Paul, Nathan and I had a trouble free drive to **Ipswich Town's** revamped Portman Road, with its Sir Alf Ramsey and Sir Bobby Robson statues. Little did we know that later on it would turn into a motoring horror show. We arrived early in pouring rain and parked in Ipswich's car park opposite the ground. We went inside onto the undeveloped Cobbold Stand upper tier where bizarrely there was a wood cabin next to the large executive boxes on the stand directly opposite to us. Pre-match the groundsman used agricultural equipment to pump standing water off the pitch and remove the plastic sheets covering it.

The covering did its job because the game went ahead despite being played in a continual downpour; unfortunately, it resulted in a very flattering 4-1 Ipswich victory. Despite the score, Ipswich fans were strangely quiet so we sang 'No Noise From The Tractor Boys!'. We also sang the Norwich reference 'There's Only One Alan Partridge!'. A marvellous observational Millwall Dennis Wise chant got its first airing today: 'He's Small, He's Hard, He Likes A Yellow Card, Dennis Wise, Dennis Wise!'

For our entertainment Millwall favourite, Joe 'Mr Potato Head' Royle was now Ipswich's manager and we serenaded him with the following to the tune of *Speedy Gonzales*; 'Oh! Fat Joe Royle, Has Got A F...ing Big Head, He's Got A F...ing Big Head; He's Got A F...ing Big H-E-A-D!' Just a thought, but why doesn't he join TV's *The Royle Family* as Joe 'Penalty My Arse' Royle, the relative with an excuse for everything?

The funniest moment came when Ipswich's cleaner decided that midway through the second half was the best time for a spot of cleaning, so armed with a mop and bucket he happily mopped the stairs in the away section and was serenaded with 'Cleaner, Cleaner Give Us A Song!'. We didn't get as much as a 'whistle while you work 'out of the miserable carrot cruncher! Following the match, we headed to our car stunned that we had played well but got technically hammered.

Some while later we emerged from the car park and headed to the motorway, which itself was like a car park due to a road closure. We had to take a massive, if scenic, detour through leafy country lanes to get closer to London. Consequently, it took us longer to get back home from Suffolk than it usually takes to get back from Burnley.

Dave drove Ted and I to **Cambridge United for the FA Cup 3rd round game on 4/1/2003**, with Paul, Nathan, Simon and Pat in a second vehicle. Driving on the M11 our car was 'wankered' by an irate driver who had manoeuvred in front of us so that he could gesture us through the rear windscreen. As we had not done anything wrong it took us a while to twig that we were the target of the signalling. Dave then indicated that he pull over to discuss the matter further, as it were. The driver dropped back, pulled alongside, saw we were Millwall and sloped back with an apologetic wave of the hand; lucky for him, as it was 6 to 1. it was very strange, as was having a Spitfire whizzing overhead shortly after.

We soon found ourselves lost in the city centre. We asked two different sets of people for directions to the football ground and were twice directed to Cambridge City! We eventually found United, where the away end was now a brand new all-seater stand miles from the pitch. Strangely, the home parts of the Abbey were still a tip. There were a couple of humorous incidents: We gave a classic rendition of Mark McGhee's *Daydream Believer*, fine if you are riding high, but a bit difficult to sing when you're not. The DJ put the tune on and when we got to the 'Top Of The League' part everyone mumbled incomprehensibly through it, marvellous.

It was one of the first real cold winter days and we sat there frozen to the marrow. Near the end of the match Cambridge's announcer gave out a nanny state message about the nature of the conditions. He said something like 'Will all the Millwall fans leaving the ground be very careful, it's cold, it's wet and DARK, and there could be sheet ice, be careful!' He repeated this to much derision, but he put the wind up me to such an extent that I asked a steward if he'd hold my hand and walk me back to our car - just joshing. I know why he was warning us, because the stairs to the new stand were metal and had probably iced up, but we're not a crowd used to being treating like Private Pike in *Dads Army*. We fortunately scraped a 1-1 draw in a drab game and managed to negotiate the exit successfully.

None of the usual London crew were going to **Grimsby Town on 18/1/2003** so I travelled with the Essex contingent, my first trip with them. There were seven of us; my cousins Paul and Gavin, their cousin Nigel, brothers Andy and Mark Bell, Glyn and myself. I travelled to Chelmsford and found on arrival that it was to be a beano. Paul drove us in a people carrier he'd hired on the cheap from the company his girlfriend works for. We set off and after consuming several 'light ales' we unanimously requested a relief stop. We pulled in to an American Diner, marched in, did what we had to do, dumped our empties in the sink and walked out without buying as much as a bean. We had another essential roadside slash before stopping at a pub outside Grimsby for a nosh. We parked up near the ground and headed to the away Osmond Stand. I was lured by the sexual wiles of an attractive lottery girl into buying a ticket as soon as I walked through the turnstile; I'm a sucker for a pretty face and the attendant bits that go with it. The only entertainment laid on by the fishy folk came before the game when Grimsby's Muppet, The Mighty Mariner, did that old sailor's tradition of showing us his arse, thankfully fully costumed.

During the kickabout, a ball was kicked into the away stand, it was grabbed by some kids who played with it whilst the spoilsport stewards vainly tried to get it back. The kids did a piggy in the middle game with the stewards who were getting very agitated. To cheer them up we sang 'Jobsworth - No Life!'. Eventually the ball was thrown higher into our stand. We won 2-0 and the ball disappeared back to London as the few hundred of us sang 'Two Nil And We've Got Your Ball!'.

We left the ground and headed back to our vehicle. We noticed that unusually not only were the pubs open but so were the off licences. Our first port of call though was the chip shop. I bought pie and chips and then went into the offy to stock up on Stella for our return trip. As I stood at the counter I managed to upset the offy owner by eating a meat pie in his shop. He said to me 'I don't know, you come to a bloody place world famous for fish and you eat meat!' I explained that I had a medical condition that required that I eat at least one meat pie when up north and he let me off.

We overcame Cambridge in the replay and Clive, Nathan, Ted, Simon, Patrick and I went to **Southampton on 25/1/2003** for the Fourth Round FA Cup game.

Clive drove the lead car with Nathan following; we easily got to Southampton, before getting lost in the town centre, despite all the signs with footballs pointing the way to the ground. Perhaps we should've used the park and ride portion of our ticket after all. Obviously getting lost isn't unusual but it was unique in that we asked four different drivers/motorcyclists for directions and managed to receive conflicting instructions, indicating that the ground was in four different directions.

Eventually we pulled up beside a taxi driver who knew the way to the ground. He kindly also told us to park in a car park, as there was no parking near the ground. Paul was already in Southampton with Helen who is a Saints fan and, by a fluke, we parked in the same NCP as Paul. We then took a short walk to the new dockside St Mary's stadium, number 89 in my ground count. Outside the away Northam Stand, we met up with Paul as well as Colin, who'd travelled down from Bridport for the match.

We went inside to our seats and I looked around at the large new red stadium. Whilst it's a vast improvement on The Dell, like many new identikit stadia, I found it a bit soulless. Millwall received only 3200 tickets i.e. 10% of the ground capacity, though the % away allocation for FA Cup games usually goes out the window when Millwall are concerned.

As it was a big game against a relatively local Premiership side, we could have sold a couple of thousand more tickets at least. There were plenty of empty seats, especially in the areas next to us. St Mary's was in fact 9000 down on capacity, that's the Millwall effect for you. Most of us sat in the correct seats next to the home fans in the lower part of the stand behind the goal near the front;

unfortunately, the sun was directly in our eyes for the entire first half. Paul and Nathan had sat higher up in the stand so didn't have our problem. Cahill and Sadlier sat a few rows behind us where they were lauded and pestered by their adoring Millwall public. Paul's girlfriend Helen became a home matchday prize-winner when her face was flashed up on the video screen at the opposite end. It's a bit surreal when someone you know suddenly pops up on a bloody great screen.

Many fans appeared to have travelled without tickets. There were about a hundred Millwall standing in our section without seats; presumably, the police thought it better to have them inside the ground where they could see them than outside. Before the game, the police moved them to the home seating to the left of us, despite heated protestations from the home fans sitting there.

In the game the home fans continually barracked ex-Pompey man Steve Claridge. When he scored in the first half in front of us, we sarcastically sang 'Claridge For England!', aimed at Southampton's England hopeful James Beattie who had an anonymous game. The funniest incident of the day followed Claridge's goal; a Lions fan ran onto the pitch in celebration and the police grabbed him. Two burly coppers were escorting him around the cinder track in front of the wildly celebrating away fans and even though they were holding both his arms he was still trying to do the arm pumping 'EIO' that we were all doing, very comical to watch. Before the second half the police decided to bring the overspill Millwall fans back into our section and they stood at the front of the stand for the remainder of the match. It's very unlike a big Millwall match to dissolve into farce.

We held our 1-0 lead for 90% of the match and Saint's fans were streaming out in droves long before the end. To highlight this we nicked their theme tune and sang 'Oh! When The Saints, Go Streaming Out, I Wanna Be In That Number, When The Saints Go Streaming Out!'. We also sang 'Shit Fans - Nice Song!'.

To burst our bubble Lions reject Kevin 'Donkey' Davies came on for Beattie and scored Southampton's late second half goal, right in front of us. Isn't that always the bloody way? We gained a very commendable 1-1 draw, though the home side had gotten out of jail in truth. We made our way back to our cars via a crowded bridge/walkway in the midst of hundreds of home fans. Southampton are not hostile but I thought to myself, this route would be quite jolly if Pompey ever play here.

I went to **Preston North End on 8/2/2003** with Andy, Mark and Glyn. It followed the pattern of Grimsby - beer/piss stops/lunch/beer/good laugh. For entertainment we had Derek and Clive and Millwall singalong tapes. It was an easy journey and we stopped at a pub near Wigan for lunch.

We arrived in Preston early, parked up and walked the short distance to the ground. Deepdale has changed radically since my first visit in the 1990s when it was very much an old style terraced ground with a hotbed crowd. There was only one newly-built large stand then, The Sir Tom Finney Stand, with his head depicted on the seats.

By my next visit in April 2000, their Division 2 Championship game, Finney's head had been joined by Bill Shankly's on a large stand behind the goal. There was now the head of Alan Kelly (who?) on the eponymously named stand that has replaced the home terrace behind the other goal, completing Preston's answer to Mount Rushmore. Only the decrepit Pavilion Paddock side terrace/stand remained unchanged. Since April 2000, the away section had moved from this open side terrace to the left hand corner of the vast Bill Shankly Kop stand. Unfortunately, Preston's bloody annoying band were in the opposite corner of our stand. To accompany their sodding racket they sang this observational ditty; 'You're Shit And You Talk Funny!'. Rich coming from people who talk like Coronation Street's Ashley.

Preston's Michael Jackson played in this game only a few days after Martin Bashir's controversial interview with the King of Pop. In honour of this, the 283 gathered Millwall sang 'Michael Jackson Sex Offender!' all afternoon.

In the game the team looked shagged following their Southampton FA Cup replay exertions and we lost 2-1. If truth be told we should really have got a hiding.

Paul drove Ted, Nathan and I to **Brighton on 22/2/2003**. On arrival, the only available parking space was among an impromptu used car sale on the main road. We parked up and worryingly noticed that our car was the only one without a price on the window. Hopefully it wouldn't be priced up and sold in our absence.

We walked the short distance to Withdean where we met up with the Essex Boys, etc. Palace, Ipswich and Norwich had stitched us up, but Brighton was the most scandalous case of overcharging ever, an outrageous £20 to sit on a makeshift wood and scaffold pole erection, with an entrance like a timber yard and Portaloos. I thought that maybe our ticket included Shirley Bassey or Barbara Streisand as half-time entertainment, pleasuring the home fans leanings, but thankfully it didn't.

The small away section is so ragged that they hadn't even bothered to name it as far as I could see. It is also so rickety that whenever we rhythmically stamped our feet, as we 700+ did frequently, it seemed in danger of imminent collapse. What happened when West Brom 'boinged' on it God knows. To add to the fun there was a running track around the pitch, which meant that it was miles from our stand. We had the sun in our face for an hour and the surrounding fields were shrouded in mist. The view was so bad that one bloke sitting behind me said 'I can't see a bloody thing; I'm going to call Clubcall in a minute to get a commentary to see what's going on!' Millwall lost 1-0 although luckily we were unable to see much of it.

After the game, we nervously went back to Paul's car, which fortunately hadn't been sold.

I went to **Walsall on 8/3/2003**, with Andy, Mark and Glyn. We had an uninterrupted drive up, arrived early, parked in a side street and walked to the Bescot. From the William Sharp away stand behind the goal I noticed that they had built a large new stand behind the opposite goal, thus ruining the ground's B&Q imitation forever.

As we stood up all afternoon trying to generate an atmosphere, unlike the home fans who were as usual very quiet, the Old Bill and stewards surrounded us for much of the game, especially the second half. Nothing unusual there then. What was unusual was Millwall won 2-1, a first win at either Walsall ground for me.

I WAS BORN UNDER THE COLD BLOW LANE

Simon, Patrick, Ted and I went to **Wimbledon on 15/3/2003** via Norwood Junction. We arrived very early and had a wander around the shops before making our way to the ground. The lack of home fans was very noticeable. It's always low key but today it was ten times worse. We went into the ground and on to the Arthur Wait stand where we watched the groundsman empty Lake Windermere on to the pitch, late comers commented on how bad the pitch was, it had been fine before he started.

Continuing the feel of the streets, the game was played in the most surreal atmosphere that I've ever been in at a match. There was an alarming lack of home fans, we had an official turnout of 1785 in a crowd of 2952 meaning there were vast acres of empty seats. How they managed to beat us 2-0 with no support God knows. It was like watching the death throes of the former top-flight club and I found the whole day depressing.

My final trip with Andy, Mark and Glyn was to **Bradford City on 5/4/2003**. For any horror fans out there, we saw a badger splattered all over the roadside on the way to Bradford. It didn't put us off our food though because we stopped off for a pub lunch at Sir Jack's in Rotherham before setting off to Bradford, which was a real culture shock - it was just so Northern and Asian. We had seemingly entered the land of the curried ferret.

We parked near the ground at the foot of an incline and made our way to the ground up a street that couldn't have been more Yorkshire if it talked like Geoff Boycott, wore a cloth cap and walked a whippet. To highlight the *Emmerdale* nature of it all, during the game we sang 'There's Only One Zak Dingle!'. Bradford was my 81st League club and 90th ground.

From the upper tier of the South Stand behind the goal my first impression of Valley Parade was that it was bloody garish, everything was maroon and yellow. It was also a hotch potch, with two large new co-joined stands at the opposite end and to our left and two shabby old stands, our stand, which had metal posts obstructing our view, and a low old-style stand to our right. Premiership relegation had stopped them turning the stadium into an impressive edifice, as they were now skint.

In the game cuddly lino ND Swarbrick, puffing his way up and down the touchline to our right, riled the home fans with away town decisions. They naturally abused him and to help them out we sang 'There's Only One Dodgy Linesman!'. In the second half Bradford's ex-Millwall keeper Aiden Davidson got a schizophrenic response when he took up position in front of us. He was applauded and lambasted with 'There's Only One Kasey Keller!' and 'You'll Never Play For Millwall!'. For the record, in the second half Denzil was racially abused by the home fans.

Most importantly we won 1-0. Our very late winner prompted us to go bonkers and we sarcastically sang 'One Nil And A Long Way Home!'. We four sang a variation, 'One Nil And A Big Mixed Grill!', in homage to our pub lunch. We headed back down T'hill happy, but glad to be heading back to civilisation.

I would like to say to the Essex boys: Big up Millwall, sing along and Derek and Clive tapes, that great forward line of Carling, Stella and Fosters, train and piss stop spotting, the Banana Splits, apple crumble and smothered chicken, they will understand. Not forgetting the Cambridgeshire town of 'Trumpington', which we drove past on every journey, appropriate given the flatulent nature of the trips.

The final permitted away trip of the season was the rearranged game at Pride Park, **Derby County**, ground number 91 for me, on **Wednesday 16/4/2003**. Paul drove Nathan, Dave and I to our first ever visit to the new place. We had an easy journey, arriving very early and parked as instructed in Derby Tertiary College's car park, miles from the stadium before trudging wearily to the ground past a gasholder and quarry.

Pride Park was another Madejski-style ground with pubs, shops and restaurants, in the surrounding area. There was also a large Rams Superstore club shop. We had a wander around until the turnstiles opened and then took up our positions in the McArthur Glen Stand behind the goal. Whilst Pride Park is an obvious improvement on the ramshackle edifice that was the old style Baseball Ground, it was yet another identikit stadium, like a monochrome St Mary's. In comparison to the Baseball Ground, it wasn't as good for atmosphere although the home fans did sing a couple of sarcastic original chants; 'Millwall's Got No Football Hooligans!' and 'You're So Poor You Sound Like Forest!'.

I WAS BORN UNDER THE COLD BLOW LANE

To highlight how widespread sponsorship has now become, Derby's Muppet Rammie the Ram did a kids penalty shootout competition with a banner behind him saying 'Mitchell Sports sponsors of Rammie's boots and gloves'. Ye Gods, is there no escape from commercialism? We won 2-1, left the ground in the dark, got lost and bumped into Robbie Ryan's Irish relatives who were equally astray. We eventually all found our way back to the car and Paul drove home.

Over the years I've seen numerous examples of 'Debbie Does Barnsley' style cheerleaders. 2002/03 was a vintage year with two great examples of the art form - Coventry's cleavage flashers and Bradford's scantily-clad, busty, gyrating 'City Slickers'. Coventry just win the title of most buxom lovelies, in my humble dirty old man opinion.

We finished a respectable ninth, despite a horrendous injury list. If the League positions in 2001/02 and 2002/03 had been reversed, it would have been seen as progress however, because of the play-off semis, many saw anything short of automatic promotion as failure. 2002/03 was notable for beating 1986 European Champions Cup Winners Steaua Bucharest 4-1 in a friendly only to lose 6-0 to Rotherham in the first League game, with Rotherham's goal-scoring hero Darren Byfield sarcastically awarded the 'Millwall man-of-the-match' award. This was my worst home defeat, as it was for everybody else under 60.

The subsequent 5-0 thrashing by Pompey was the first time that I had seen two such heavy home defeats in one season and I don't want see it again! Low-key season or not, I still thoroughly enjoyed myself; the camaraderie, the funny chants, comments and incidents are what it's all about.

10.

The Lion Roars
Back To Life
Season 2003/04
Division One

FOLLOWING IN THE WAKE of the very low-key preceding season, this was to develop in to one of the most interesting and eventful campaigns in my Millwall-going lifetime; it was to be a highly emotional experience.

To begin with, even though there were only a handful of arrests throughout 2002/03, the pre-season friendly at Colchester United was cancelled on police advice. Due to the financially damaging implications of the away fan ban, despite their seeming effectiveness, the policy for 2003/04 was for no away fan bans no matter what. Only four obvious potential aggro games were designated as Teamcard/Members only all-ticket home games - Cardiff, West Ham, Stoke and Forest. Every away game remained all ticket for us. Division 1 contained not only us and the above four but also Sunderland and Burnley; it was a season ripe with potential flashpoints, only time would tell what would transpire. With the lifting of the crippling ticket restrictions, the new season began to take on a more normal air. The crowds very slowly crept back up although still well down on our first season back in Division 1. However, it seemed that the gloom was lifting. To top up our most loathed status, and complete the unholy trinity with Millwall and Dennis Wise, we added Kevin Muscat to our squad.

During the season having Wisey as manager, Muscat as captain, the Ashikodi/McCammon incident and Stan Ternent's racist accusations, it gave the less charitable element of the press an excellent opportunity to slag us off, which they naturally did.

The Games - 2003/04

In this section, I have included all of the away trips that I went on and the more important home games in one of the most exciting seasons in Millwall's history.

The first away game of the season was to a new ground for all of us, a trip to the newly-relegated **Sunderland on 16/8/2003 at The Stadium of Light,** my 92nd League ground. This was the day after my birthday and for the first time in my adult life I went totally without alcohol on my birthday itself, I didn't fancy a stonking hangover followed by a 600 mile round trip; my liver must have thought there was a draymen's strike.

Glyn, Andy and Mark managed to get EasyJet tickets at bargain basement prices and flew from Stansted to Newcastle Airport for this match. Dave, Paul, Nathan, Simon, Pat, Dave Murray, Ted and I looked into various means of transport:

1) Plane - now far too expensive because we had left it late and Pat would be full price.

2) Train - too expensive with most trains sold out anyway.

3) Automobile - Dave's new works van was too slow and uncomfortable and we couldn't find a minibus company willing to hire us a vehicle either economically or without the correct people-carrying license.

In the end we settled for the Junior Lions coach. Dave picked us all up in the early morning sunshine and we drove to the New Den to catch our 7am coach. We boarded the King's Ferry coach and Dave S and I took up seats above the toilet where there was more legroom, though we hadn't legislated for the loo backing up on the way up. I think you can guess what it was like up close on a hot summer's day.

That aside the coach trip to Wearside was lengthy but uneventful. We arrived early outside the Stadium of Light and it looked very impressive; it had Black Cats all around its outer walls and was situated on raised ground overlooking an industrial area beside a stream. Our coaches went through a narrow gate to get into the car park and we pulled up behind some buildings close to the away end. As soon as we stopped the police boarded our coach and informed us that they didn't eject people at the ground they simply arrested them, presumably why the Mackems had such a high arrests per season record. Suitably lectured, we got off the coach, bought a programme and made our way into the Metro FM South Stand behind the goal where we met the Essex jetsetters. I had been to Roker Park several times and never seen us win, in fact Simon and I were there for a 6-0 hiding several years back, which was great fun I can tell you.

Whilst Roker, with its famous roar, was a real football ground in the Old Den mould, the new ground is a modern, plush, huge but ultimately characterless edifice in the manner of St Mary's and Pride Park. The Roker Roar was largely absent thanks to relegation, a bad run of biblical proportions and the fact that the ground was half-empty. Sunderland, like most modern grounds, had designs depicted in the seats; there was their Black Cats badge and 'Ha' way the lads', whatever that might mean, in the seats opposite us. They also appeared to be sponsored by *On the Buses'* Reg Varney (?). I must change these glasses!

Pre-match and at half-time in the centre circle a boy combo and then a girl combo performed karaoke pop renditions that made the acts on *Phoenix Nights* look like Las Vegas' finest. They initially played Republica's *Ready To Go* before the teams came out to Prokofiev, far too posh for me. There were Millwall 1570 in the left hand corner of the stand with segregation meshing to our right. Not a bad turnout for such a long trip, I thought.

Swelled by the fact that it was the first away game of the season, we had the dubious pleasure of remaking our acquaintance with Mick McCarthy and there was a largish 'Firm'. During the game, there were the usual verbal exchanges with the locals either side of us with several close-up abuse-hurling encounters between both sets of fans across the segregation meshing. When we took an early lead we sang the following intentional misidentification Newcastle references; 'Geordies, Geordies What's The Score?'/'Toon Army!'/'Are You Geordies In Disguise?'/'You Ran From The Geordie Boys!' and 'Shearer!'.

These didn't go down too well, as you can imagine. In response, Sunderland's relatively quiet fans sang the following delusions of grandeur chant; 'Hello, Hello, Mickey Mouse Club!'. That's Palace surely? They also sang the regional stereotype chants 'Southern Shite!' and 'Soft Southern Bastards!'. Not the usual descriptions for Millwall fans.

Mick McCarthy was overseeing a disastrous run of Sunderland defeats, so we sang the sarcastic 'There's Only One Mick McCarthy!' and 'There's Only One Keano!'. In addition, we sang the Millwall management era chants of 'F… Off Mick McCarthy!' and 'Mick McCarthy Is A Wanker!'. Despite a second half Sunderland onslaught, we held out and won 1-0. We applauded Millwall off the pitch and elatedly left the ground. On the floor outside near the exit, beer bottles were strewn about as the home side had sold beer in glass bottles inside the ground. Amazingly, these weren't hurled at the police or home fans. To our left police were pushing the massed home fans of a hoolie persuasion back whilst our contingent were encircled by riot police and corralled by police cavalry near the away exits. Our 'Boys' tried to break free of our cordon to get at the Mackems. The Firm chant 'Bush, Bush, Bush!' filled the air and everyone, willing or not, surged towards the home supporters behind the police lines. Eventually, after a few surges and minor scuffles, the situation quietened down and most of the home fans were dispersed. It was nothing major but without heavy policing it could have been.

As we were being held outside the ground a Kings Ferry coach came out of the area where we were parked and drove up the road. Naturally we thought this was our coach and that we were stranded. After several more minutes we were allowed to get back to our transport, which thankfully was still there. The other coach had been the team coach. The Essex flyers managed to get through the police lines before the cordon had been set up and boarded the Metro to Newcastle early. They stood out like a dog's bollocks because they didn't have Sunderland shirts on. Nevertheless, they got back to Newcastle airport unscathed. They rang me from Stansted at a time when we still had hours of our trip to go, cheers! Sunderland's league record was now 17 straight defeats. Well on the way to breaking Darwen's (?) 1899 League defeats record, sadly for the record books, they spoilt it by beating Preston in the vital game.

The next away match was **Stoke City on Tuesday 26/8/2003,** usually very 'interesting' to say the least, as my previous report testified. Unlike the previous season, we were allowed to travel to the match. I went on my own on a club coach and met Glyn, Andy and his twelve-year-old son Alex in the ground. Alex, like Pat, has been to over 30 away grounds. My 2.30pm coach had an uneventful journey and we arrived at the Britannia relatively early.

The first thing that struck me was that they had added additional layers of segregation fencing at the usual trouble spot outside the away stand, now called the South Stand, creating a no man's land between the away exits and the side fence. They had also put caging in the surrounding car park to stop aggro spreading out across the whole area, as it had done in the past. Presumably, because of the above and our relatively low turnout of a hardy 366, there was no trouble, the first time that I had not seen aggro at either of Stoke's grounds.

The game was a coma-inducing goalless draw; there were a few oddities though -

1) There were bouncers inside the refreshment stall for a start. This is the only ground where I've seen this; I didn't think the food was that bad.

2) There's a road near the ground called 'Gordon Banks Drive' which I thought was a tad tactless as Gordon lost an eye in a car accident!

3) They had two gender colour-coded LSD trip hippo Muppets. A pale blue boy one called Pottermus and a pale pink girl one called Pottermiss, truly bizarre.

Next up was the caravan park at **Gillingham on 6/9/2003**, the day of the Macedonia v England Euro 2004 qualifier. Simon, Pat, Ted, Paul, Nathan and I drove there in Dave's huge bright green van, which said 'Hackney Health Authority' on the side. Not exactly inconspicuous, it may as well have said 'Londoners On Board' on a windscreen sticker, certainly not ideal for a trip to Wolves or Pompey. We drove to Kent in brilliant sunshine, squinting against the sun because the van's sunshades were about 8ft up so were useless.

We reached Gillingham, parked up a distance from Priestfield and had to cross a level crossing to get to the ground. When we got there we met the Essex contingent and found that the old away terrace now had seats and had been renamed the Brian Moore Temporary Stand. It was like a giant's open air Meccano kit, making it on a par with Withdean; thankfully, it was a very hot afternoon. Priestfield cannot expand much due to its residential position; as long as there's ample parking for caravans I'm sure they'll be blissfully happy. There was the usual London/Gypsy exchanges of abusive and we sang one up to the minute chant to the tune of *Harry Roberts*; 'Tony Martin Is Our Friend, Etc, He Kills Pikeys! Let Him Out To Kill Some More, Etc Tony Martin!' Nothing much else to report other than we lost again, 3-4, this time by clutching defeat from the jaws of victory.

We left Priestfield crestfallen and walked back to find the van. We tracked it down easily by homing in on its kryptonite-like green pulse in the distance. We then drove home whilst attempting to listen to England's game on Dave's radio, which Simon had to hold together to stop the batteries falling out.

Watford, 13/9/2003, a 12.30pm kick-off, live on Sky. Paul drove Simon, Pat, Ted and I to Hertfordshire, on my God knows what number visit.

There were a few points of note. In attempting to limbo through the narrow turnstile, I destroyed my brand new mobile phone in my pocket, crushing it between the turnstile and myself and leaving the screen looking like the burning map at the beginning of *Bonanza*. Gianluca Vialli was no longer manager, so we asked Sir Elton 'Where's Your Boyfriend Gone?'.

Kevin Muscat had a pre-half-time psychotic episode resulting in an injury-time penalty for Watford and Muscat getting a straight red. Despite cruising at 1-1 leading up to half-time and looking comfortable, we then lost 1-3, cheers Kev.

West Ham United at Upton Park on Sunday 28/9/2003 was the most eagerly anticipated away game for many a season. I've never found Upton Park particularly hostile; it certainly isn't like the Old Den that's for sure. However, even though my Hammers mate Ian said that Spurs, not us, were their sworn enemy there was obviously massive potential for aggro.

There is a long history of problems - a dockers strike donkeys years ago, the infamous Harry Cripps' testimonial at the Old Den, many recent clashes between the two sets of fans including a death on both sides and the fact that we hadn't played each other for over a decade. Hence the unprecedented 800 coppers on duty including riot police, cavalry, numerous hoolie vans and police helicopters hovering above. Unsurprisingly the match was switched to a Sunday noon kick-off. In an effort to prevent trouble, Millwall organised a live beam back to the New Den to stop ticketless fans travelling and West Ham had a policy whereby you had to have a previous Hammers booking history to get a home ticket. I agreed to get our East End contingent's tickets, enduring the customary several hours leg-numbing wait, thankfully there were more ticket windows open than usual.

Mark was in the queue several hundred people behind me, and I agreed to get the Essex boys' tickets with ours so we practically had a row to ourselves. Mark took their tickets and I distributed most of the London contingent's tickets in the build-up to the game, because we were travelling separately to the ground. I gave Paul his ticket at Watford; however he doesn't use a wallet and lost it. He spent the week before the match dismantling his home and car in a frantic and desperate search for it. He had no joy so his dad Dave sacrificed his own ticket and watched the match on the New Den Jumbotron instead. In the interest of paranoia, as I still had Dave's ticket Paul asked me to hold on to it in case he also lost this one. As I live in the East End, I decided to travel by bus, a journey that usually takes about 30 minutes.

However, I had no idea how restrictive the police would make the area so I left myself a couple of hours to do the trip. My bus pulled in to Canning Town Underground/Bus/DLR station, at around 10am and it was like a riot police compound. Numerous Hoolie vans were massed there with others rapidly heading towards it from all directions, sirens blaring. There were scores of riot police clad in black like ninjas disembarking from vans and heading down on to the platforms of the Jubilee Line tube.

I continued my journey and later heard that hundreds of Millwall were taken off the trains, searched for tickets/weapons, unarmed and sent back south if there was a problem, before the police marched the remainder many miles to the ground, presumably the reason why so many Millwall arrived late at the ground.

As with the ludicrous Highbury clock stories years before, the local media had been full of speculation that we were going to desecrate or cut the head off Bobby Moore's statue in Barking Road. Obviously we didn't. However, when I arrived, I found it covered in Millwall blue tarpaulin and encircled in a metal fence. Why didn't the police just keep their eye out for someone with a spray can, an oxyacetylene cutter, heavy lifting gear, a wheelbarrow or fork - lift truck and they'd have their culprit. The Boleyn pub close to the ground was also boarded up and closed for the day.

Paul and Nathan drove to the game and I arranged to meet up with them opposite this pub. I arrived first and waited near Bobby Moore's statue where several small groups of West Ham 'Boys' were scouting the road. We sensibly wore no colours so when the brothers arrived, we walked towards the ground unimpeded. En route, we passed the Castle outside the Dr Martens Stand and then waited for the rest of the East London contingent. Simon, Pat and Clive came by tube and joined us soon after. Mad Ted had exhibited a previously hidden sensible streak and decided not to go to this game because he thought there would be trouble! The away section was now in the old home North Bank, renamed The Centenary Stand, and the opposite end to our other trips. Presumably, as it's nearer to the tube station it's easier to police.

We wandered along back streets and past a bus garage before arriving at the away turnstiles, where a wall of stewards thoroughly searched us before we were allowed into the ground. Unlike many years before we didn't have to go through metal detectors this time. We met up with everyone else inside and sat in our real seats near to the corner flag and Chicken Run on the left hand side of the lower tier beneath West Ham's Junior Enclosure, which actually contained juniors. Our 2500 allocation was less than other sides due to the segregation worries.

I had heard rumours that Millwall's 'Boys' were going to block-buy tickets in the home areas, although in the end this hadn't happened. Richard Sadlier, sadly now retired, again sat among us in the away seats receiving a hero's welcome. Upton Park was vastly improved since our last visit, except for the Chicken Run. Bizarrely there was a huge area of grass between the touchline and this stand as the pitch had been moved across to accommodate the new stands. It looked peculiar and was very similar to a pre-renovated Molineux where they had pre-match five-a-side matches between the stand and the pitch. The home fans were very quiet apart from a few intermittent 'Bubble' bursts. I think that they felt that playing teams like us was somehow beneath them.

Naturally, there was still the usual macho posturing and offering out invitations between our section and the home fans. Irrespective of the home atmosphere, we made a hell of a racket, serenading the locals with all the customary anti-West Ham and Bobby Moore abuse. A friend of mine told me sometime later that someone he knew living a mile or so from the ground had to turn up their TV when we were singing, as they couldn't hear it above our roar! There were a couple of amusing incidents; prior to the game, the officials warmed up at our end and referee MR Halsey did his pre-match routine in front of our seats. As he held on to the corner flag and kicked his legs in the air like an arthritic Tiller Girl we sang 'Oh! Oh! The Hokey Cokey, Etc.'. He seemed to find this amusing and gave us a twirl, he didn't give us any decisions but at least he found us funny, which is something I suppose.

At half-time, the screen at the opposite end of the ground projected advertisements for corned beef. As nearby Dagenham used to be known as 'Corned Beef Island', due to the local's dietary habits, I thought it was funny, perhaps it's just me. I'd never seen Millwall win at West Ham, I missed the Simod Cup game, but today Millwall were very unfortunate not to win. We had outplayed them, nonetheless, a 1-1 draw has to be seen as a good result I suppose.

I WAS BORN UNDER THE COLD BLOW LANE

After the match, we were locked in for one and a half hours as police helicopters hovered above the opposite end of the stadium indicating the police's efforts to clear the streets of the hostile natives. Unsurprisingly riot police and stewards had surrounded us all afternoon. Despite our protracted wait, it was all very good-natured and we stood providing a vocal backdrop to the videoed post-match interviews.

One of the stewards in the massed ranks strung out across the away end was a Rasta with dreadlocks tied back. As he walked along in front of us got 'There's Only One Bob Marley!' and 'Bobby, Bobby Give Us A Song!'. We didn't get so much as a 'We're Jammin' out of him. We also serenaded the numerous police with the obligatory 'Harry Roberts'/'Laurel And Hardy' and 'Old Bill, Old Bill Give Us A Song', etc. I noticed in Richard Lindsay's book that a Harry Roberts played for us in the 1930s!

We also sang the following to imply that Sunday afternoon duty was a nice little overtime earner - 'Double Time!' Eventually we were allowed out and, close to the bus garage, someone let down the tyres on a police van. As a hissing sound filled the air the police were helpfully told that Kwik Fit was their best bet, though they didn't find this funny. Everyone headed to Upton Park tube save for Nathan, Paul and I who had to get back to the main road. Unfortunately, opposite Green Street Market, a mass riot police presence prevented this and we were forced to wait behind their lines before being allowed to proceed, much to the bemusement of the passing Asians. We were told that we would only be let through in dribs and drabs because West Ham would attack any large group. Following a long wait, we were gradually let through, although not before drivers had proved that they actually had a car by showing them their car keys. Eventually Paul and Nathan set off home and I waited for my bus as police vans hurtled towards Canning Town in a blur of sirens and flashing lights.

We saw no trouble at all and went the whole day unmolested. However, Ian later told me that a sizeable group of West Ham 'Boys' had had large-scale clashes with truncheon-wielding riot police on their way to confront Millwall at Canning Town, with missile throwing and cavalry charges aplenty. One of my Millwall mates has a police officer brother-in-law, based in the East End. He said that the local police had been on trouble-watch north of the river from 7am until 9pm on the day. He said that whilst Millwall had been mostly contained, due to being in large trackable groups, the police ran around all day tracking numerous smaller groups of tooled-up Hammers trying to prevent them from massing and attacking us, largely confirming what Ian said. None of this negative West Ham information was mentioned in the press as it would have been had it been us. I had the impression that the media were disappointed that it wasn't carnage.

Paul drove Nathan, Ted and I to **West Bromwich Albion on Tuesday 30/9/2003** completing a run of five 'W' team games - Watford, West Ham away Wimbledon and Walsall at home. We had an easy trip and were sitting in McDonald's opposite the ground just after 5pm; we then parked in a designated club car park just off the main road. The ground wasn't officially open so we had a wander around the outside of the Hawthorns with Ted as our trailblazer. Suddenly he disappeared via an open door into the Smethwick End; we followed him and found ourselves in an empty floodlit stadium. The stewards were still being briefed and they initially ignored us until Jobsworth Number One and his henchmen threw us out. We then waited outside WBA's club shop for Andy, Mark and Glyn to arrive. As we waited, Steve Claridge, there for a speaking engagement, walked past and we exchanged hellos.

When everyone had arrived we walked to the away turnstiles where they had installed new fangled scanning machines and had a steward in attendance showing the more stupid among us i.e. me, how to use the bloody thing. West Brom came out to the stirring Old Spice music, amongst other things, then ripped into us from the off. 437 Millwall watched a very one-sided match with the Baggies 'Boinging' and singing all night, creating an excellent atmosphere. Millwall were lucky to only lose 2-1. After the match, police marched us through an alleyway at the back of the away section, totally in the dark save for the glow coming from their luminous yellow coats. It was like an SAS night training exercise and one old boy in our party fell over, to the police's total indifference. Following our walk, we were miles from our car and we walked back to it with Ted abusing any Baggie within earshot; fortunately, we got back to it unscathed. Paul decided to fill up with petrol before hitting the motorway; unfortunately Mark, driving the Essex Boys, did not. They ran out of petrol on the M11 and had to push the car on to a hard shoulder until his and Andy's dad rescued them. We arrived home at 1am; they arrived home several hours later.

As England were playing a vital Euro 2004 match in Turkey, none of the London contingent fancied a trip Oop North on **11/10/2003**, but I did. English by birth, Millwall by religion; anyway, how can anyone possibly refuse a trip to picturesque **Rotherham United**?

For the first time this season, I joined the Essex boys for the trip to Yorkshire. I met driver Mark and Glyn at Chelmsford and we picked Andy up en route. I bought my ticket from Millwall separately from the others and when I texted them in the week to say that the tickets were 'strange', they didn't know what I was talking about. At Andy's we had a 'you show me yours' session and I found that my ticket bore no relationship to theirs. My one was a Millwall ticket with 'Rotherham United Gen Adm Away Game!!!' typed on it. I thought it was odd when given it but convinced myself that due to the low turnout because of the Turkey game, Rotherham hadn't printed tickets and Millwall had provided their own, more of which later.

As soon as we were on the way the three non-drivers naturally made numerous sarcastic petrol references to Mark, which we continued all day. We set off North listening to the usual stuff. Andy's newly-acquired *99 Greatest Farts* tape also got its first airing, if that's the right phrase. We planned to have a leisurely lunch at Sir Jack's outside Rotherham but, for the first time ever, we encountered traffic jams on the way out of Essex and were running slightly late right from the start. Eventually the roads cleared but we had to make an urgent stop because Glyn, in particular, had been giving Monsieur Artois a seeing to. We stopped at the fantastically named Ram Jam Inn.

We set off again and with the road now fairly clear we made good progress and were on track for our nosh-up in Rotherham when suddenly one of the back tyres blew and Mark pulled on to the hard shoulder to replace the tyre. We set off again reaching the pub late, but still with time for two courses, or so we thought. Usually they serve both courses at the same time; naturally, as we were running late they didn't today. Nevertheless, with a skinflint's determination Glyn, Andy and I refused to budge until the apple crumble we had paid for arrived, which it did at 2.35pm. We bolted it down before racing towards Millmoor. Unfortunately, they had changed the road system and we had to drive all around town to find the car park they knew from previous trips. We parked up at 2.55pm and raced past the scrapheaps and steel yards, arriving just as the game kicked off.

At the turnstile the others went through successfully. When I handed the turnstile man my unique ticket he said 'I can't take this mate, it's a Millwall ticket!'. I explained the situation to him and offered to pay and he said 'I'll have to ask a steward'. I told the others to go in as my stupidity shouldn't affect them. I felt like a right Yorkshire pudding I can tell you.

A steward arrived who unfortunately looked like a Picasso painting, nose for an ear, ear for an eye, you get the picture. He said 'This is a Millwall ticket mate! I'll have to get the head steward.' He used his walkie-talkie and within seconds a dozen stewards were hurtling in my direction. My unfortunate looking steward said 'What the f… are you lot doing here? I only wanted to sort out this bloke's ticket query!'. They sloped back inside and the steward very kindly said 'F… it mate, go in!'. I thanked him and joined the others with about ten minutes gone. I told them what had happened and they said that they thought it was all going off when the stewards hared out, but now they understood. Millwall = trouble in most stewards' eyes.

After a goalless match where my turnstile shenanigans were the high point we headed back south whilst trying to listen to the Turkey match on a radio that we couldn't get a decent signal on. In the end we listened to Terry 'We're All Doomed' Butcher's Five Live punditry leaving us with the impression that the game had been dreadful and that England had been piss poor. Not true at all as the TV highlights later confirmed. I hate listening to football on the radio, I don't have a clue what's going on, call me thick by all means but there you are. We had an easy trip back and thankfully England qualified.

Working on the third time lucky principal, I joined the Essex Boys for the trip to **Burnley on 25/10/2003**, another ground that we had been permitted to travel to having been banned in 2002/03. Burnley is a long trip and a bit of a nightmare at the best of times, however this was a horror show of epic proportions. I'd go as far as to say that it was the worst ever away trip I have been on, outstripping even my previous worst, the FA Cup trip to Hartlepool in the dark days.

I arranged to meet Mark and Glyn at Chelmsford at 9am. I got there early and Mark arrived soon after. Unusually Glyn, coming via Colchester, was late. We didn't have Glyn's mobile number so asked Andy to call him and then call us back. We found that he was on his way and he arrived 7 minutes late, not especially late but eerily significant, as you will see. Glyn had been on a Stella bender at a leaving do the night before and due to his delicate condition he left his match ticket on the sideboard. His wife had dropped him off at Colchester station and he only discovered this after she'd driven off. He got a cab back to his house, passing his wife on the way, before setting off hell for leather back to the station. With Glyn aboard we picked up Andy and set off.

I had an internet map that advised us to go via the M6, but Andy said that we should use the Huddersfield/Hebden Bridge route instead; unfortunately, we decided to follow the map. Glyn likes a few sherbets on away jaunts but today he sat in the back with a stonking hangover and went teetotal. He'd certainly picked a very bad day for it though, as it was to turn out. We reached the M6 with its numerous 'Toll Road Opening Soon' signs, it was like a car park and we pootled along surrounded by cones, with the motorway signs optimistically flashing '40' - if only.

After what seemed like an eternity, the traffic magically cleared, Mark hared off at breakneck speed thinking it was now okay, only to quickly run into the next wall of congestion. After a very fraught non-stop five and three quarter hour drive, we parked up in the cricket ground behind Turf Moor, just as the PA man announced the teams. We dashed to the Cricket Field End Stand behind the goal and were in our seats a prophetic 7 minutes late; the club coaches arrived about ten minutes later. There were only 345 travel-weary Millwall there and there was no atmosphere from the home fans, very unusual for Turf Moor. Millwall dominated the game and missed a hatful of chances. It should have been 5-1 but ended 1-1. We went back to the car and were quickly on the motorway.

If you wanted to produce a postcard that epitomised Northernness, a snapshot of the countryside, housing and industrial area around Burnley would fit the bill admirably. The postcard could simply say 'The North' and you'd have no argument from anyone.

After a couple of hours Mark was beginning to fall asleep at the wheel so we pulled into a services for about half an hour. We then set off and all was well until we reached the M11 at about 9pm. We heard and felt a bump from the back wheel, could smell burning and thought we had run over something. We continued a short distance before pulling off on a hard shoulder. There was no dead animal, the tyre was intact but the wheel arch was covered in fluid. Even though steering was becoming difficult Mark drove on a bit further until we reached a convenient garage, Mark replaced the original wheel with the spare and we set off again. The steering was now if anything worse, especially on the winding badly-lit country roads just outside Chelmsford. We had to stop again and pulled up outside a country pub. Mark called his dad, whose car it was, but he was reluctant to come out following the West Brom debacle and informed Mark that he'd only had the car MOT'd the week before, but the tyre in the boot was buckled and shouldn't be used. Brilliant! His insurance policy also didn't cover our rescue. Mark called his own insurance company, but unfortunately his insurance only covered his car and not him so they wanted a mortgage to come out and get us. To make things worse it was now pitch dark and pissing down.

Despite my last train out of Chelmsford rapidly approaching we decided to dump the car in the pub car park and pick it up in the morning. To show how bad the steering was, in order to push it we had to replace the tyre with the original one so that we could direct it properly, and all this palaver without the aid of a torch. Andy then called his wife to come and get us, which she did. Andy drove her and Mark to his home and Glyn to Chelmsford Station to get his train, before driving me to Shenfield where with a couple of minutes to spare I caught the 11.35pm final train to London.

17 hours door to door for me, a f...ing nightmare and no mistake. We found out later that the brake cylinder had broken and we were lucky that the back tyre hadn't fallen off as Mark mimicked Michael Schumacher on the motorway. Bugger Chris Rea and the M25 - the M6 is the real *Road To Hell*.

The next trip was **Norwich City on 8/11/2003**. I boarded an empty 'dry' train at Liverpool Street and arranged to meet the Essex Boys en route at Colchester. We expected the train to break down; amazingly, we had a trouble-free trip, arriving at Norwich station at 12.30pm. We headed straight for the nearest pub filled with Millwall and although nothing was happening, we shortly had a visit from the local constabulary. Dave Murray and his cousin, who lived locally, came in shortly after this. We had only been allocated 270 tickets, which we had to apply for via a lottery. We got our tickets separately but when we checked them in the pub we were surprised to find that we all had tickets in row B, why was to later become apparent. At about 2.30pm we left the pub with Dave remaining behind as he was walking his cousin to the home part of the ground. We walked to the stadium via a new area that looks like Romford, full of clubs, restaurants and bars. En route, we encountered the customary home collection of elderly gentleman farmers, their wives and young kids.

Inside the ground we met Dave and Johnny Lynch who travelled down with him on the train. The ticket mystery was solved because the old South Stand was being replaced by a new stand that was still under construction and they had erected a wooden wall in front of the building site with two rows of seats, A and B, stretched out in bloody great lines along its extent. There was only one way in or out so you had to 'Excuse Me' your way to your seat. It also meant that we had a dugout eye view of proceedings and couldn't see anything apart from the lino's arse. We had to stand to see anything, which led to numerous arguments with the jobsworth stewards trying to get us to sit, though they didn't have much luck. There was no proper singing from us, despite Grandad because it would have been a Chinese whispers affair. The home fans were quite vocal though continually stinging Muscat's ears with abuse, I find them unthreatening, but then I'm not a gypsy burglar. Highlighting their 'Get Orf My Land!' mentality they sang 'We Shoot Burglars!'. I've never seen us win at Norwich, we haven't won there for donkey's years and this game was no different. We had old boy Darren Huckerby tormenting us all afternoon and lost 3-1. The Essex boys, Johnny Lynch and I headed back to the station and we spent most of the train trip reminiscing about the good old days when we actually used to win away.

Paul, Nathan Ted, Simon, Pat and I drove to **Reading on 15/11/2003**. We arrived early, parked in the huge club car park and Ted had his obligatory row with a parking steward, before we took up our position on the newly named Fosters Stand. In total contrast to my lino's arse view at Norwich, Simon Pat and I had to move twice before eventually ending up in someone else's seats in the penultimate row underneath the roof beams. Whilst the others were okay our policy of sitting where we liked came unstuck due to a 2000-plus away turn of a 'Don't Go Away Very Often - You're In My Seat!' variety. Wise and Wilkins had now taken over the reins so there was no 'Judas' McGhee edge to the game and overall it was very low key. Apart from our musical chairs episode, nothing much to report other than we suffered yet another defeat, 1-0 this time.

The next match at **Bradford City on 29/11/2003** was a 5.35pm kick off on Sky, an odd time for a match and a first for me. As none of my London mates were going, ordinarily I'd have gone with the Essex Boys but due to the late kick-off I wouldn't be able to guarantee getting back to Essex in time to get a London train, so I went on the club coach on my own. Our coach together with a half-empty Junior Lions coach, bizarrely left at 10am, leaving seven hours to get there. Bradford must have moved further North since my last visit.

The trip consisted of a lengthy cloudburst, steward John doing a mammoth quiz in aid of a local hospice and a *Vote for Jim* Jim

Davidson video which managed to offend every woman on board. We stopped at Donington for three quarters of an hour and arrived at the newly named Bradford & Bingley Stadium at 3.20pm. As it was so early the ground was shut so I headed off behind the stretched out Millwall coach contingent looking for a pub. We did this via an archetypal Northern street with a bloody steep gradient. The area appeared to be largely Asian, with Bangladeshi youth clubs dotted about. As I breathlessly struggled up the incline several Millwall youths ahead of me were confronted by local knife-wielding Asians. Thankfully, apart from making dire threats, nothing happened. At the top of the hill was a pub, the Bradford Arms, and although there were some local fans we made up the bulk of the clientele. I was pleasantly surprised to find that a pint of Fosters was only £1.75; being used to London prices I practically fainted at the cheapness.

This first pint was served in a glass, however, to highlight the Millwall factor perfectly. After we had been in situ for a few minutes two police officers came in and did a tour of the pub, after which my second pint suddenly shot up to £2 and was served in a plastic container, a coincidence I'm sure. I spent an hour in the pub before setting off to the ground to meet up with the others in the upper tier of the renamed TL Dallas stand, behind the goal. Due to the kick-off and TV this match was what I'd call a hardcore enthusiasts-only affair with only 244 making the effort. On the entertainment front Bradford's Muppet was called Billy Bantam, a bloody great maroon and yellow cockerel - we agreed that it was the biggest cock we had ever seen! There was also a prat wearing a Bradford kit with a bowler hat, briefcase and brolly, mimicking Bradford & Bingley's logo; jobs must be hard to come by up North. Thankfully the 'City Slickers' were still there for me to nonce at.

When we took a seemingly unassailable 2-0 first half lead, to salute managerial debutante Bryan 'Captain Marvel' Robson and Bradford's directors we sang 'We Want Robson Out!'/'Robson Out!' and 'Sack The Board!'. Bradford got a goal back in the second half and their fans began to sing, in response we sang 'You Only Sing When You're Losing!'. I should've known the game would end how it did, it had all the right ingredients; Bradford hadn't beaten

Millwall for something like fifteen years, they hadn't won since September 16th 2002 and they had a brand new manager. A last minute defeat was a cast-iron certainty, and we lost 3-2, with the added bonus that we threw away a 2-0 lead. At the end of the game the PA blasted out *That's The Way I like It*. It's not the bloody way I like it, I can tell you. I boarded the coach in a state of shock and the home fans took the piss from the street.

The next match was **Cardiff City on 20/12/2003**; a 12.30pm kick-off, again live on Sky. It was our first visit since the heavily publicised aggro at Ninian on 7/8/1999 and followed Millwall and Cardiff starring in the BBC2 *Hooligan* documentaries. Unsurprisingly it was a Category C game and we were given only 600 terrace tickets. We had to buy a ticket voucher, which could only be exchanged for a match ticket in transit on a 7am club coach.

Nearer to the game, Millwall announced that fans could travel under their own steam to Wales, although they still had to buy a match voucher and coach ticket, albeit at a reduced rate, and then board a police-escorted coach with the rest of us. We were to gather at Cardiff West services J33 on the M4 by 10.45am. The draconian measures were an alternative to banning us from the game and theoretically meant that the Heddlu were able to stop anyone travelling directly to the ground separately. There were rumours that coach companies didn't want to take us to Cardiff, not because of us, but because of violence encountered when they had taken other sides there. I can honestly say that I've never seen Millwall cause any damage to our own coaches. I got the tickets/vouchers for Andy, Mark, Glyn, my cousin Paul and me on the first morning that they went on sale so we had tickets 1-5 on coach one, there's keen for you. Apart from Glyn, this was to be their first taste of the delights of club coach travel. I had a lie in until 5.30am before getting the tube; the others had to get the first train out of Colchester/Chelmsford at 5am.

We met up at the New Den and our half-dozen coaches left in convoy in a pre-sunrise gloom. For the entire journey, it was pissing down and misty, in fact it was dark all the way there. Andy brought enough food to feed the whole coach and we ate it between the five of us - it was good practice for the Christmas pig-out. We stopped at services in the West Country before continuing to the tolls on the Severn Bridge and bandit country. As we went through the tolls our coach nearly went into a full-blown skid but thankfully the driver contained it and we continued into Wales singing our pro-English/anti-Welsh repertoire with gusto whilst waving St George flags and inflatable sheep. We arrived at Cardiff West where several police meat wagons and mobile video units were parked outside. The Metropolitan Police were also there. Inside the services it was like an England rugby shirts, Stone Island and Burberry fashion parade and everyone eyed each other suspiciously, but surprisingly there were no Soul Crew there. We picked up the car drivers, before our coaches left under police escort at 11.15am. Millwall ticket staff then handed out match tickets in exchange for our vouchers. I sat in the aisle seat for the bulk of the journey up next to Paul. He hadn't had the pleasure before so I told him what it was usually like at Cardiff/Swansea.

When we left the services I sat by the window so that I could head any bricks away; joking aside, I was fully expecting an attack at any moment, but unusually nothing happened and within half an hour we were on the outskirts of Cardiff with the Millennium Stadium in the distance. In 1999, we drove through the city centre, this time we left the motorway and drove straight in to Ninian Park. We pulled up outside the ground at 11.40am and I was glad to see that the 'Millwall Scum' luminous graffiti was still on the car park wall from our last trip.

There was now a segregated fenced-off coach area near the away section. We disembarked and sang to announce our arrival; there was still no sign of the home Boyos. The police then confiscated every inflatable, fluffy sheep or anti-Taff item and we went in. There were only 274 of us there, which the Taffs implied was due to cowardice; whatever the reason we were here and we made our way on to the John Smith's stand to the left hand side of the goal. This was the same open Grange End terrace that we occupied last time; however, it was now a covered terrace with seating at the front and terracing at the back. There were metal roof posts obstructing our view and we stood above the seating trying to get an angle to see the game. The FA told Cardiff that they could take the pitch side perimeter fencing down after this game, though it seemed that most of the fencing had already gone, save for the area in front of the Popular Bank section to our right, the main area for home hoolies last time. To the left of us were home seats and to the right of us there was an all-standing area filled with Cardiff fans reminiscent of the old away/home end at Filbert Street. The home supporters were behind segregation fencing and roof-high missile meshing, with a no man's land manned by police and stewards on their side of the fence. We fully expected a late influx of unticketed Millwall Boys to turn up at the ground at any minute to start the hoolie festivities, but they didn't and it was very flat compared to last time. The bar was open so Mark and Glyn decided to give it a bloody good seeing-to, downing five pints before the match and two at half-time! Sam Hammam was conspicuous by his absence so there was no pre-match walkabout, although the home fans still mimicked his strange head-patting gesture. The pre-match music consisted of a Harry Secombe-style operatic version of *Men Of Harlech*, which the home fans also sang all afternoon.

The game started on a sodden pitch and Andy Roberts scored after four minutes directly from a wind-assisted corner right in front of us. To highlight this we sang 'One Nil And Your Mum's A Sheep!'. The first half finished 1-1 in the freezing cold and wet. As we stood there discussing how cold it was at half-time a streaker suddenly burst from the Cardiff section to our right dressed only in a blue and white Santa hat and a smile, mad wasn't the word for it. Naturally every man commented on how 'small' he was, implying that we were all better equipped than him. In truth, he was lucky to have anything on show considering it was bloody freezing. He was covered up and led away by the stewards to much laughter.

There were signs around Ninian saying they didn't tolerate racist abuse. This obviously doesn't include anti-English or Welsh abuse, as you will see from this selection of chants/banter.

From Us To Them: Highlighting Russia beating Wales in the Euro 2004 qualifiers, someone unfurled a Russian flag and a banner that said something like 'We're Off To Portugal With All Our Pals' was positioned on the fencing facing the home fans to our right. We also sang 'We Love You Russia!'/'I'd Rather Be A Russian

Than A Taff!'/'Portugal!' and 'We're Going To Portugal, You're Not!'. To accompany the glut of English rugby shirts and flags in our section we did sheep bleating noises, our sheep-shagging repertoire, pro-English chants and the usual 'I Can't Read' plus the political 'You Can Stick The Welsh Assembly Up Your Arse, Etc - Sideways!'/ 'You're Just A Third World Country!' and 'Where Have Your Coal Mines Gone?'. In response to Cardiff's hooligan claims we sang the usual plus 'Cardiff Ran From Grandad!'. To the home fans behind the segregation fencing we sang 'It's For Your Own Protection!' as we went 2-1 and then 3-1 up we sang 'Ole, Ole, Ole You're Shit!'/'3-1 And A Long Way Home!' and 'Jingle Bells, Etc, Oh What Fun It Is To See Millwall Win Away!'. When Cardiff fans chirped up we sang 'We'd Forgotten You Were Here!'.

From Them To Us: To be honest I couldn't understand everything Cardiff sang but here's a selection ;'Always Shit On The English Side Of The Bridge!'/'London's Full Of Gypos, La, La, La, La!'/'Fight, Fight, Wherever You May Be, We F...ing Hate Millwall FC And We Don't Give A F... Whoever You May Be, We F...ing Hate Millwall FC!'/'You've Only Got Ten Boys!' and 'You'll Run Like The West Ham Fans!'.

The only crowd incident apart from the streaker came in front of the home Popular Bank side terrace following a discussion between Wise, Earnshaw and the linesman about a non-returned ball. The home fans tried to hit Wisey with coins and hit the lino instead. The match was stopped whilst the Old Bill emerged, video cameras in hand, and walked around the pitch to their section, to which Cardiff sang the splendid 'It's Just Like Watching The Bill!'.

There was no trouble in the ground so at the end of the match we were only held back for a short time before stewards and police led us out. Outside, the police had blocked off a small road to our left where a few Cardiff were waiting. They had also blocked off the car park to our right where a considerably larger group of home fans were being held back by the massed police ranks, consequently there was no trouble outside either. Singing all the while, we were soon on our way, wankering anyone who looked vaguely Welsh. We stopped at the services to drop off the drivers before heading back to London.

The media highlighted the coin-throwing incident and I would imagine they were very miffed that it had been a trouble-free day, largely due to excellent policing, which isn't something you'll hear me say very often! The police were unusually polite and good-humoured all day and although we were surrounded for the whole game, there were surprisingly no riot police on open display, which made a nice change. The match ticket said 'Enjoy Your Visit To Wales' and we sure did.

Boxing Day 2003 was a trip to **Crystal Palace** for a noon kick-off. Due to the Bank Holiday, Paul, Nathan, Dave and I had to go all around the train network to get there. It was Iain Dowie's first game in charge and to welcome him we sang 'Dowie You're An Ugly C...!'. For some reason we weren't as vocal in the ground as usual although unlike Palace at Millwall, we were still there in numbers with 4313 of us in the Arthur Wait Stand. As per usual, we took the piss out of the suburbanites, singing our customary repertoire. Specifically, there was one bald eagle who gestured to us from the Holmesdale who was naturally picked out for special treatment receiving 'Baldy, Baldy What's The Score?' and 'Baldy Takes It Up The Arse!'. The home fans were again especially mouthy in the ground, they sang 'You Live In A Tower Block!'/'One Nil And You Still Don't Sing!'/'One Brain Between Ya!' and 'Where've Your Home Crowds Gone?'.

For the record the home cheerleaders gyrated about fully-clothed for winter; where is the noncing value in that? There was one oddity in the programme, an interview with the match referee Peter Walton called 'Who's Whistling?'. What it should've been entitled was 'Who's Whistling Whenever Millwall Go Near A Palace Player?'. Whether the interview had anything to do with it, I don't know but he was a Home Town Harry par excellence. A new manager usually means a defeat, as at Bradford; however, in this instance, despite the ref we gained an extremely fortunate 1-0 win thanks to a Neil Harris goal and a Denzil penalty save, made even more exceptional because it was only one day after a piles operation on the *Only Fools And Horses* Christmas special. Never mind - Ho! Ho! Ho! and all that.

I WAS BORN UNDER THE COLD BLOW LANE

I missed Wigan away, so my next game should've been to Telford but it was postponed so my next trip was to **Crewe Alexandra on 31/1/2004**, only my second visit. I went with the Essex Boys on a busman's holiday for Andy because he's a train driver. To celebrate Andy brought his Ivor Biggun tape to entertain us.

Mark drove there in his new car on the week of the big freeze. It was raining continually and with the spray from the lying water it was like driving blind. There were also very bad side winds.

Only our combined bulk and the weight of the Stella that we had on board stopped us being blown over. We continually checked the radio and with friends/family to see if the game was on. It was, so we continued via the empty M6 toll road and, despite everything, we arrived early in the trainspotter's paradise that is Crewe, parked and headed for Gresty Road.

Inside we found that the pitch was in seemingly mint condition. Previously we sat behind the goal; today we had the whole of the side Bluebell BMW Stand despite only having 467 fans. Unfortunately, near where we sat it appeared to be a pigeon bombing range as the floor and seats were covered in bird droppings. They had added a large side stand since my last visit, which looked totally out of place in a stadium that resembled a Conference ground. Due to the stadium and family club home fans, Crewe reminded me of Division 2; the atmosphere was poor, with all the passion of Charlton/Palace. A drummer sitting behind the goal to our right accompanied what noise they did make.

Despite the home atmosphere we were in good sarcastic chant mode. For example, to the home fans/ground we sang 'Sunday League!' and 'Are You Charlton In Disguise?'. To highlight the fact that Telford had knocked Crewe out of the FA Cup we sang 'If You're All Going To Telford Clap Your Hands' and 'We're Going To Telford, You Ain't!'. In our eyes the home fans were Scousers so we sang 'You're My Scousers, My Only Scousers, You're Only Happy On Giro Day, It Doesn't Matter How Much They Pay You, Please Don't Take My Stereo Away!'. Despite the horrendous conditions one Millwall fan standing at the front took his shirt off to display his chubby physique so we questioned him about his identity; 'Are You Jordan/Geordie/Andy Fordham In Disguise?' Our main target though was the cropped-headed lino PJ Groove running the line in front of us in the first half, he was certainly a fat groove if you get my musical drift.

Among the more polite chants he got were 'Have You Ever Seen Your Cock?'; only with a mirror on a stick. 'Linesman, Linesman Give Us A Pie!'/'There's Only One Phil Mitchell (Grant Mitchell)!'/'Mitchell, Give Us A Wave!' and 'We Thought You'd Died In The River!'. In the second half, a thin linesman replaced him and was greeted with 'Where's Your Belly Gone?'. We led 1-0 at half-time and despite the abuse Mr Groove disallowed a home goal in the second half, bless him. Crewe did get an equaliser and the home fans woke up. We sang 'You Only Sing When You're Drawing!'. Crewe's only songs of note were 'You're Just A Shite Town In London!' and when we got a bit excitable in the second half they sang 'Sit Down And Behave Yourself!'. With practically the last kick of the match, Danny Dichio scored our winner and we four went berserk, running to the front like ten-year-olds to celebrate. The whistle blew to notch up our first ever win at Crewe and we left the ground singing in the rain.

My next trip was the rearranged fourth round FA Cup tie at non-League **Telford United on Wednesday 11/2/2004**. The preamble to this game was a farce from start to finish, there were two cancellations, with the first so late that most people had already left, with some even reaching Shropshire. People had lost money on non-refundable coach/train tickets and time off work. Travelling to this game was also a farce; to get there by train meant going all around the Midlands and West Ham were playing at Wolves so Euston would have been fun, in the end their game was switched to Sunday. There were also rumours that Shrewsbury fans were trying to get tickets to have a pop at us. Reacting to this, West Mercia Police tried to impose ridiculous travelling restrictions, which Millwall wouldn't accept. I believe they wanted it to be similar to the Cardiff match with everyone travelling by coach. However, this would have required 30 coaches or so, which wasn't practical. It all smacked of Leigh RMI away hysteria to me.

I WAS BORN UNDER THE COLD BLOW LANE

We were eventually allowed to travel under our own steam and Paul agreed to drive Simon, Patrick, Nathan and me to the original game, leaving Walthamstow at 10am. Everyone had been looking forward to the game due to Telford's disrespectful attitude and our 1450 allocation sold out very quickly. Their third round victory against Crewe was lauded as a giant-killing whereas drawing us was met with disdain. The reaction of Telford's players to the draw on TV and their manager's subsequent TV and press comments was what really wound everyone up, including Millwall's players. Telford's website also seemingly implied that beating us was something of a formality. On there I noticed that their home match on January 10th had been postponed due to poor drainage, so I told everyone to check before setting off. I checked Teletext at 8.50am, which said nothing about a pitch inspection, let alone anything else. I set off happy all was well and then had a nightmare trip arriving 15 minutes late. We were due to pick up Nathan in Chingford but heard on the radio that it was off before we got that far. Paul dropped us back at the station and we headed back home.

The Essex Boys had also set off and were already into the beers when I called them and they too turned back. Still, at least we were in the fifth round draw for the first time since 1994/95 when we knocked out Arsenal and Chelsea, before losing to QPR in the fifth round. We drew Burnley at home; I don't know whether they were sufficiently big for Telford. We didn't know until practically the day of the rearranged match whether it would be at Millwall, Telford or a neutral ground. Eventually, thanks to the home club's valiant efforts, a £15,000 hot air balloon, dozens of helpers and 40 tons of sand it eventually went ahead a few days before the fifth round. Telford must have lost a fortune with the costs of the above, stewarding, catering, etc and the loss of the money from the BBC, scheduled to show 30 minutes highlights of the first game on *Match Of The Day*. Many Millwall fans also returned their tickets for a refund with the original sell-out allocation reduced to 997 on the night. Despite their losses, Telford turned down Theo Paphitis' offer to play the game at the New Den and for them to keep the takings. We had been hitting

Telford's website for days prior to the go-ahead. My cousin Paul had become a phone stalker, calling Telford practically every day. Having confirmed it was on, Nathan drove Paul, Simon, Patrick and I to Shropshire.

We had an uneventful journey and arrived at 'Telford - Birthplace of Industry' at 5.30pm. We noticed that most car parks were shut so we parked in the car park at the Bucks Head Stadium, which looked like a smaller scale Sixfields from outside. We went to get some food on the main road and noticed that the pub closest to the ground was shut and local police were already patrolling the streets augmented by London police. The best comedy moment came as we walked back towards the away end - four police were walking in front of us, stopped outside the away end and began knocking on the doors to get in, accompanied with the customary phrase 'Open up, it's the police'. After a couple of fruitless attempts to gain access, they said 'Open up it's the police - honest!' We all found this highly amusing; perhaps you had to be there.

Once The Frank Nagington Stand turnstiles opened at 6.30pm, we went inside. In the programme, there was a picture of Telford's players looking elated at the Cup draw, a bit of spin there I think. The match ticket was equally odd because it had a seat number but also said 'Standing Only'. Inside we found that it was going to be a throwback to the joys of terracing. We took up a position on the top step of a covered terrace right behind the goal with the Essexites. Apart from the DJ's dubious musical taste Telford's ground wasn't too bad - there was one seated grandstand, two covered terraces at each end of the ground and one open side terrace with a large luminous scoreboard/clock centred above it. Telford had apparently spent £12million on renovating their stadium though they seemingly had spent nothing on the pitch, a bit like building a pub and forgetting to put a bar in. The pitch looked like it was only suitable for sandcastles and donkey rides; I was rather hoping that they were going to have women's beach volleyball as pre-match entertainment, unfortunately not. Naturally, we pointed out the state of the pitch, one bloke near me shouted out 'You'll be alright to start the building when the cement turns up!'. Naturally, we also sang the obligatory 'Oh, I Do Like To Be Beside The Seaside!'. As per usual we abused the officials running around the cinder track in front of us pre-match and the cuddliest one of them, a linesman, conducted our abuse. Home Muppet Benny The Buck, was the thinnest I*t's A Knockout* effort I'd ever seen and fell flat on its face right in front of us on a particularly sandy part of the pitch, just as we were stinging his ears with the usual abuse.

At half-time Benny threw sweets into the crowd and managed to hit a policeman full in the face, after which we warmed to him. In schoolboy prank mode someone let off a stink bomb in the away toilets but the strangest thing was a bloke sitting in the seats to our left in a sixties West Ham shirt, oddly not the first time this has happened away. He got the full gamut of West Ham abuse and responded by standing up and kissing his shirt, until the stewards threw him and his friends out and we cheerfully wankered him on his way. The vast majority of the home fans were fairly quiet and contentedly waved their white balloons. One fan even waved the obligatory silver foil FA Cup. There were about ten home 'Boys' to our right who gave us the odd rendition of 'Who The F...ing Hell Are You?' and 'Division One? You're Having A Laugh!'. We countered with the customary piss-poor opposition abuse, plus 'Sheep, Sheepshaggers!' and 'You're Welsh And You Know You Are!'. Telford's team didn't go for us in the gung-ho fashion that we thought they would and we comfortably won 2-0. To highlight our victory we sang 'Shit Pitch - No Cup!'.

In truth the match was an anti-climax following all the rigmarole we had been through. We left the ground and had to take a police-inspired detour through streets full of officers and with a police helicopter circling above us. There seemed to be a few local 'Boys' hanging about but we saw no trouble ourselves and got to our car unscathed. Telford was only my second trip to a non-League ground with my only other one being a visit to Dagenham in December 1981, which had also been an on-off affair.

The next away trip was the long journey to **Preston North End on 21/2/2004**. I made my fourth visit to Deepdale with Mark, Andy and Glyn. We had an easy lager and food-filled trip and parked in the exact same spot as last season. We again sat on the left hand side of the Bill Shankly Kop, with the mouthy home youths and the enormously irritating band to the right of us.

For the record local crooner Stephen Bayliss sang two songs from the centre circle before the match and Preston's Muppet was a strange bird thing called Deepdale Duck, but strangest of all was the home fans going in to raptures when they got a corner, singing 'We've Got A Corner!'. There were quite a few exchanges between our section and the home pubescents to our right. To their monotonous drum/bugle accompaniment we sang 'Craigy Brown Sex Offender!' Yet another hapless manager to join our sex offender register. On the boasting front they sang 'You Think You're Hard, You're Having A Laugh!', in response we sang the usual crap opposition chants and 'Have You Ever Been To Millwall? Have You F…!'. To mimic their 'P.N.E.' chant and hoolie boasts we sang 'A & E!'. They sang that London was 'A Town Full Of Faggots!'we replied that Preston was 'A Town Full Of Orphans!'.

As at Crewe a bloke in our section, seemingly possessed by a Geordie, decided that although it was freezing he'd take his shirt off; cue a torrent of fatist abuse from the home fans. The stewards and police then came onto our steep stand to castigate a bloke for having the audacity to stand up and sing! We knew that they couldn't eject us all so with typical Millwall petulance we stood up and sang 'Stand Up If You Love Millwall!'. They buggered off and left us alone. It was a good day in all and we won 2-1, my first ever win there.

I went to **Sheffield United on Tuesday 2/3/2004** on my own on a club coach. I arranged to meet the Essex Boys in the ground. There was one club and one Junior Lions coach and we had an easy, sun-filled trip up featuring another exceptionally moody video, *Monster* starring Charlize Theron, for which she'd won the Best Actress Oscar on the previous day.

There were a couple of signs that it would be a 'turn the coach around and go home' game: Wisey had been awarded Nationwide Manager of the Month for February - the kiss of death - and United were going through a rough patch.

Tonight's match was like *Groundhog Day*. We stopped at Donington services and met our police escort at the Catcliffe roundabout. It was my third consecutive Tuesday night trip to Bramall Lane and third consecutive defeat by a single goal, having largely dominated the game. The home crowd atmosphere had been quiet/loud/quiet. The teams again came out to *Star Wars* and their Muppet was still a Captain Pugwash thing. An unlucky female walked past us and received the obligatory sexual innuendos, the only difference being that tonight the girl was what we in London call a 'Right Doris' i.e. very attractive. We again chanted 'cheat!' at the home side.

Referee Frazer Stretton was so bad that the home fans booed him at half-time and we booed him during the second half and at the end of the match. Probably due to him, there was a large-scale punch up between both sides and as the ever-loveable Neil Warnock stuck his not insubstantial hooter in, we sang 'Sit Down Pinocchio' and the less cultured 'F... Off Warnock!'. To be fair to the ref the home side theatrically rolled around after every tackle; I think that some of the five minutes injury-time at the end was to allow them to do their curtain calls.

There were a few changes:

1) The PA worked and the home side were introduced as the 'Red Wizards'.

2) The Arnold Laver Stand to our right had the third of its length near us covered in netting due to previous aggro.

We sat in the front row of the alarmingly steep upper tier of the same stand as before, now called the Gordon Lamb Stand. Unfortunately, you cannot see the goal beneath unless you stand up or dangle over the front wall.

As both sides were in the FA Cup quarter-finals, the match was very tentative. Despite Paul Shaw playing for United he amazingly didn't score, but we still lost 2-1. I'd still not seen us win at Sheffield United. The homebound trip consisted of seeing Shaw at Watford Gap, karaoke renditions over the mike and a Happy Birthday salute to Larry on the stroke of midnight. Unfortunately, the coach went to and from the M1 via the West End and I was stuck south of the river. I decided to walk from the Elephant rather than the ground as Rotherhithe Tunnel was closed. I set off at 1.30am and arrived home an hour later - I could have done without it in truth.

THE LION ROARS BACK TO LIFE

Having beaten Burnley, we reached the FA Cup quarter-final for the first time in 19 years. When we drew **Tranmere Rovers at home** we appeared to have our easiest passage to the semi-finals ever following Walsall and Burnley at home and Telford away. That said, we hadn't reached the FA Cup semis since 1937 and ominously I'd never seen Millwall win a major cup quarter-final. To date I'd seen two losing League Cup quarter-finals, Norwich City and Swindon, and two losing FA Cup quarter-finals, Ipswich Town in 1978 and Luton Town in 1985, the last two also ending in a 'riot'. In the build-up the media naturally majored on our previous misdemeanours and following Stan Ternent's ill-founded Mo Camara rant they portrayed a visit to the New Den as something akin to a Nazi Rally.

The game was live on BBC's *Match of the Day* on **Sunday 7/3/2004** at 1pm so we were graced with the Scouse Mafia of Hansen, Lawrenson and Reid. Not to mention the sarcastic Gary Lineker, who dissed a lunchtime trip to Millwall on a West Ham v Fulham Cup highlights programme shortly before this game. I'm sure they must have relished their trip to the New Den.

The crowd was swelled but the atmosphere diluted by a large glory-hunting contingent. The big flag got an airing and people dug out their Wembley and Division 2 Champions flags. I thought it was comical when PA man Les explained that the East and West stands had seat numbers and people had to sit in the correct seats, adding 'For those who have not been here before, these are the two big side stands' - no need for sarcasm, not bloody much! There was also a couple of thousand Tranmere fans who sang a very sarcastic chant 'It's Only Millwall - Come On Tranmere!'. The club pointedly had anti-racism adverts in the programme and there was a huge banner across the empty Lower North stand, with continual references over the PA about not blackening the clubs name further, no pun intended.

I found the game very flat, save for Kevin Muscat's penalty miss and although we should've won comfortably we drew 0-0. Tranmere Rovers black forward Eugene Dadi's likely racist reception was the main point of focus in the days prior to the game. With the press probably sending not only their sports reporters but also news reporters and war correspondents to the game, they must have been miffed that the worst Dadi got was hairdo abuse and nothing violent happened. Prior to the replay, we found ourselves in the semi-final draw. We avoided Man U and Arsenal and drew Sunderland in a repeat of the game 67 years before, continuing the seemingly easier route to the final and Europe!

On **13/3/2004** we went to **Ipswich Town** for my sixth visit. Paul drove Nathan, Simon, Pat and I on a very easy trip to Suffolk, with Millwall on a cup run and in play-off contention. We arrived very early and parked in a car park close to the ground that resembled a gypsy site. Oil drums, skips and tyres littered it. We wondered if we would have any wheels left or a car at all when we got back, nevertheless we left it and walked past the huge Planet Blue Ipswich club shops en route to the town centre. Pat appeared to be possessed by Mad Ted because he greeted every local we passed with 'Ooo Ar!' as though it was a normal greeting; luckily, the rustic home folk were too docile to take offence.

In the shopping area, we wandered around in Millwall colours and I was glad to see that there was not a bandwagon-jumping football shirt in sight with only Millwall/Ipswich merchandise on view. We had a McDonald's before heading to the ground; we went inside and again took up position in the still unrenovated Cobbold Stand upper tier among 1195 Lions. Portman Road used to have a good atmosphere, when the away end was a covered shed behind the goal next to the home fans; sadly, the home atmosphere in the all-seater ground is now very quiet.

The PA played *Papa's Got A Brand New Pig Bag*, *The Great Escape* and *No Limit* as the teams came out, which failed to rouse the home fans from their slumber. On the entertainment front Ipswich had two mad Muppets in the guise of politically correct *My Little Pony* horse creatures, one black and one white, naturally we abused them in time-honoured fashion. The ever-lovely Joe Royle had numerous colour pictures in the club programme for us to treasure. The most bizarre thing though was the half-time competition to win a DVD of Ipswich's 1978 FA Cup win against the Arse, where the contestants tried to re-enact Ipswich's winning goal *Phoenix From The Flames* style, managing to make complete prats of themselves in the process.

THE LION ROARS BACK TO LIFE

The game was a great performance by both the team and us resulting in an excellent 3-1 win against one of our main play-off rivals. We were loud and sarcastic all afternoon, singing the usual rustic/farmyard repertoire. The PA played *Tom Hart* when Ipswich scored their consolation goal and we E.I.O'd our way through it to take the piss. We repeated this performance each time the home side had a wayward effort. After the game we went back to Paul's car, which, thankfully, was still in one piece and we drove off before being caught in traffic. Suddenly Neil Harris walked up the side of us in a Millwall tracksuit; everyone of a Millwall persuasion greeted him enthusiastically for his two goals in the game. Pat was still hyperactive and insisted that he needed to greet some more yokels before we left Ipswich. He stuck his head out of the sunroof and 'Ooo Ar'ed' everyone that we passed, several of whom gave him the finger.

Paul, Nathan, Dave, Simon, Pat and I went to **Tranmere Rovers for the FA Cup Quarter-Final Replay on Tuesday 16/3/2004**, on one of nine club coaches of varying quality that departed at 1.30pm. We had never won at Tranmere and they hadn't lost an FA Cup replay at home since 1929, so the portents weren't good.

Our coach was of the older vintage, with a video but no videos. It had a toilet but unfortunately it became full on the way up. It was to be an aromatic trip because our journey also took us through umpteen muckspreadings. We stopped with another club coach at Stafford services where two police cars immediately arrived and parked right next to us, a coincidence I'm sure. We continued north to the land of the almost Scousers - Birkenhead - past Port Sunlight's Industrial City of lights, very impressive if a tad smoky. We drove unescorted through the leafy suburbs around the ground and road signs suddenly appeared when we were only a few hundred yards from the stadium.

We arrived outside the away end at 7pm and for some reason the police then forced us to drive right around the ground to empty out our coaches in the home car park. We stood up to get off only for a Mersey Beat WPC to get aboard and demand that we sit down so she could gives us the usual tosh. Having delivered her address, which we totally ignored, she disembarked and let us do the same. As per usual, the local police carried massive billy sticks; they were also accompanied by barking Alsatians and 'Caught on camera CCTV' mobile vans. At the away entrances we were searched before being allowed on to the peculiarly shaped Cowshed Stand (?) behind the goal.

It was my third trip to Prenton Park and since my visit in the 1990s it had been completely revamped and is now all-seater. In addition to our covered end there was a huge stand, The Kop, at the opposite end, one large side grandstand to our right and a smaller side stand to our left. Naturally, we ignored our tickets and took up the best position we could on the crowded stand with 2023 Millwall. Emotionally I felt fine until we were in the ground before the nerves set in. To offset this I psyched myself up for a night of primal screaming, which worked a treat.

Continuing the day's aromatic theme, many people appeared to be smoking copious amounts of soothing ganja to calm their nerves. Tranmere's on-pitch announcer, aided by their Muppet, a dog thing called Diane, was trying to whip the home fans into a frenzy and a drummer in The Kop accompanied their 'Super White Army' chants. Alarmingly, Uriah Rennie was our comedy ref for the evening, ye Gods!

The teams came out to the theme to *The Rockford Files* for reasons best known to Tranmere and the game started as we made a hell of a racket from inside our police/steward cordon. We scored two early goals through Cahill and Harris, prompting wild celebration among us and quietening the home fans. The Wirral appears to breed posher types than your average stereotypical Scouser, but despite the family club home support there were a few foolhardy locals to our left who tried to rile us when we went 2-0 up, strange timing I thought. Although strictly not Scousers, we still greeted them with our usual Liverpool abuse. Having made themselves the focus of attention the Home Herberts were unceremoniously dragged out by stewards and we waved them goodbye.

Against the run of play Tranmere got a goal back on 40 minutes and *I Got You (I Feel Good)* blasted from the dicky PA, which sounded on the verge of blowing at any minute. Millwall as per usual put us through the emotional wringer in the second half with a rearguard action after having been cruising in the first half, which was made more fraught by Rennie's eccentric display. With injury-time seemingly going on for an eternity we whistled cacophonously to try to get him to blow the bloody whistle. We had been loud all night but when the final whistle eventually blew we went ballistic. The players and Wisey came over to acknowledge our support and celebrate to our backdrop of arm pumping 'EIO'/'No One Likes Us' and pro-Wisey repertoire. We also sang 'Are You Watching Mark McGhee?'/'Now You're Gonna Believe Us, We're Gonna Win The Cup!' and 'If You're All Going Old Trafford Clap Your Hands!'.

We stood stunned at making the semis and Tranmere fans applauded us as they left the ground, so we returned the applause for their side's spirited display. We boarded our coaches, now outside the away end, and the driver tried to get a confession from the arch criminals who'd brought six tins of beer aboard, which he fortunately found before the police. No one 'fessed up so he gave up. It was strangely subdued on the coach, I think everyone was in shock.

As our loo was broken we stopped at services in the Midlands and ended up staying for 30 minutes as everyone queued for provisions. A couple of my immediate number, no names no pack drill, decided that the food was free and we 'inadvertently' acquired a couple of china plates as well. Still, serves the buggers right. I eventually arrived home after a fifteen-hour day at 3.30am. 'FA Cup semi-finals! Quick nurse, the smelling salts!' The press were beginning to realise that there was a real possibility of our appearing in the FA Cup Final and the UEFA Cup, a prospect that they viewed with horror and no little trepidation.

In an already fantastic week, we now had the mouth-watering visit of **West Ham United on Sunday 21/3/2004**. As an East Ender, this was my most eagerly awaited game of the week. On Bolina Road's railway arches near the North Stand there are these cheery messages; 'B Whackers Kill West Ham'/'WHU R.I.P'/'Welcome 2 Millhell - Treatment' and 'Turn Back Or Die!'. The latter featured in *The Football Factory*, which should make them feel welcome. Naturally, the game was all-ticket/members only and a noon kick-off.

It was the Happy Hammers first ever visit to the New Den and they were given the whole of the North Stand, an allocation of 3700, of which they took up only 2869. A shortfall presumably due to Mother's Day, the threat of aggro and the safer alternative of watching the beam back at Upton Park. The New Den game had the largest British football police operation ever costing £270,000, with 1100 police apparently orchestrated personally by Scotland Yard. The Essex Boys saw hundreds of Hammers boys bundled on specials at Stratford station by dozens of riot police, my usual East End mates saw police aplenty at both Whitechapel and Canning Town stations and I saw numerous meat wagons flying along the A13, confirming the widespread nature of their operation. We arrived early and were luckily able to park in our normal spot; strangely, we didn't see many police near the ground.

For the record, Andy's son George had been the mascot against Gillingham in December and today his son Alex was Millwall's mascot. Although the crowd was only 14,055, due mostly to the Membership requirement, the Millwall areas were roaring like the Old Den and there were numerous police, including cavalry, in the four corners of the ground. To welcome our loathed neighbours we booed their team as they came out for the pre-match warm-up and sang 'Miiiilllllwaaaalll' through their team announcement, naturally we also sang our usual abusive Hammers repertoire.

With the way that the game was to pan out, we were able to take the piss in response to anything that they sang, very similar to the Palace home game in 2001. The West Ham fans now massed on the away end sang 'I'm Forever Blowing Bubbles'. In response we sang 'You Can Stick Your F...ing Bubbles Up Your Arse - Sideways!'. Why are they forever blowing bubbles? Did someone write it whilst sitting in a bath after they had eaten a tin of baked beans? West Ham also sang the bizarre 'Where's Your Caravan?', famous for its caravans, Bermondsey is. To highlight the large Asian area around Upton Park we sang 'You're Just A Small Town In Bengal!' and in homage to their relegation manager we sang 'There's Only One Glen Roeder!'. To rub in the ease of our victory we sang 'You're Shit And

THE LION ROARS BACK TO LIFE

You Know You Are!'/'Can We Play You Every Week?'/'West Ham Are Going Nowhere!' and 'Don't Cry West Ham, Don't Cry!'.

It was a very windy day, although not as windy as West Ham's defence, epitomised by Christian Dailly, Hammers captain and famous religious newspaper, who scored a cracking own goal and received a Tony Norman style selection; 'We Love You Dailly Oh Yes We Do!'/'Dailly, Dailly What's The Score?'/'Dailly Plays For Millwall!' and 'There's Only One Christian Dailly!'. We also screamed 'Shoot!' each time he was anywhere near his own goal. More bizarrely, on the Hobbit-spotting and fashion front he got 'There's Only One Frodo Baggins' and 'Dailly's Got An Afro!'.

At 3-1, with West Ham's team wilting in the atmosphere, their goalie Bywater was sent off after clattering into Neil Harris, giving away a penalty in the process, at which point a couple of hundred West Ham 'Boys' in the North Lower attempted to invade the pitch. Presumably trying to get the game abandoned they surged towards the front of the stand, clashing with stewards and tearing up the massive anti-racism banner stretched across the front couple of rows behind the goal and then pulled up the segregation meshing. Millwall's 'Boys' in the West Lower greeted this attempt to get a riot started by verbally abusing them but not making any concerted efforts to get on the pitch. Perversely, the fact that Millwall didn't attempt to confront them was probably seen as a Hammers Hoolie victory. Hooligan or not, why would any Millwall fan risk getting a match against the enemy abandoned that we were strolling?

The New Den echoed to Millwall chanting 'Scum!' and the CBL sang the ironic 'We're The Best Behaved Supporters In The Land - When We Win! We're A Right Bunch Of Bastards When We Lose!' chant. Eventually stewards, police, riot police armed with shields and batons and cavalry, encircled the Hammers. We sarcastically greeted their deployment with 'Laurel And Hardy' and 'Nee Naw!'.

We eventually won 4-1, my best ever win over the 'Academy'. However it could easily have been six or seven with Millwall missing two penalties, our third in a row. Still, mustn't be greedy. To rub it in Millwall did an 'Ole' ball-keeping performance in the second half that consisted of 27 unopposed passes. This Mother's

Day massacre was one of my Millwall-supporting highlights. It does not get any sweeter than this. At the end of the match, we saluted the team, Theo, Wilkins and Wise. I was delirious, I even found myself enjoying *Rockin' All Over The World* blasting over the PA as we gleefully headed out of the CBL.

The unhappy Hammers were held in the ground for over an hour, giving them ample time to destroy the toilets in the away stand, whilst the streets were cleared before being herded back to their transport by the police. Clive gave me a lift home and the radio was alive with calls about West Ham's attempted invasion. Amazingly, the tabloids at least, referred to the troublemakers as West Ham thugs, complete with colour pics; wonders will never cease.

I went out in the East End on the night for a celebratory light ale, grinning from ear to ear like an idiot. This emphatic win gave all us East End/Essex people piss-taking rights for many weeks after and did we milk it? Oh, yes! Happy days.

I gave my West Ham chum Ian a few days mourning before going in to his shop to wind him up and apart from trying to throw me out, he told me that there had been a pitched battle between a hundred or so riot police and a large West Ham 'firm' at Shadwell station early on Sunday morning. He said West Ham had pelted the police with bricks and bottles as they were preventing them from entering the station. This wasn't mentioned in the media, not even the local press.

Our next match was on **Wednesday, 24/3/2004 at Wimbledon** in their passionless National Hockey Stadium, Milton Keynes - a town most notable for its concrete cows. It was a new ground for all of us, taking my League ground tally to 93.

Just prior to our visit Wimbledon were given permission to change their name to Milton Keynes Dons, which sounds like a speedway team to me. Whatever I think of the merits of the name, it finally severed any tenuous link that they had to the original South London club. I think the relocation was a disgrace and Koppel was lucky that Wimbledon have such inoffensive fans. Can you imagine what would have happened if he had to face our type of supporters, having tried to move us 50 miles away? Rather like the end of Mussolini I'd imagine. I don't think he'd have liked the outcome much.

Dave drove Simon, Patrick, Nathan and I the short distance to North Berkshire. After crossing nine roundabouts (!) we parked in the stadium car park at 6.30pm; the area around the ground was like a small retail park and we had a McMeal before going into the West Stand behind the goal, where we met the Essex deputation and various other away day regulars. It was a peculiar stadium, like a scaled up Subbuteo ground. The two end stands were temporary erections, as was the side North Stand; however, whilst the two end stands stretched the length of the pitch, the side stand only took up about a third of one side. These three stands were open to the elements and despite the fact that we were in the open air they were 'No Smoking'. The remaining stand to our right was an impressive and large covered grandstand. To complete the temporary nature of the stadium the toilets were Portaloos.

Rather like Brighton the tickets were an outrageous £20, although it was also a 'Kid for a Quid' night, as fellow pot-less club Bury did a few years back. The game was allegedly all-ticket although we found that you could pay on the night and there were also Millwall in the North Stand to our left. Lecherously I was hoping that as we were in a hockey stadium we would be treated to St Trinian's style schoolgirl hockey as pre-match entertainment but sadly there were no jolly hockey sticks. The home side came out to *Who Let The Dogs Out?* and *U Can't Touch This*. The way they played it was more like *U Can't Watch This*!

Abusively in the second half every time Wimbledon's cropped-headed beanpole goalie Scott Bevan went near the ball he got 'Freak!' and 'There's Only One Uncle Fester!'. Despite this, he gave us a cheery wave after the match. We stood up all night watching a non-event, no atmosphere, a Division 3 level crowd of 3037, including 944 Millwall, and it was so bloody cold that we had to stamp our feet to try to stop them freezing. Wimbledon were effectively already relegated even at this early stage and we continued our fantastic run by winning 1-0. The most entertaining event on the night though was a girl in a pink top and coat standing by the Millwall stand to our left. She appeared to have had a few and kept trying to show us her breasts, accompanied by the usual requests from us men. In the end, the police took umbrage and tried to eject her. She didn't go quietly, knocking one of them over the advertising hoardings surrounding the pitch, then put up spirited resistance as burly coppers tried to drag her out. Eventually the police won and threw her out and we sang 'Bring Her Back!'. Sadly they didn't. Our win meant that we again rose to fifth, elbowing West Ham out of the top six in the process. That joy aside, it was a very depressing evening especially in the wake of the Hammers game.

I missed Walsall away, only my second missed game home or away all season, so my next game was the **FA Cup Semi-Final against Sunderland at Old Trafford on Sunday 4/4/2004** at 1pm, a repeat of the 1937 semi-final and another encounter with Big Mick. It promised to be the noisiest semi-final ever between two passionate clubs famous for their 'roars', particularly at Roker and the Old Den.

Despite the club seemingly getting their ticket office shit together this season, the semi ticket arrangements were a bafflement. We had an allocation of 30,000 tickets so by my calculation if it had been two tickets per Teamcard/Membership our 'official' fans would have filled the allocation easily. Millwall's decision to make it one ticket only was always doomed to fail, the maths just didn't add up. There was also a pecking order for the tickets and our problem was that in our combined group some were only members, requiring several visits or a wait of several days to get the tickets. In the end my cousin Gavin got his and his kids junior season ticket enclosure tickets on Wednesday 24th March. I got the London/Dorset contingents' tickets on 'season ticket holders only' day on Thursday and Gavin's brother Paul queued on Sunday straight after a nightshift for the Essex Boys' and Dave Simms' ticket as he didn't have a season ticket. Millwall subsequently panicked after this and abandoned the policy of having to have a Tranmere ticket to get extra tickets; even so, we still undersold our allocation by 9000, told you so! Why they didn't adopt the two tickets per Teamcard policy in the first place I don't know.

THE LION ROARS BACK TO LIFE

In the build-up to the match we received more publicity than we ordinarily did although there seemed to be a policy whereby if they mentioned us in a good light they had to counteract it with something negative, particularly prevalent in the tabloids. They were also keen to point out that our fans' behaviour would be under the spotlight, with a warning from Greater Manchester Police about the huge operation that they were putting in place, both inside the ground and in the town centre. Strangely, Sunderland, who as I said have a very large arrest record, weren't mentioned at all - there goes that balanced reporting again.

With rail works on the day of the game, people had various methods of getting to Manchester. Some even chartered planes, others stayed the weekend up north. Gavin drove up on Friday with his son and daughter and stayed with friends in Leeds. Colin managed to book a hotel room in the city centre, and drove up on Friday with his brother-in-law, his son and one of his friends. Colin's son Chris is at Music University in Manchester and coincidentally his band were doing a gig there on Saturday night, which he was able to see. It seemed that most people chose to drive or go by official or unofficial coach on the day. The Essex contingent left at 6am on Sunday in Andy's people-carrier, laden to the gunwales with cases of Stella, cracked into before the sun was up, let alone over the yardarm. In honour of the special occasion, Mark penned an adapted 'Oh Wisey' drinking song 'Oh! Stella, Wowo, Etc, It's Only 5 Point 2 But It's A Lovely Brew! Etc!'. For the record Mark and Glyn managed to polish off 48 small bottles of Stella between them during the whole trip, accompanied by three pints of Budweiser in the ground! Bravo!!! Dave S arranged a 12 seater minibus and driver for our East London group. None of us fancied the club coaches as it was bound to be carnage at the New Den, with dozens of unnumbered coaches setting off at the same time.

As we were leaving early, Clive stayed at my flat on Saturday night so we went out for a few beers to calm our nerves, got in at midnight and I woke him at 4.45am after a few hours' fitful kip. We set off in the dark, save for a full moon beaming down, to walk to our meet in Hackney. There were 10 of us in total - all the usual

I WAS BORN UNDER THE COLD BLOW LANE

East Enders plus Dave Murray and his mate Tony. Everybody was in Millwall clobber of one sort or another, Pat wore a blue and white 'Cat in the Hat' style titfer, ridiculous unless you are in the Cup. He put a Millwall St George's flag in the rear window and we set off, with the sun now up, at 6am. Our driver should've been a Hammer's fan and unsurprisingly he cried off a few days earlier. Our replacement driver came from Sunderland but wasn't a football fan so we couldn't take the piss out of him either.

We travelled North via the M40/M6 on largely empty roads for the early part of the journey. To add a bit of adventure our driver drove like Juan Pablo Montoya's more reckless brother. He continuously tailgated and pulled out of other car's slipstreams at 80mph. We were so close to the cars in front that I could practically reach out and open their boot. To add to the terror, he looked at Dave and me, sitting in the front with him, whenever he spoke to us, which he did continuously, forcing Dave to feign sleep to try to get him to concentrate on the road. It was a bit hairy, I can tell you. Despite everything, we stopped at a trucker's café near Cannock at 8.30am, had a fry-up and continued north. As we neared the M60, it was like a Millwall parade; limousines, coaches, minibuses and dozens of cars surrounded us, draped in Millwall colours. There was also a smattering of Sunderland vehicles, allowing us to hoot/wave in recognition or give them a damned good wankering as applicable. We passed numerous Millwall travellers having impromptu roadside 'comfort breaks' and every fellow Lion that passed leant out of their window and greeted them with encouraging remarks. The camaraderie was fantastic with the atmosphere building long before we arrived in Manchester.

Despite our dyslexic driver sailing towards Stockport at one point, we arrived in Manchester at 10.30. He dropped us off on a main road and we joined the massed chanting Millwall throng gathered in front of two pubs with Old Trafford forming an impressive backdrop behind us. Standing near us was practically the entire cast of *The Football Factory*. I'd watched it on a moody video the week before so being next to them was surreal. Dave, Paul and Nathan went into a Wetherspoon's pub that resembled a madhouse, the rest of us decided not to bother. I had Colin's ticket and I went to meet him at Sir Matt Busby's statue before we rejoined the others. We stood amid hundreds of fellow Lions and there were a couple of funny incidents. An open-backed truck suddenly pulled off the road, edged through our throng and stopped. It's back laden with numerous crates of lager. Everyone did cartoon-style double takes before several people thought 'Ah free booze' and began to help themselves, much to the bemusement/anger of the four black blokes on board. Ted was one of the looters and was confronted by one of the larger black blokes, Ted fronted him and it resulted in a tug of war between them for a case of lager until the police arrived and surrounded the truck, allowing them to unload their booze, albeit a few cases light. Clive stepped in to pull Ted away before he got nicked. I've seen some daft things but this beer delivery was well up there with the silliest ever.

A short while later a Sikh band came along dressed in Sunderland shirts and red turbans, with some draped in St George flags. They walked through us banging their drums and we greeted them with 'Are You West Ham In Disguise?' and 'Sikh Army!'. Ted booted one of them up the arse, a traditional East End greeting, and threw a tin at them. He is mad, you know. Nathan, Paul and Dave missed most of the fun and eventually emerged from the pub having smuggled us some bottles out past the bouncers. We stood outside the pub drinking until the spoilsport fuzz told us that we had to go inside to drink. One WPC even confiscated my beer but we couldn't be arsed to argue so we set off to the ground. Dave M and Tony were sitting in the East Stand and remained outside the pub. They told us later that it kicked off shortly after we left. Overall, though, the vast majority of fans were too busy enjoying the moment to cause any aggro.

We walked to our stand and on the way we met several fellow Lions we knew and greeted each other warmly. We also took some photos of our group with the huge glass-fronted East Stand and Sir Matt's statue as a backdrop. Dave S went to join the Essex contingent in the North East Quadrant and the rest of us went into the massive North Stand. We were in the second tier and the tickets said anyone in this tier was in for an arduous ascent and they weren't bloody wrong. Ominously, there was a seat halfway up for anybody who couldn't go any further. The ticket also said that anyone with tickets in the third tier who was a vertigo sufferer shouldn't even attempt it. There had been a report that the upper tiers at Old Trafford were unsafe, as the barriers weren't sufficient to prevent a plunge into a tier below. Yet another example of the nanny state in action and merely an attempt to stop people standing up at matches; everyone was up and down all afternoon and no one plunged over the edge from what I saw. I bought the tickets an hour after they went on sale and I asked for £35 tickets in the North Stand 2nd tier, on the halfway line near the front. The girl handed me tickets in row 30. Not knowing if the row numbers went from the pitch up or whether each tier had its own numbering, I said to her 'Are these tickets at the front of Tier 2?'. She said 'Yes'. Having scaled the staircase, we breathlessly arrived at the concourse and asked a steward where row 30 was. He said 'Four rows from the back'. Bollocks! We continued our ascent to just in front of the executive boxes with the third tier floor a few feet above our heads. Although the view was excellent, we were a long way from the pitch, thank God I'm long-sighted. Sunderland fans were practically next to us, so at least it promised to be an afternoon for close-up banter.

Old Trafford had been vastly improved since my previous two visits in the late 80s/early 90s when there were still large areas of terracing behind each goal. It's now an enclosed all-seater arena and really is fantastic. Looking around the ground before the kick-off every Sunderland fan seemed to be wearing a club shirt. It looked like a sea of red and white sticks of rock, though we out-did them in the flag department. Our section also included tickertape, balloons, silly wigs, hooters and horns. There was even someone near us made up as the Lion from *The Wizard of Oz*, with a Millwall shirt on. The Mackems outnumbered us heavily and from our position we could see empty seats in the East Stand with the second tier totally empty. There was also an empty section in the South East corner. Sunderland naturally sang 'You Couldn't Sell All Your Tickets!'. True enough, but there was a good reason as I explained earlier.

THE LION ROARS BACK TO LIFE

The teams came out for a pre-match kickabout and were greeted loudly. The teams were then announced and we 'hoorayed' ours and booed theirs. The DJ played Prokofiev and Republica, mimicking Sunderland's Stadium of Light, and played a reggae megamix of 'Let 'Em Come!' for us. He also played Frankie Goes To Hollywood's *Two Tribes*, all good stirring stuff. Unfortunately, he had the annoying modern habit of continually repeating that it was the FA Cup semi-final between Millwall and Sunderland, which got on my pip. The teams came out for real to a fantastic ovation, the game kicked off and the first half atmosphere was really good. The Mackems were very loud in full flow and so were we. Sunderland hit the bar early on and gave us a scare, Neil Harris then had a goal disallowed for a marginal offside before Cahill sent us into raptures with a goal. I was so animated that my watch flew from my arm and ended in the row in front, truly time flying. Unfortunately, Paul Ifill was stretchered off and Kevin Muscat limped off, which put us on the back foot. Prior to Muscat's departure, he was fouled and trampled all over by that prat McAteer, prompting a mass brawl; consequently there was 6 minutes injury-time, seemingly every game at Old Trafford must adhere to the strict rules of the Time Lord Fergie.

We had been up and down like a whore's drawers on pay night throughout the first half. At half-time we sat down only to continue the first half exercise regime throughout the second half. During the match the stewards surrounded our section pitchside but didn't do the same to the Mackems, strange that. The second half was very much a backs to the wall effort, although Dichio had a great chance, which he headed straight at Mart Poom. Whilst we had been loud in the first half, in the second half we pumped up the volume to back Millwall's rearguard action, continuously singing our Millwall repertoire, with a 'Millwall' version of England's 1966 samba-style clapping chant for some strange reason being very popular. The Mackems, by comparison, were largely quiet. I'd been concerned that a large glory-hunting contingent would require song sheets and step-by-step idiot-proof drawings showing how to do the 'EIO' goal celebration, though thankfully, this wasn't necessary. Wembley had disappointed me but today was infinitely superior. It was a real Lion's roar and what the Autowindscreen should've been. Naturally it was a much bigger game, but there were also far fewer glory boys, one good thing that perversely came from not selling all our allocation.

With 5 minutes left McAteer was sent off, for stupidity I think. Ten men or not at only 1-0 every minute seemed like an hour especially as we had two bloody scoreboards counting down the minutes either side of us, a situation very reminiscent of our 3-2 FA Cup win at Chelsea in 1985. To torture us, 4 minutes injury-time was announced and we created a wall of whistling to try to get the ref to blow up. After what seemed like an eternity Paul Durkin blew the final whistle, Colin, and I bear-hugged each other with tears in our eyes as 38 years of supporting the 'Wall came pouring out of both of us. The curse of McCarthy's Manager of the Month award had struck again and we beat Sunderland for the third time this season. The team did an emotional lap of honour whilst the PA pumped out the 'Let 'Em Come' megamix. We sang 'Oh Wisey!'/'EIO'/'No One Likes Us'/'We're Proud Of You Millwall!'/'And Now You're Gonna Believe Us, We're Gonna Win The Cup!'/'Grandad's Going To Cardiff!', 'Who The F… Are Man United?' and 'The 'Wall Go Marching On, On, On!'. By now I was a wreck my voice, was cracking and tears were running down my face.

We eventually left the stadium. To meet Dave S we navigated through a throng of delirious Millwall fans and found him. He came running towards us, jumping on Paul, Nathan and then on me. He's been going even longer than I have and was in the same emotional state as me. In truth, it was too much for all of us to take in - Millwall were in the FA Cup Final and Europe!!!!! As we walked back to meet our driver I told Patrick he should appreciate how lucky he'd been in his twelve years. He'd seen a Wembley Cup Final, two Divisional Play-Off Semi-Finals, a Championship season and an open-top bus trip to Parliament. He now had an FA Cup Final and a UEFA Cup adventure to look forward. The only major thing that I'd seen that he hadn't was a couple of seasons in the top flight. He must think this football-supporting lark is a doddle. We reached The Trafford pub that was our rendezvous point and waited for Dave M, Tony and our minibus outside. All around flags were waving and everyone was singing and hooting their car horns, like Wrexham but on a grand scale. Bob Peeters limped by on crutches accompanied by Joe Dolan and Pat dashed over to get their autograph. Our driver then arrived, we got aboard and instantly cracked open the Stella. It then took us almost 2½ hours to get on to the motorway proper and heavy traffic continued all the way back. Ted suddenly announced that he'd broken his diabetes needle, was overdue his injection and was naturally worried. Simon works in a hospital and called the NHS Helpline number to discuss our options, thankfully everything was okay as we had food and chocolate on board. Our only entertainment, apart from our hysteria, was a 'Whinging Scouser FM' phone-in where every Liverpudlian caller moaned about beating Blackburn 4-0! Pat announced that he was desperate to go to the loo and as the queues to get in to the services were horrendous, we pulled on to the hard shoulder. Everyone relieved themselves on the grass verge, but Dave S suddenly announced that he had to do a big job urgently! So he ran to the top of the verge and proceeded to do just that. What he hadn't realised was that his lofty position meant that everyone inching along had a full view of what he was doing and he received numerous cheers from fellow Lions. As a backdrop Pat sang 'You Dirty London Bastard!' You don't get this sort of quality everywhere. We drove on and eventually the traffic cleared, so our driver was able to drive as he had on the way up, with the added peril of heavy rain. Still, I thought, if I'm going to die at least I'd die happy.

Fortuitously we got back to London in one piece. I had a few sherbets in my local where coincidentally the game was being replayed on a large video screen, before going home. Indoors I rewound my video of the game and pressed play. It came on just as Martin Tyler said 'Millwall in the Cup Final!' at which point I burst in to tears; for some reason hearing it on TV made it sink in, we really were in the FA Cup Final, although it may just have been a reaction to surviving the drive home. I don't think fans like the moaning Scousers on the radio really appreciate quite what this means to a club and fans like ours. I was deluged all the way back from Manchester and all the following week with congratulations from all quarters, even West Ham fans, and trying to get back to normality wasn't easy because Millwall were in every newspaper, on every phone-in and London TV news programme. In some sort of parallel universe the extremely unlikely became reality - we were in the 2004/05 UEFA Cup even if we lost the Cup Final, because our opponents Manchester United had already qualified for the Champions League. Millwall's website even posted details about the format of the UEFA Cup the day after our semi victory. My God, it was true! Summing up how surreal it was, Simon emailed me and wrote 'I think my radio's on the blink; they keep talking about Millwall, Manchester United and Europe in the same sentence!'. Naturally, our success had to be tempered by much of the media mentioning the negatives as well. The *Daily Mail* even managed to print a picture of the Luton riot a mere 19 years after the event. Strangely, the fact that there were no arrests among Millwall's 21,811 fans wasn't widely mentioned. There was also a consensus in the media that having Millwall in the Cup Final somehow devalued the competition; so much for the magic of the cup.

On **Wednesday 7/4/2004, we played Cardiff at home**, a real after the Lord Mayor's Show affair with 11,500 of Sunday's fans mysteriously disappearing. They'll reappear for the Cup Final, bless 'em. It finished scoreless but there was the usual volatile atmosphere thanks to 816 mouthy Taffs. However, the only point of note was the last minute dismissal of Tim Cahill and the fact that the point took us back above West Ham in the top six.

There were however plenty of chants about the Cup Final, the most surreally sarcastic being 'We're Going To Cardiff, You're Not!'. The other chants were about our appearance in the UEFA Cup; 'We're All Going On A European Tour!'/'Europe, Europe Here We Come!'/'Grandad's Going On A European Tour!' and 'Grandad's Going To Belgium!'. There was also a classic Europeanised adaptation of an old favourite, 'Bonjour, Bonjour We Are The Millwall Boys, Etc, And If You Are A West Ham Fan Surrender Or You'll Die, We All Follow The Millwall!'. As it was Cardiff, they sang their usual hooligan-boasting repertoire and also sang 'Shall

We Sing A Song For You?'. We replied 'Shall We Shag A Sheep For You?'. On a similar inter-species breeding tip there was a marvellous adaptation of 'I Can't Read'; 'I Can't Read, I Can't Write, But I Can Drive A Jeep, I'm A Cardiff City Fan And I Love Shagging Sheep!'.

Following this game, we had now played the three most volatile teams - Stoke, West Ham and Cardiff - and there had been no major aggro at home or away, although for the Hammers and the Taffs in particular, not without radical travel restrictions and hundreds of riot police.

I went with Mark, Andy and Glyn to the first away trip since Old Trafford, **Coventry City on Easter Saturday 10/4/2004**. We had an easy journey and arrived early. On the corner of the road outside the stadium there was a Millwall memorabilia stall selling a glut of both West Ham Mother's Day Massacre T-Shirts and FA Cup Final memorabilia.

We took up our position in the usual side stand now called the Mitchell and Butler North Stand. We had only been allocated a portion of the away area for some reason and had less than 600 fans there. Dave Murray joined us in the seats at the top of the stand, next to the gobby home fans. Strangely, despite their provocation, only our response interested the stewards positioned between them and us. Mind you, one of the home stewards was so cross-eyed that he could have been keeping an eye on us and the home fans behind him at the same time. For added security, police surrounded our section for the whole match; I'm getting déjà vu again. If the Cardiff game had been lacklustre then this was Millwall in a coma; not one player appeared to want to tackle any of the opposition for fear of getting either injured or booked.

The game ended in a 4-0 defeat thanks to some comedy defending and we dropped out of the play-off zone. The situation in both this and the Cardiff game hadn't been helped by injury or Cahill having a disciplinary Sword of Damocles hang over his head. Nonetheless, it wasn't a good attitude with a play-off berth there for the taking. Despite the game, there were still some points of interest, there was a notice behind the refreshment counter which was truly a sign of the times - 'All staff must speak English when working behind the counter'. Well, at least what passes for English in the Midlands, anyway. Sadly, the gyrating girlies had disappeared.

Coventry's goalie Shearer wore one of the vilest kits known to man. It was beige, orange and black and a real throwback to the 90s, keeping up Coventry's proud tradition of horror kits. Coventry's programme contained a three-page article on their first team coach Archie Knox, which we acknowledged with 'Archie Knox Is A Wanker!'. A pitchside sign facing us had a sentiment borne more out of hope than likelihood, which said 'Thank You For Not Using Foul And Abusive Language'. Yeah, righto. Behind the stewards Coventry were bravado personified and as we capitulated they sang 'FA Cup, You're Having A Laugh!' and 'You're Gonna Win F... All!'. So much for their pitchside sign. In response we sang Cup Final/European/sarcastic chants including 'Millwall's Going To Cardiff, La La Etc!'/'We're Going To Cardiff, You're Not!'/'We're Going To Europe You're Not!'/'Get Your Passports Out!'/'Three Nil And We Still Can Sing!' and 'You're So Loud It's Unbelievable!'. There was a fat mouthy City fan in the home section behind the goal who got some new fatist abuse; 'Fat C... Takes Up 2 Seats, La, La, Etc!' and 'You Only Sing When You're Eating!'. Finally there was a classic, if bizarre, chant about black player Mark McCammon: 'Posh Spice On A Diet, She Eats A Lot Of Salmon, And When She's Shagging (F...ing) Beckham She Thinks Of Mark McCammon!'

We set off south listening to Gary Newbon badmouth Millwall's' right to be in the final on the radio. The air in Mark's car went very blue and Glyn wanted us to drive on to London to kill him. We calmed him with a horse tranquilliser and were back in Chelmsford by 7pm, an easy trip but a God-awful performance.

Paul S and I went to **Nottingham Forest on 17/4/2004**, a ground we had been banned from in 2002/03. We went on the club coach, which formed a convoy with a Junior Lions coach. Larry was our host; strangely, though, we had no moody videos.

Our trouble-free trip up included a pick-up at Milton Keynes Coachway. We continued to Forest without a police escort, in total contrast to my last visit. Thankfully Paul didn't have a broken foot now, either. We pulled up in Forest's car park and instantly a policeman got on board and attempted to give us his speech without a mike whilst we took the piss out of him, he was then given the microphone and repeated the usual Old Bill Spiel; 'Ejection Policy, No Swearing, No Racist Abuse…' We all yawned, he then humorously said 'If anyone has got any alcohol on board, I suggest you drink the alcohol and eat the tin, because we're going to search the coach when you get off!' Blimey, a copper with a sense of humour, we should've had him stuffed for posterity.

Paul and I went into the ground where we met Mark, Andy, Glyn and Lawrie, a young Essex away regular, who travelled up with them. We sat together on the lower tier of the Bridgford Stand, to the right of the goal in the impressive City Ground. There was a no man's land of empty seats to the left of us and in the Brian Clough Stand to our right, although we had Forest fans in the tier above us. It was a poor turnout with only 670 Millwall, around a quarter of our last visit there.

Before the game, the home fans passed a gigantic Forest home shirt across the Trent Bridge Stand lower tier. It appeared that Forest's DJ had done a Tony Blackburn course in 'How to be a DJ' as he exhibited all the modern traits - formulaic footy anthems, tension building/rabble-rousing patter and the team's entrance was heralded with 'This Is Nottingham Forest', just in case anyone had lost track of where they were, though he didn't play 'Robin Hood'.

The game was vital for both sides with us still trying for a play-off spot and Forest not far off relegation. In the goalless first half Forest had a goal disallowed and hit the bar and Millwall missed several good chances. The second half was a complete turnaround. Livermore scored a fluke from a free kick so quickly that several Lions were still in the bar. Forest then equalised and went ahead through our handballing chum David Johnson, before sub Nick Chadwick scored a very late leveller. Danny Dichio and Forest's Wes Morgan were also sent off for a handbags affair. It was certainly action packed. This 2-2 draw continued my lengthy run of good fortune in Nottingham with my only defeat in the city at Forest in our old First Division days.

Forest's fans above us were unusually very vocal all afternoon. They sang 'Forever And Ever, Red Flag Flying High' about hating

I WAS BORN UNDER THE COLD BLOW LANE

'Cockney Bastards' i.e. us. 'You Must Have Come In A Taxi!'/'Worst Support We've Ever Seen!' and 'We Bet You Ran From The Hammers!' etc, you get the picture. They also sang 'Sit Down Shurrup!', the pronunciation of which had us rolling in the aisles. Grandad got particular attention; 'There's Only One Jimmy Saville!' and 'Where's Your Zimmer Frame?'. When they went 2-1 up they sang 'Grandad, Grandad, Give Us A Song!' and 'Grandad, Grandad What's The Score?'. More bizarrely they sang '2-1 To The Football Team!'.

We had been singing 'European Tour' all afternoon, together with many anti-Hammers chants for some reason, I cannot see the point of singing anti-West Ham songs outside London, it's not as though they will hear them is it? In response to the home chants, we sang the old chestnuts 'Going Down!' and 'You're Going Down With The Derby!'. In defence of Grandad we sang 'There's Only One Grandad!' and 'Grandad's Going To Europe!' at which point he stood up, faced the Forest in the upper tier and pointed at himself.

Stoke fans had caused trouble at Forest the previous week and consequently the stewards and police were very keen to bugger us about today. They continually lectured our fans, including Lawrie, for standing up or making gestures. The Forest above us and in the old Main Stand to our left were doing exactly the same. In fact the upper tier threw coins and a plastic bottle down, which landed close to our disabled fans, though they went unpunished. In the second half as the goals rained down the barracking went up a notch and the police started throwing people out of our section indiscriminately, whilst again ignoring the equally animated Forest. I asked one Plod why they had a 'Millwall only' policy, suggesting that they should have a look upstairs too. He told me to 'watch the match!'. I continued my enquiry but as usual I may as well have saved my breath. The stewards then made the mistake of picking out Grandad for particular attention, which led to the response that I had predicted previously as we rose in his defence and the stewards sensibly skulked away before it got out of hand. The policing and stewarding was very OTT and our response only got more hostile when the police started randomly dragging our

258

fans out. Despite everything they let everyone out together although I saw no problems outside.

Paul and I got on our coach and as we waited to leave the car park we saw the police crash one of their meat wagons into one poor sod's car, which was good for a laugh. We had an easy trip back listening to a procession of whining Scousers and Spurs fans on *606*. We dropped the Milton Keynes two off, and drove through London via the East End, where we passed a West Ham-stickered van and a bloke wearing a 60s Hammers shirt; obviously we abused them. Despite this spirited draw, we were outside the top six.

The final away League game was a Sky Xtra 5.35pm kick-off at **Derby County on 1/5/2004**. Ordinarily I'd be morris dancing or dancing around a maypole on Mayday obviously, but instead I chose to go on a Millwall pervs outing to Derby along with 414 fellow Lions. Following two home defeats, we had successfully taken play-off qualification out of our own hands. Derby, though, were still in the relegation mire.

I went on my own on a club coach arranging to meet the Essex Boys there. There was only one coach, which wasn't full, and one large and one small Junior Lions Kings Ferry coach also travelled up. Our coach had a placard in the front window that said 'Grandad's Barmy Army On Tour' along with a rampant Lion, 'Coach Number One, Bermondsey SE16, No One Likes Us' and 'Millwall FC'. Lottery Larry was our steward and he was serenaded with his own song, 'Oh Larry Wowo, Etc, He's Only Five Foot One, He Takes It Up The Bum!'. Away regular Pam said 'That's a bit harsh; he's much taller than that!'. En route we picked up the same two Milton Keynes Lions at the Coachway as per the Forest game. On the road in to Derby, we went past a scrap yard and caravan site, which prompted numerous Gillingham/Kent comments. We followed the 'Away Supporters' signs and ended up going in to, and then out of, Derby Tertiary College car park, before driving into the large open area around Pride Park and parking up. I went in to the ground at around 4.20pm where I met up with Andy, his two sons, Mark, Glyn and Lawrie. We then stood together on the concourse watching *Gillette Soccer Saturday*. It was surreal as we knew all the results before going into our match. We sat to the left of the upper part of the renamed away section, the Cawarden South Stand. Due to the importance of the game, the home side generated a good noise, especially the East Stand to our right who were accompanied by drummer boys.

The teams came out to Queen's *One Vision* with Millwall looking more like the youth team than the first team. Again, the stewarding was OTT; dozens of them stood facing us, continually pointing out supposed offenders. Numerous police, including Met officers, backed them up; there were even three police dressed like a SWAT team, in black boiler suits and luminous yellow baseball caps. These three continually took stills and video footage of our section, even though nothing was happening.

Early in the match, Derby's Marcus Tudgay did an Olympic quality dive in the area, prompting Mark Cowburn to give them a penalty. Several Millwall fans near the front of the upper tier lambasted the referee for this and the stewards tried forcefully to drag some 'offenders' out. Many in our section took umbrage and a fracas erupted, with the stewards getting quite a few punches and kicks for their trouble. Lawrie hared into the fray despite being warned previously about his behaviour and fortunately he didn't get pinched. The police flooded our stand and calm was restored. Amazingly, the trouble didn't appear in any of the media that I saw. Justice was done when Andy Marshall saved the penalty. Shortly after, the home side did score and it finished 1-0 at half-time. Andy's sons were then involved in a penalty shootout against Rammie and the Derby kids. They came back to the seats clutching their awards and we all settled down to suffer the second half. Derby got a second goal and we managed to have no meaningful efforts on their goal all afternoon in yet another 'After you Claude!' performance. In fact, the only efforts on goal in a Millwall shirt came from Alex and George in the penalty shootout.

Here are some of the original Derby chants to give you a feel for the day. To our low turnout: 'You're So Quiet You Sound Like Nottingham!'. and to us Londoners they sang a mock Cockney 'Wanka!'. With their second goal, they made themselves safe and they sang 'Stand Up If You're Staying Up!'. Sarcastically, we stood up with them. As they cruised to victory they sang 'Two Nil In Your Cup Final!' and 'That's It For Millwall!'.

Our only chants consisted of their relegation plight: 'Derby Going Down Like A Russian Submarine!' and 'Going Down!'. Obviously, we abused their new forward Paul Peschisolido with his usual Brady abuse and responded to practically anything they sang with 'We're All Going On A European Tour!'.

Following a home whistling deluge, the ref blew his whistle and the DJ played *Glad All Over* and *Celebration*. Relieved Derby fans streamed on to the pitch despite pleas not to and several of them gestured towards us, an invasion and provocation ignored by the police/stewards who continued to face us. As the celebrations continued we left the ground. I edged through the police lines strung out across the away exit and got back on board the coach. We then set off under police escort through delirious home fans who waved and wankered us. Someone behind me said 'No sheep will be safe here tonight!' With our defeat any lingering play-off hopes had now completely disappeared. When we dropped the MK2 off many of us went into a very small and smelly gent's toilet, it smelt so bad that when Grandad broke wind in the queue it acted like an air freshener! Just thought I'd mention it.

Our final League game was a meaningless 1-0 home win against relegated **Bradford City**. Our first win since the semi-final thanks to a Harris penalty - our first successful penalty in four attempts - and we finished a disappointing 10th, having blown a comfortable 5th place and a two home games in hand advantage; Cardiff here we come.

11.

'Millwall In Your Cup Final!'

FA Cup Final v Manchester United, Millennium Stadium, Cardiff, 22/5/2004

WHO WOULD HAVE thought it? Millwall flashed to a worldwide TV audience of billions! In a final between two of the most hated sides in English football. Perfectly explained by my mate Simon who said to the Manchester United fans that he works with 'No one likes us, but everyone f…ing hates you!'. Consequently, for the first time ever every neutral was on our side, especially United's rivals. On Sky in April and May I heard Arsenal and Chelsea both sing 'Millwall, Millwall, Millwall!'.

In the build-up to the game, I had best wishes from fans of West Ham, Spurs, Southend, Chelsea and Arsenal. Being so popular was an odd sensation. Naturally, we had to have a Cup Final song, in our case *Oh Millwall*, a bastardisation of 'Oh Wisey'. Mick Brown conducted the recording and videoing of the CBL, in particular at the Reading game on 24/4/2004. The lyrics were printed in the programme and the Jumbotron did an old style 'follow the bouncing ball' version as well. We sang various chorus parts very loudly, including the PG Wisey version. This was the first time a crowd had ever appeared 'live' on an FA Cup song with the team. I'm still awaiting my performance and video royalty cheque. In typical Millwall fashion, EMI's LA publishers, who held the rights to the backing tune *Volare*, refused to allow its release. Apparently, other sides, including England, had tried to use the tune in the past and had also been refused. In the end, they relented and it was released shortly before the final, charting at number 41!

MILLWALL IN YOUR CUP FINAL

Whilst I found the banning of the song quite funny, the FA's handling of the tickets was a scandal. I heard the final referred to as Prawn Sandwiches v Jellied Eels, a bit fishy, as was the FA ticket allocation. The FA arranged a meeting regarding ticket allocation, told us it was cancelled, held the meeting anyway and gave Manchester United 28,000 to our 21,400, the dodgy buggers. The FA implied that South Wales Police had voiced concerns about hooliganism and the ticket allocation was amended for security/segregation reasons. This didn't hold water because whilst Millwall had only 18 arrests in 2002/03 with no arrests at our semi, United had 186 arrests and 16 fans arrested at their semi. United fans themselves had previously had clashes with the Soul Crew in Cardiff; see BBC's *Riot Cops*. Such was the sense of indignity surrounding the FA's ungentlemanly conduct that it was raised in Parliament by several MPs, resulting in the FA doing nothing other than promising to look into future ticketing and security arrangements. The phrase 'bloody lot of good that will do us' sprang to mind. *The Independent* had a report saying that of the 13,000 'neutral' tickets, 1000 would go to London/Kent associations i.e. they would effectively be Millwall tickets, whilst the other 12,000 would go to Manchester and other associations i.e. they would effectively be United tickets.

Ticket holders had to be 'genuine' neutrals or fans of one of the specified clubs because they have their allegiance printed on their ticket and would be policed within the two clubs' segregated sections. The FA intimated that this was again on police insistence, which the Heddlu denied. As far as I know, it was the first time that two sides in the final received differing allocations - one rule for Millwall and one for everyone else as usual. Many people implied that we were moaning unnecessarily because United fans lost out more than us. True enough, but they must lose out at every other Cup Final. Anyway, I was under the impression that the FA Cup Final was a national sporting institution and not a United home game. Not exactly an example of the FA persecuting United, as Sir Fergie always implies. As one 'Old Time Musical' philosopher once wrote, 'It's the rich what gets the pleasure, it's the poor what gets the blame, ain't it all a bleedin' shame!'

I WAS BORN UNDER THE COLD BLOW LANE

Once the allocation arguments had been papered over, they went on sale at one per season ticket/member. I decided not to go on the 'season ticket only' day on Sunday but to get Dave's members' ticket together with the eight season ticket holders' tickets on May Bank Holiday Monday. When I arrived at the ground at 6.45am, Bolina Road was crammed with Millwall stickered cars and even at this early hour, the queue stretched back past the club shop, I joined it just outside the football cages. The car park opened shortly after 7am and we made our way into the ground concourse, past many professional queuers with portable chairs and other comforts of home. I eventually came to a halt three-quarters of the way along the North Stand. As we queued stewards handed out maps and gave ticket info, as they had for the semi. The refreshment cart went along the line and the refreshment points were open. Merchandise was on sale on the concourse, including the West Ham *Hammered* video and numerous FA Cup Final flags, T-shirts, pom-poms, big blue pointing fingers, blue wigs of varying designs, blue and white plastic boaters, rosettes, jester hats, blue and white grease paint and spray-on hair dye. To cheer us up the concourse TVs had Sky Sports on, who were repeatedly replaying tearful scenes of Leeds fans/players following their relegation the previous day. Never mind, Elland Road will be another new ground for me.

The ticket office opened at around 9.30am and shortly afterwards stewards brought around revised maps showing the rapidly disappearing available blocks. When I emerged outside, blinking like a mole at 10.30am, it was pouring with rain and a Sky crew were filming interviews with the queue, getting people to strike the customary 'I've got a ticket!' pose. When I got to the window at 11am the second tier blocks behind the goal I wanted were gone, so I bought nine £65 tickets, four in one row and five in another row two behind on the lower tier of the North Stand.

My cousin Paul had been a couple of hundred people behind me and continually popped down for a chat. He'd heard stories of smart cards not being swiped on Sunday with some people going around twice. Rumours are rife in queues so I told him to ignore them. There was an element of truth this time though because the club later admitted that some swiping machines had broken down on Monday, not Sunday, but insisted all Teamcard numbers had been taken either via machine or manually and every member would get a ticket. In the end, our allocation was sold in 5 days prompting even the *Evening Standard* to question the inequality of the ticket allocation. Subsequently Millwall tickets changing hands for several hundred pounds each.

Strangely, Sir Fergie had not engaged in his customary mind games in the build-up, probably thinking that United didn't need his psychological warfare tactics to beat a side who were the biggest underdogs in FA Cup history. Millwall were the first side from outside of the Premiership to reach the final since its inception and we would be the lowest ranked side from the First Division ever to win the Cup should we do so. The omens for victory were far from good.

The media were their usual self with most reports mentioning the hooligan possibilities of the game. On the eve of the game the ITV News Channel implied that many people wanted neither side to win and to prove why we shouldn't have anyone's backing they showed footage of the Birmingham riot as the start of their report, business as usual yet again. The game was Category C and there was the added possibility of a terror attack, meaning there was a huge police operation with 1000 officers including 50 armed police on duty. They had been searching lorries in the days leading up to the game but stressed that this was a terrorist rather than football hooligan deterrent. They also put a massive city centre security operation in place from Friday onwards and said they would be searching the bags, etc of anyone entering the stadium.

I didn't expect us to win so I'd been relatively calm all week until bizarrely I saw *Question Of Sport - FA Cup Final Special*, at which point for some reason the nerves began to kick in. I watched this at my mum's before walking home at 8pm. On the way I saw numerous cars and vans on the A13 and coming out of Rotherhithe Tunnel, heading westwards with Millwall flags flying - the Cardiff invasion had begun.

Although the club had laid on a 'special' train and dozens of coaches, we again plumped for making our own way to the game on the semi-final minibus. We had the same driver as Old Trafford so it was St Christophers and rosary beads all around. I went to the pub on Friday night for a couple of beers to steady my pre-trip jitters. In the end, I had a good night's sleep and woke up at 5.45am feeling slightly nervous, although I was nowhere near as bad as I'd been for the semi because I expected us to beat Sunderland. I had the radio on as I got ready and the news reports were practically speaking of Millwall as though we were a pub team, made up of plumbers, brickies and electricians, etc rather than a pro side.

I know we were outsiders in the extreme and are nowhere near the massive corporate entity that United are, but we've been in the top flight ourselves. The way they were speaking it was as though Telford had reached the final not us. Naturally, I found it all a bit patronising, I must remember to get a thicker skin for my next birthday.

The driver lived near Clive and picked him up first before picking me up en route to Hackney. Our party consisted of the usual East End group plus Dave Murray and his friends Rocky and Martin, he of the 4-3 Reading match, who was armed with a case of Stella. Rocky and Martin are Millwall members who had journeyed over from Ireland especially for the game. We set off at 7.30am, again resplendent in Millwall merchandise, but without Pat's flag this time because Simon was flying it outside his Millwall outpost in Hackney.

We had a Manchester United mug on the dashboard on the driver's side, as we had had for the semi-final trip. We didn't like this much but agreed that we could always use it for on board relief later on if necessary. We had Five Live on, which was solely about the final. It spoke of Millwall in the customary 'David and Goliath' tones and they referred to the game as being between 'Worldwide Icons and the Salt of the Earth'. The nicest comparison I heard, much better than the usual 'Scum of the Earth' reference anyway.

We sailed up the M4 with little traffic, in bright sunshine and in high spirits. Fortunately, despite my and Clive's reticence about sitting in the front with the old boy racer, he didn't tailgate anyone this time; pointedly we made sure that we didn't speak to him and he largely kept his eyes on the road. In the West Country, it became similar to the semi trip; there were a few Man U cars but there were numerous Millwall vehicles, with flags, window stickers, scarves and the *Standard's* Dennis Wise semi-final poster, etc, on show. There was even one newish-looking car that had Millwall comments painted all over it in blue paint including 'Hoot if you follow Millwall', which we did. I didn't fancy the owners chances of getting the paint off. Once again, stretch limos and roadside pisses were popular. At one point, a convoy of camouflaged Army vehicles also passed us heading west. More alarmingly, several tanks on trailers were heading out of Wales; jokingly we said 'Blimey, tanks! How bad is the security going to be?!!'.

We decided to cross into Wales before stopping at services and as the Severn Bridge and Wales came into view our driver gave out a yell and we veered off the road onto the hard shoulder; our brakes had gone, f...ing brilliant. Our driver said he'd get us into Wales and would stop at the first services we came to. He hand-broke his way through the tollbooths, stopping to pay our toll fee and then drove a short distance before pulling into services full of fellow Lions shortly after 10am. Peculiarly, at the services there was a Filipino woman or somesuch flogging Lions merchandise whilst intoning 'Come On Mirrwarr', which was bizarre to say the least.

Our driver phoned the man who owned the minibus and discovered that he didn't have cover with anyone, no RAC, AA or Green Flag, no one!!! Luckily, the Essex contingent had also been driven there in a minibus and I'd kept in touch with them all morning and knew they were only a short distance behind us. I called Paul and asked them to come into the services with us and ask their minibus driver if he would take us into Cardiff after he'd dropped them off. Fortunately he agreed to do this and said that they had four empty seats as they had a 16-seater rather than the 12-seater they had booked, so four of us could go with them now and he'd come back for the others if they couldn't get our minibus fixed.

I got on board as I had Colin's ticket, along with Clive, Simon and Pat. We told the others the plan and dished out the tickets to the people remaining behind at the services. We set off, abusing a Man U limo that pulled up the side of us with a hearty chorus of 'You're Gonna Win F... All!' whilst Lawrie waved a Millwall flag at them.

I WAS BORN UNDER THE COLD BLOW LANE

The Millennium Stadium was very well signposted with roadside signs indicating which team should take which turn off and with only minor traffic delays we were soon in Cardiff proper. At around 11am we parked up outside the police headquarters, disembarked and Andy took some ironic photos as we posed in front of a police meat wagon. A local copper came over and asked if we would like him to take the photo so that Andy could be in it, which he did.

The police we met here were very friendly and chatty, as per the League game at Ninian Park. The Essex minibus driver asked if he needed to go back to get the others so I called Paul S to see what the situation was. He said that they had set off again using the same handbrake tactic and were almost in the town centre. I told him to call us when they had parked up and we would arrange a meeting place. We gave our driver a score for helping us out and started walking into the city centre.

The Essex lot set off to the pub and we went into the main shopping centre, which was full of Millwall and ticket touts. There were wandering T-shirt sellers and makeshift merchandise stalls aplenty, including the Filipino women, selling every item you could think of including bloody annoying air horns.

We bought a couple of throwaway cameras and stood outside the main arcade to soak up the ambience. We told Paul S where we were and they agreed to come to us. The atmosphere in the shopping precinct was excellent, very friendly in the main with both teams' fans mixing, although it was massively Millwall biased as the area was at our end of the ground. We did hear a few challenging chants being exchanged with any Man U that came along, but mostly everyone just sang pro-Lions chants.

There was one bloke in the precinct wearing a T-shirt that perfectly summed up the nation's feeling; it said 'I Support Two Teams, Millwall And Whoever Are Playing Man United'. The most bizarre thing in the shopping area was the sight of bemused Japanese tourists taking photographs of anything that moved. I'd never seen Cardiff proper before due to security restrictions at my two Cardiff City visits, but without the local hoolies to worry about I thought it was a really nice place.

MILLWALL IN YOUR CUP FINAL

After a while Paul, Nathan, Dave S and Ted arrived with Dave M etc setting off to find the rest of their Irish contingent who had travelled via other means. We set off to get something to eat at a Burger King near to Cardiff Castle. Inside, Ted was getting into a real lather about a very busty Man U blonde whose breasts he was loudly complimenting and trying to photograph. I said that if he didn't calm himself I'd pour the ice from my Coke on to his vitals. He gradually calmed down and we discussed how they had got in to Cardiff and where they were parked. They said that they parked near the Man United end where the police told them to move the vehicle off the road or they would tow it away. They explained what was wrong to the police and were told to push it to a side street, which they did as Man U fans in a nearby pub took the piss. Naturally, Ted rose to the bait and gave them the finger. Pushing was becoming too arduous so the driver said he'd try to drive the minibus a short distance. They got on board and drove off at which point 50 Mancs came out of the pub and charged up the road after them, though fortunately they managed to outrun them and escape unscathed.

Due to the bus owner's lack of cover, Dave S then had to use his RAC membership, which had unfortunately just run out, to try to get it fixed. He updated his membership and paid £65 to get them to come out and tow the vehicle to a garage. To be continued...

The atmosphere had been great in the shopping precinct but was even better nearer the ground, which had been pedestrianised by the police. Our end of the street was a mass of blue, with people in Lions costumes, silly hats, face paint and wigs. There were also some people with inflatable FA Cups. I saw one Lion-costumed bloke with a ripped-up Man U shirt in his mouth, funny and effective. I even saw some 70s throwbacks in butchers coats, I hadn't seen these in an eon.

Colin stayed in Bristol on Friday with his wife and daughter Hannah, who is at university there, and travelled by train to Cardiff on the day. I'd been calling him to see how he was getting on, which hadn't been easy as everyone appeared to be using their mobiles at the same time and the signal was very erratic. I eventually got him and we all set off towards Cardiff station via the

I WAS BORN UNDER THE COLD BLOW LANE

United end of the ground, where they were playing football in the street. On the way I lost all the others because they stopped to try to get their mug on TV as a crew were filming in the middle of the street.

I continued on and texted the others to say that I'd meet them at the ground as I still had Clive's ticket. I reached the quaint Cardiff Central Station just as Colin's train pulled in; we met up and walked back towards the Millwall end. As per the semi, on the day we met various home and away regulars and greeted each other warmly. I met one regular, Paul, outside the ground, who I'd stood with on the terrace at Blackpool on the day when we thought that it would be Millwall's last ever game. He said to me 'Who'd have thought when we were in Blackpool all those years ago that we would be in the Cup Final?', perfectly summing up just how far the club had come.

Colin and I bought our mega-expensive programmes and waited for the remainder of the East Enders who were waiting to see Millwall's coach arrive at the ground; they then joined us and we went through the entrance to North Stand Gate 2 having had our tickets and bags checked. We also met up with the Essex Boys who had not wasted their spare hours, as they were well bevied up. We wished each other well and made our way inside and into our sections, them to an upper tier and us to the lower tier.

The Millennium Stadium was very impressive from the outside and even more so inside. I thought it was an excellent ground, far better than Wembley, with the stands surprisingly close to the pitch, very much a football stadium although built primarily as a rugby ground. The Millwall areas of the ground were filling up nicely, even before 2pm; the United sections by contrast were largely empty. I got the impression that the final to them was just another game; after all, they had been there and done that numerous times before. To further highlight this Millwall's team came on to the pitch in their designer suits, United didn't bother.

Our nine seats were almost directly behind each, other near to the back of the lower tier in line with the left hand corner flag, and although we were low down the view was excellent. Many people were taking pictures on cameras and digital phones of our spectacularly blue section; it was a sea of blue flags, Millwall shirts and silly hats.

Zampa was also there and there were fluffy lions, balloons and beach balls, etc being bounced about as well as a blow-up doll and other inflatables. One huge beach ball had on it 'The F… Up Cup - We Beat The Scum 4-1!'. There were also the customary witty Cup Final banners; just behind us there was a large banner that said 'Dennis Wise Has Laid On More Balls Than Jordan', Simon or Katy Price version I do not know. I also saw 'Prawn Sandwiches 0 Jellied Eels 1' and 'There Were 3 Wise Men, Only 1 Little Den'. We continued to stand and watch the build-up; we booed and 'Miiiilllllwaaaallled' through Man U's team announcement as their faces flashed up on the video screens and naturally cheered our team's names and rapturously applauded our players as they came out to warm-up.

Cardiff's PA man was the customary rabble-rousing type of prat, stating the bleeding obvious and playing the normal footy anthem music. The video at the other end of the ground was showing the goals from the games that got the two teams to the final, though I thought the overall build-up to the match was subdued.

There was a large podium in the middle of the pitch, which had the FA Cup itself plonked on top. Army bods surrounded this podium as young children laid out adverts, or somesuch, on the pitch. The roof was open and there was a strange flying camera on a wire hovering above the pitch. With less than twenty minutes to go the Royal Engineers Band came onto the pitch in a sixties football ground-style and played *The Great Escape*, which we sang our way through.

At about this time our driver phoned to say that the minibus couldn't be repaired until Monday and we were, to put it technically, f…ed! So, in addition to worrying about how we would cope against United's internationals, we also now had to worry about how we would get home.

There was a running order in the Freeman's catalogue of a programme that said *Abide With Me* would be sung at 2.48 pm.

I WAS BORN UNDER THE COLD BLOW LANE

With military precision, precisely on time, buxom blonde Katherine Jenkins walked seductively to the podium to a chorus 'Get Your Tits Out For The Lads!'. Unfortunately she didn't, nonetheless it must have made her day.

I'd never been to an FA Cup Final, none of us had and I'd been looking forward to singing the football hymn in situ for the first time ever. Unfortunately, from our position we couldn't really hear it as it was too noisy and she was halfway through it before I twigged where she was in relation to the words on the video screen. She also sang *God Save The Queen*, which we sang in the customary football fashion i.e. too fast, so we males finished before she did, I'm saying nowt!

The teams came out for real in a flurry of flags, tickertape, cheers and the Old Spice music. Sven-Goran Eriksson was the guest of honour and he walked on to the pitch to a chorus of 'One Ulrika Jonsson!'. He was introduced to the teams as we booed the Man U handshakes and cheered ours. The ticket allocation was brought into sharp focus with the ground full: 'neutrals' weren't in evidence at all, our third of the ground was surrounded by a wall of red in the other two thirds. It reminded me of an election chart following a Labour landslide with our section the Conservatives. The split was more like 49,000 Man U and 22, 000 us, in the crowd announced as 71,350.

On the football front Millwall did very well from a containing point of view in the first half and we had looked set fair to reach half-time scoreless. Cristiano Ronaldo, who had been continually lambasted with 'There's Only One David Beckham!' chants because of his showboating, then scored at our end a couple of minutes before half-time. If we'd reached half-time goalless we may have had a chance to cause an upset; sadly, it wasn't to be.

From a fan perspective one idiot ran on from the United end shortly before this and someone ran on from our section when their goal went in. Both were unceremoniously dealt with by the security and dragged off the pitch. Unusually for us, pre-match we applauded referee Jeff Winter and his assistants as they did their warm-up run. It was his last ever match, so to thank us in the second half he gave United what I thought was an early but debatable penalty and allowed an offside goal, ta very much. I'm a bit biased so, right or wrong, for each decision he made against us I had a serious bout of referee-specific Tourettes. Unusually the video screens showed everything again, controversial or otherwise.

People were standing near the front of our section all afternoon forcing us to stand up for practically the whole game. The PA made announcements about sitting down which naturally prompted 'Stand Up If You Love Millwall'; you must know how truculent we are by now. Our support had been loud, colourful and mostly continuous, whereas the United fans, from where we stood anyway, appeared to be living up to their prawn sandwich reputation, the support discrepancy seemed to be confirmed by various mates watching the game on TV who texted me to compliment our backing whilst slating United's.

Due to our perception of their support we sang 'You're Just A Bunch Of Wankers'/'Shall We Sing A Song For You?'/'You Only Sing When You're Winning!' and '3-Nil And You Still Don't Sing'. Most pointedly, 'Your Support Is F...ing Shit!' echoed around the ground. United replied with 'Who The F...ing Hell Are You' and in response we sang 'You're Not Champions Anymore!'.

Refereeing aside United dominated most of the second half and we chased our tails. Even so, we sarcastically 'Ole'd!' when Millwall had a short keepball patch. Whilst I was obviously disappointed, United are a top European side and as such losing 3-0 was no real disgrace, particularly when you consider that some of their players individually are worth more than our whole team combined. Additionally, although Wisey played, we missed Dichio and Muscat and I would estimate that our squad was collectively the youngest ever in a final. We had three 19-year-olds - Sweeney, Elliott and Cogan - all making an appearance and not forgetting the very late introduction of Curtis Weston, the youngest ever player in an FA Cup Final at 17 years and 129 days.

The BBC posters for the Final featured Keane and Wisey with the headline 'The Bigger They Are...'. This reminded me of a quote by former Boxing World Champion Charlie Magri who once said 'The Bigger They Are, The Harder They Hit You!'.Unfortunately, in this case Charlie was right. If we had won I was going to get a picture of Fergie apoplectically tapping his watch and use it as wallpaper but, sadly, in the end I didn't have the pleasure.

They always say that the game flashes by and this was certainly true for me, so what it was like for the players I don't know.

With no Royal Box at the final whistle, the army boys brought the bloody great podium back on and once it was erected the medals were brought out by Grenadier Guards on what looked like silver trays, in a manner like the ambassador's ball on the Ferrero Rochet advert. Millwall received their runners-up medals before the winners and we sang 'We're Proud Of You Millwall!' which I certainly was.

Man U then went up to get theirs and when they lifted the cup there was an explosion of red and white streamers as the PA played *Beautiful Day* and *Rockin All Over The World*. Both teams did a lap of honour, as the PA played Man U's *Glory, Glory, Man United* which only goes to prove that, biggest club in the world or not, they still couldn't commission a decent bloody cup song. No one left our section from what I could see, choosing to stay put and salute our team. By contrast, United's section had many empty seats. We again broke into 'Your Support Is F...ing Shit!'. The fact that we remained to the bitter end was apparently practically a first, usually the losers' fans bugger off pronto. In truth, Millwall reaching the Cup Final in the first place was reason enough for us to celebrate and it certainly didn't feel wrong to salute Theo and the side parading on the pitch in front of us.

We eventually left the ground, Colin headed to the station and we went to meet our driver. We had to go back to our kaput minibus because we had left our gear, including Ted's insulin, on board. I arranged for Dave M and his Irish companions to go on my cousin's minibus and we took up a position on the main road to await our driver. He arrived soon after and we set off in the general direction of the station.

Outside a pub on the opposite side of the road to the station United fans were raucously celebrating and police soon surrounded them with officers and horses. Thankfully, there had been no terrorism problems and, obviously I can only speak from my own experience, but the policing certainly didn't seem to be heavy-handed or intrusive at all. We certainly didn't see armed officers on the streets as I had thought that we might from how the media had portrayed it. We saw no trouble but my cousin said that there was a punch-up outside the McDonald's he was in. He said it looked like escalating until being calmly and quickly nipped in the bud by the Heddlu.

Returning to our journey, we skirted around the police horses and headed away from the city centre towards the M4 on foot, crossing main roads, going through an industrial yard, wading through rubble and climbing a grass verge. It was like a bloody assault course. We eventually made it on to a very narrow footpath, which had overgrown hedging all along it. We edged along in Indian file whilst trying to avoid being hit from behind by speeding cars.

As we walked several United vehicles passed us, including a stretch limo, and they all took the piss so we responded in the usual fashion. After a lengthy trek we emerged at a park and ride. Unfortunately, it was a United park and ride and our thin blue line stood out like the proverbial dog's nadgers. Nonetheless, we had to stand there because our driver was now lost and had to call the salvage company for directions. Fortunately as we stood there a couple of parking stewards saw that we were lost and said that they would ask a bus diver if he'd take us to our destination which turned out to be at Cardiff Heliport. They said it was miles away and inaccessible on foot.

Fortuitously a double-decker bus driver agreed to take us and nine of us got on board. We were the only passengers and the driver turned down several roadside requests for lifts. We then drove around and around the outskirts of Cardiff, took a scenic if pointless tour around Cardiff docklands and got caught up in heavy traffic before eventually arriving at the heliport.

We emptied out the minibus, including opening the untouched case of Stella. We then bribed our bus driver to take us back into town, which thankfully he agreed to do. We eventually arrived at Cardiff station, passing the celebrating Man U pub that was now surrounded by police with an additional convoy of meat wagons parked along the main road. We walked towards the main part of the anachronistic Cardiff Central station and were then redirected to a side entrance. The station was sectioned into London, Bristol or Manchester platforms and seemed well organised.

As we made our way towards the London platforms a couple of young girls were walking ahead of us. Ted, in his infinite wisdom, decided to tell one of them, a blonde, that she had a big bum. Naturally she was apoplectic; she was a local and went into one about how insulting her arse was somehow related to insulting Cardiff per se. She looked like she was going to lamp Ted so he tried to say that it was only a joke. I pointed out to Ted that women don't ask if their bum looked big only for someone to tell them it did without even asking the question! The offended girl walked towards some blokes standing on the corner and told them of the insult. We thought they were locals and that we were about to have a totally unnecessary ruck with the Soul Crew, but luckily they were Millwall and merely told Ted that he was a naughty boy.

We made it to the London entrance in one piece and joined a queue of fellow Lions. We had no tickets, obviously, and we had found nowhere to buy one, we shuffled along with everyone else and boarded a Millwall train at 7.30pm. Due to our traipse around Cardiff the rush hour had already taken place so our train was full but comfortable and we managed to find seats with tables. For the record, on the platforms at Cardiff station there were trainspotters.

Colin was by this time in Bristol and rang to check our plight. I told him that we appeared to have found a way home, unless the train derailed or we were thrown off for being ticketless. Although it was a 'dry' train we smuggled the Stella aboard and offered them around the carriage. The steward warned us not to drink as we could be turfed off the train. The trip was painless, despite the fact that the train was of a vintage that you only see for football specials. We arrived back at Paddington just after 10pm.

Our minibus driver had come back with us and Clive and I managed to cadge a lift with him and his mate, who had come to pick him up as they were driving back to Dagenham via where I live. We shook hands with the rest of our party, who were travelling home by tube, thankful that we had somehow managed not to get ourselves killed. It had been a relatively cheap trip in all because we didn't pay for our minibus or our train.

Whilst the day had been an adventure of epic proportions, the game had been disappointing because the Giant beat Goliath and Millwall left their slingshot and pebbles at home. Nevertheless the occasion was always going to be more than the game. It was a once in a lifetime experience, that was for sure, with the day in total capturing in microcosm what football travelling is all about. It seemed somehow appropriate that the biggest horror trip of all time, even eclipsing the Burnley match earlier in the season, came on Millwall's biggest day.

The club organised an open-topped bus parade for the team, stopping in Surrey Quays shopping centre and Lewisham for the day following the game, to celebrate reaching the final at worst. Whilst I truly appreciated the achievement, I felt a bit flat after the final and didn't fancy going, although some of my mates went as did an estimated 30,000 others.

Despite the season petering out from a play-off perspective, if someone had told me at the start of the season that Millwall would beat West Ham 4-1, make the FA Cup Final and qualify for Europe then I'd have called the local mental hospital for the men in white coats to take them away.

The prospect that everybody, Millwall and other sides' fans alike, had talked about after we qualified for Europe was the possibility of the draw bringing up the dream pairing of Millwall v Galatasaray, giving us a jolly jaunt to the former Turkish capital, Istanbul, as highlighted by one bloke we saw outside Old Trafford chanting 'Turkey, Turkey Here We Come!'. Sadly, Galatasaray didn't qualify, which must have pleased the UN peacekeepers no end. We had been guaranteed our European spot when Charlton beat Liverpool to confirm that they couldn't catch United, which must have pleased the anoraks no end and struck terror into the dodderers at FA HQ.

As a seeded team we went straight in to the first round proper with the real big boys, however, as I thought we would be, were drawn out against an Eastern European team, in our case Ferencvaros a trouble club from Hungary. A team that I had actually heard of, it should be fun. I never thought I'd see Millwall in Europe, Hungary here I come!